VIEWS TO DIE FOR

VIEWS TO DIE FOR
MURDER, ANARCHY, AND
THE BATTLE FOR SYDNEY'S FUTURE

MARK SKELSEY

TRAFALGAR
PUBLISHING

Published 2025 by
Trafalgar Publishing

www.viewstodiefor.com.au

All rights reserved. No part of this publication may be reproduced, stored in a retrieval system or transmitted in any form by any means, electronic, mechanical, photocopying, recording or otherwise, without the written permission of the publisher and copyright holder.

The moral rights of the author have been asserted.

Copyright text 2025 © Mark Skelsey
Copyright photography 2025 © Mark Skelsey unless otherewise noted

Book production
Longueville Media
PO Box 205 Haberfield NSW 2045

While the publisher has made every effort to obtain all relevant copyright licences, any parties with further information or claim to copyright are invited to contact the publisher directly.

 A catalogue record for this book is available from the National Library of Australia

ISBN Print: 978-1-7637410-0-3
ISBN eBook: 978-1-7637410-1-0

Contents

Preface: "He was terrified – he was yelling" ix

Part 1: The rise and fall of Sydney's first suburb 1

Chapter 1: From windmills to 'high status' villas 3
Chapter 2: Upstairs, downstairs 9
Chapter 3: "One of the finest streets within the city" 13
Chapter 4: "A stodgy old maid" 26
Chapter 5: Follow the artists 34

Part 2: Ripe for redevelopment 49

Chapter 6: Business comes first 51
Chapter 7: "Fairylands and Hollywood" 58
Chapter 8: The planner who was "not fond of research" 64
Chapter 9: All the pain and no gain for Woolloomooloo 66
Chapter 10: A suburb "ripe" for change and development 74
Chapter 11: "The rest of the development industry has always followed me" 84
Chapter 12: Transforming an "ugly step-daughter" 97

Part 3: Urban warfare 107

Chapter 13: From a "black night" to a green ban future 109
Chapter 14: "If ever I saw an example of visual pollution, this is it" 115
Chapter 15: Naughty nuns outside court 125

Chapter 16: Inner Sydney – "a region in transition" 131

Chapter 17: An unwanted South Coast holiday 145

Chapter 18: "None of us were really the sort of people
who were going to back off" 148

Chapter 19: Strangers in the street 153

Chapter 20: "He was in big trouble" 161

Chapter 21: "They threatened me and prevented me
from escaping" 164

Chapter 22: "The best living quarters that I will probably
ever have" 169

Chapter 23: "Dead silence" at the auction 176

Chapter 24: "We believed in the potential for
a social revolution" 180

Chapter 25: Linked by art and blood 191

Chapter 26: "It felt very much like war" 195

Chapter 27: "Residents and developers alike
are victims of inadequate legislation" 205

Part 4: Juanita's defiant stand 215

Chapter 28: "Green ban soup" 217

Chapter 29: "There is very little of the old Cross now" 225

Chapter 30: "The whole house started to smell like
someone had thrown up into it" 233

Chapter 31: "A class war going on" 242

Chapter 32: "Let us not let the rich who live in these houses …
forget the tactics that were used to make way for
them" 255

Chapter 33: A club in Western Sydney 265

Part 5: The legacy   269
   Chapter 34: Victoria St hits the big screen................... 271
   Chapter 35: Innovation comes from warfare................ 282
   Chapter 36: "I love the plane trees ... terraces and the
                  proximity to everything"...................... 293
   Chapter 37: Sacrifices which should be recognised 299

Author's notes and acknowledgements   317

About the author   319

Note: This book, and in particular Chapter 15, contains language some may find offensive.

WHERE THE STORY IS SET

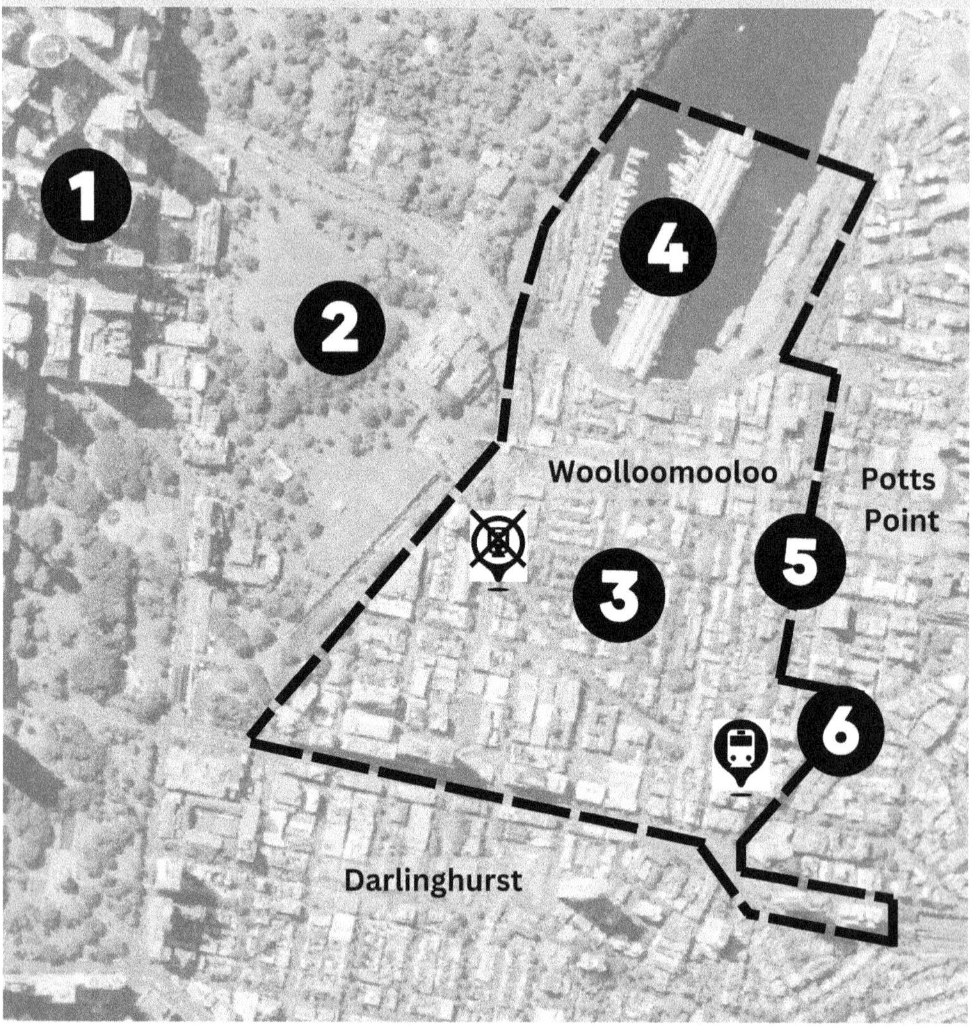

1	High-rise Sydney Central Business District	**4**	Woolloomooloo Bay Finger Wharf	▢ Boundary of 1969 Woolloomooloo development scheme
2	Domain (open parkland area)	**5**	Victoria St, on ridge above valley	Location of proposed Woolloomooloo station (never built)
3	Valley in which suburb of Woolloomooloo is located	**6**	Darlinghurst Rd, known as a historic 'red light' district	Kings Cross station (opened 1979)

PREFACE
"He was terrified – he was yelling"

As the clock passed midnight, Arthur King was pleased to finally climb into bed. It had been a long day and an extraordinarily hectic fortnight, and he needed all the sleep he could get.

During the first half of April 1973, King had found himself as the de facto leader of a nascent resident action protest movement. A teacher, he was among approximately 400 residents who, on or around 3 April, were told they would be forced from their small flats in 40 terrace homes located in the inner-Sydney suburb of Kings Cross. Some tenants were offered money to leave, at times accompanied by unsavoury tactics such as having front doors deliberately broken, bricks thrown through windows or utility services cut off.

"There were protected tenants who had been there for 20 years [and] were just getting evicted and being offered money to get out," King recalled in an interview for this book. "I objected to that; it is a terrible thing for someone who has a protected tenancy to tell someone here's $1,500 – go and suit yourself."

King said he never saw tenant intimidation but also recalled: "I heard about it, there were plenty of stories of people being handed eviction notices in an intimidatory manner".

A Sydney property developer, Frank Theeman, was behind the evictions. He wanted to demolish the historic and grand Victoria St terraces and instead build high-rise towers of luxury apartments, with spectacular views to Sydney Harbour and the city skyline. It didn't matter that an estimated 80 of the tenants were unemployed and that a further 66 were pensioners, while others had low-paying occupations such as cleaning, taxi driving, bartending or seafaring. They need to go for 'progress'.

For several months, King had suspected that a major development proposal was going to be announced. In January 1973, he and three other activists had written in an open letter that the street was "unique in the Australian urban tradition" and its "human scale and visual quality" were at risk of being "totally destroyed". "[Victoria St] was prettier than all the rest, it has got nice trees, and it is nice and wide, and it is 300 yards from all the action at the Cross. I lived there in the same flat when I was at university. I had a great affection for the street," King said.

But fighting the plans had proven to be busy and exhausting work.

King had acted quickly after hearing about the evictions on 3 April. Just two days later, he'd addressed a monthly meeting of resident action groups from around Sydney. The minutes of this meeting record that 39 action group representatives heard King speak about the "need to preserve this historic area which was under threat from development" and the fact he'd be approaching the State's heritage advocacy group, the National Trust, for support.

On Sunday 8 April, a public meeting was held in the street outside King's flat. About 50 residents attended and decided to form a residents' action group to fight for their cause.

A few days' later, on Wednesday 11 April, around 150 residents and their supporters met at a local church and voted again to continue to resist. They were joined by members of a vocal and militant building union, the Builders Labourers' Federation. King co-chaired the meeting. A decision was made for residents to patrol the terraces, particularly at night, to stop them from being damaged and to protect the remaining tenants. The residents' resistance movement was gaining momentum.

Even more importantly, King and his supporters were receiving positive media coverage.

On Friday 13 April, King appeared on the Channel Ten news, while the day before the ABC's current affairs show *This Day Tonight* (TDT) had been out on the street covering the story. The TDT footage had shown the vandalised frontages of the terraces, with windows boarded-up, doors hanging on their hinges and first floor balconies without their historic and decorative metal balustrades. It had also featured interviews with unhappy tenants, one of whom said he was being harassed, and footage of King and a group of supporters approaching Theeman's real estate agency office, seeking to discuss the issue.

"This is a deputation from a meeting we had last night; we would like to present the resolutions that were passed at the meeting," King was heard saying to a person who opened the agency's front door.

One of Theeman's agents supplied a written statement to TDT, but refused to appear on camera. The statement claimed the occupants of the terraces had been dealt with under the proper processes and at any rate were "gamblers, drunks, prostitutes and hippies".

With the public meetings and the media coverage, King was gaining attention – perhaps even a little too much attention.

This became clear on the morning of the 11 April public meeting. King was visited by a police officer who asked him if he was doing "illegal things" in the area and also made inquiries as to whether he had an outstanding divorce payment. After being taken to the local police station, King was able to explain he'd never married and so couldn't have an alimony payment, and no further details were forthcoming about the "illegal things". "You are not the right one," local residents recorded a police officer saying, before taking King back to his flat.

Late in the afternoon of the following day, King had a second visit from police, with the officers this time claiming they'd had a complaint about drugs being located at his home. King denied that there were any drugs in his possession and the police didn't even bother searching his home.

It's possible that someone was using the local police to place pressure on King, at the same time he was fighting the development proposal.

If this was the case, it was a low-ball tactic and a harbinger of things to come.

However, if the police visits were intended to stop King from his anti-development campaigning, it didn't work. Since the 1960s, King had been involved in The Push, an informal grouping of several hundred Sydneysiders who believed in anarchist and liberation ideals. Unlike many of the other tenants, King was educated and articulate and believed in the right anti-authority cause, including fighting censorship and institutional racism. Victoria St was another cause he believed in. He was appalled by the manner in which the tenants had been evicted, and the proposed destruction of the historic terraces, and it would take more than a couple of visits from the police to make him back down. "I've always been a bit of a shit stirrer and politically active," King told this author, when asked why he led the resistance movement.

King's flat had become the headquarters of the movement. On the evening of Friday 13 April, several members of the resident action group met in King's flat. They discussed the coming weekend's activity, in particular a door knock planned for the following day. According to a 15 April statement prepared by resident activist Roelof Smilde, as the meeting drifted into Saturday and the clock struck 1am, King declared he was tired and wanted to go to bed. The residents left, with some joining the street patrol.

A few hours' later, most likely around 4:45am, King was awoken when someone turned his lights on. At the foot of his bed stood a heavily built man – someone King didn't know. The man appeared to have let himself into the apartment, courtesy of a key left in the door by one of the 'resident activists' who was at the flat the previous night, and who was later expelled from the group because of suspicions that he was in cahoots with the developer.

"Who the fuck are you and how did you get in?" King demanded. The man claimed he was looking for someone called Sue and, as he shuffled back into the hallway, said he must have entered the wrong flat.

King chased him into the hallway, only to be clubbed over the head by one of the man's colleagues, before being blindfolded, gagged, forced back into his bedroom and ordered to put on clothes. He was then man-handled down the stairs of his terrace and into the street.

King did manage to get the gag free, and yelled out for help. Someone heard his pleas – a Victoria St resident named Gregory Bible, who told a 1983 coronial inquest about the incident. Bible said that, around 4.50am, he saw a man being dragged into a car on the opposite side of Victoria St. "It seemed to me he was terrified – he was yelling," Bible said.

The car sped off into the night. The battle for Victoria St had begun.

PART 1
THE RISE AND FALL OF SYDNEY'S FIRST SUBURB

CHAPTER 1

From windmills to 'high status' villas

Just 40 years after the arrival of the First Fleet, Sydney town was looking distinctly tatty. Its population of approximately 12,000 people was crowded around Sydney Cove, where the First Fleet's commander Arthur Phillip had placed the Union Jack on 26 January 1788. Many of its population regarded the settlement as crowded, disorderly and unsanitary.

As a result, by the late 1820s, New South Wales Governor (NSW) Ralph Darling was receiving applications for improved living conditions from prominent Sydney citizens.

To help solve his problem, Darling cast a lazy eye in the direction of a prominent landmark known as Woolloomooloo Hill.

At the time, the name 'Woolloomooloo' was loosely applied to the area east of the Sydney town settlement, including to parts of suburbs or places known today as Darlinghurst, East Sydney, Kings Cross, Potts Point and Elizabeth Bay. The actual boundaries of the area called Woolloomooloo were most unclear, as were the origins of the name – or even how to correctly spell it. Part of the area had been subject to a land grant in 1793, and the farm built on the site had been called 'Woolamoola' or 'Walla Mulla', based on the Aboriginal name for the area, which is thought to have been either 'Wallabahmullah' (which means black kangaroo) or 'Wallamullah' (which means place of many fish).

The Woolloomooloo area included a swampy valley closest to Sydney town, which drained to an inlet of Port Jackson, along with an elevated area further to the east, separated from the valley by a sharp cliff face. The area above the cliff was known as Woolloomooloo Hill, the valley beneath it just Woolloomooloo. The area was said to be highly significant for the indigenous Cadigal people, as a ceremonial site and camping and hunting grounds.[1]

Since the first years of the 1800s, the hill had been the location of a cluster of charming windmills, which were described as the "most picturesque" in Sydney[2] and were one of the first structures to greet visitors travelling by sea. Darling's predecessor, Lachlan Macquarie, had also set aside part of the hill and the area behind it running down to Port Jackson as a reserve for Sydney's dispossessed Aboriginal people. Macquarie ordered that huts be erected in this reserve and boats be provided to those living there.[3]

However, given the grumblings about the cluttered and messy state of the main township, Darling had a different plan for the area after coming to power in 1825.

Darling saw Woolloomooloo Hill as having the potential to set a new and higher town planning standard to inspire others to follow. He wrote that he wanted Woolloomooloo Hill to be a "high status area … which would serve as both an example and a chastisement to the debased population of Sydney town". He was also willing to dispossess the local Aboriginal people, for the second time in 40 years, to allow this dream to come to life.

Darling went to work, personally overseeing plans to release and subdivide the Woolloomooloo Hill area into 17 'town allotments', which averaged around three hectares in size, on which members of high civil society would be invited to build expensive residences. This area would be, in effect, Sydney's first exclusive suburb – a little like Point

---

1 *Woolloomooloo: A Biography*, NewSouth Books, 2017, by Louis Nowra, page 18
2 Windmills of Sydney, available at Dictionary of Sydney, published 2016
3 *Sydney: 1842-1992*, Hale and Iremonger, circa 1992, by Shirley Fitzgerald, pages 31-33

A painting of Rosebank, built in 1831, featuring one of the original villas on Woolloomooloo Hill, by an unknown artist (Source: Mitchell Library, State Library of New South Wales)

Piper or Mosman today. The colony's general hospital superintendent, chief justice, architect, sheriff and deputy surveyor-general were among the land recipients.

Regulations were drawn up for land development, including that no more than one villa should be constructed on each of the spacious new allotments and that the villa be surrounded by landscaping. In addition, those villas were required to face Sydney town (most likely to provide the educative role so desired by Darling), and had to be built to a high standard and within a certain period of time.

It was an early attempt at town planning, and also clearly a move designed to elevate Sydney's civic status and make the colonial outpost look like a more attractive place to live. "By the mid-1830s, the parade of 'white' villas down the spine of Woolloomooloo Hill presented a

The view north from Craigend, one of the Woolloomooloo Hill villas, towards Port Jackson, showing other villas and windmills, 1845 oil painting by George Edwards Peacock (Courtesy of Dixson Library, State Library of NSW)

picturesque sight, and was visible from the harbour and the town of Sydney," notes the history book *Villas of Darlinghurst*.[4]

However, as high-minded as the planning philosophy may have been, it was swept away by a more potent Sydney force – property development.

By 1838, just seven years after the last of the land grants, the landowners were already pressing the government to remove the "one villa per lot rule", to allow them to profit from the construction of additional homes on their land. The landowners' cause was helped by the colony's worst financial recession in the early 1840s, which was triggered by a severe drought, along with economic woes in England that reduced capital inflows into NSW.

---

4   Villas of Darlinghurst, State Library of NSW, 2002, in Introduction section

In fact, one landowner – Thomas Macquoid – committed suicide in October 1841 after being ordered to pay 600 pounds in a court ruling. Macquoid was the colony's sheriff and feared his inability to pay the debt would result in him losing his position. Around 8am one morning, he chose to use one of his own pistols to end his life in his heavily mortgaged Woolloomooloo Hill home.

Another landowner, Edward Hallen, was a draughtsman in the NSW Surveyor-General's office and in 1842 used these skills to draw up a new plan to subdivide the seven lots closest to Sydney town. These lots were long and narrow, stretching from the high country (where the villas were located) down to roughly halfway across the valley. With the express agreement of the landowners, this plan created six new streets running north-south towards Woolloomooloo Bay, including Woolloomooloo Rd (now Darlinghurst Rd and Macleay St) and Brougham, Dowling, Forbes, Bourke and Victoria Sts.

By running north-south, Hallen's new street alignments forever trashed Darling's vision that the fronts of homes in the area should face in a westerly direction towards the city. In fact, it would now mean the elevated and more unsightly backs of homes, particularly those on Victoria St, would be most visible from the main town.

Furthermore, the new street plan did not appear to take into account the topography of the land, which meant that the proposed new thoroughfare of Victoria St – around 600m long and 20.1m wide – was precariously placed adjacent to a cliff which provided a prominent outlook for the Woolloomooloo Hill area. In later years, this cliff would prove to be a dangerous menace for children and property owners, and an interesting opportunity for property developers.

By the mid-1840s, the grand vision of magnificent villas sitting on large lots was beginning to fade. One of the first subdivisions was that of the chief justice, James Dowling, who had passed away in 1844. In the same year, his three-hectare estate sitting around Brougham Lodge was subdivided into approximately 50 new residential lots as little as 236 square metres in size. In doing so, the subdivision created the southern entry of Victoria St.

A section of the notorious Victoria St cliff, as seen from Brougham St in the 1840s - note the 'mountain goats' enjoying the location at image left (Courtesy of Mitchell Library, State Library of New South Wales)

"Whether the [Woolloomooloo Hill] area served as 'an example and chastisement' is doubtful," noted the City of Sydney Council's official historian Shirley Fitzgerald in her book *Sydney 1842–1992*.[5] "Of far greater interest to its owners was the question of whether it would make a profit."

It was this environment of greed and rule-breaking which brought the suburb of Woolloomooloo, including Victoria St, into the world. The same environment would return to the street with devastating impact some 130 years later.

---

5 *Sydney: 1842-1992*, page 32

CHAPTER 2

Upstairs, downstairs

In the delightful 1927 silent film *The Kids Stakes*, based around the newspaper cartoon character Fatty Finn, a group of street urchin children charge up the Butler Stairs between the valley of Woolloomooloo and Victoria St, which sits on top of the cliff. In doing so, they need to sneak past wooden 'no entry' signs and a snoozing policeman, both of which have been placed at the top of the stairs to stop people and animals from the valley getting into the rarefied and more exclusive Potts Point area.

The children are looking for Fatty's pet goat, which is causing a nuisance and is under threat of the chopping block after escaping into the garden of a Potts Point mansion. The pet goat, Hector, is needed for an upcoming billy cart derby – hence the movie title *The Kids Stakes*.

The metaphor from the movie is clear – Victoria St and the valley below are connected, but different. The two areas may have been created from the same 1842 plan. But as far as their social status is concerned, the two areas are miles apart. The valley below is occupied by scoundrels and ruffians, the hill above it by the cultured and well-to-do.

Most suburbs tend to start their lives with a honeymoon period where, at least in their early years, they are regarded as wholesome, happy places. This reflects in part the fact that, in a suburb's early years, the roads and homes have just been constructed and appear fresh and new. It usually takes a generation of ownership before a suburb becomes labelled as rundown, or as a slum.

This was never the case with Woolloomooloo, which was regarded as a slum from its earliest days.

In 1858, English-born William Stanley Jevons took a saunter around Woolloomooloo. Jevons had trained in London as a scientist, but had come to Australia to work as an assayer for the Sydney Mint. Jevons' real interest, however, lay in being an amateur scientific observer and writer. He made solitary journeys on foot to various parts of New South Wales (NSW), and was interested not only in the State's geology,

Child actors in the 1927 silent movie The Kids Stakes walk up the Butler Stairs between Woolloomooloo and Victoria St (Photo courtesy of National Film and Sound Archive of Australia)

Potts Point children re-create the same scene in 2024 (Photo: Mark Skelsey)

botany and meteorology but also in the growth of new towns, and the lives and habits of the people.

This led Jevons to single-handedly construct a 'social survey' of Sydney in 1858, which in turn led him to Woolloomooloo.

To be fair to Woolloomooloo, Jevons did note that many "first-class" houses – built "neatly in a row" – were fronting Dowling, Forbes, Bourke and Palmer Sts. But he stated that most other parts of the suburb, particularly the lower lying areas, had "second and third class" houses and in some parts there was a putrid odour, no doubt linked the open sewers which drained towards the bay. "The flattest part of Woolloomooloo must certainly be unhealthy from the damp miasmatic air which must lie upon it at night," Jevons wrote. Miasmatic, by the way, means a foul-smelling vapour arising from rotting organic matter.

Jevons also noted that two and four-bedroom cottages had been built to face the suburb's service lanes "as to render the population here very densely aggregated".

Just two years later, the *Sydney Mail's* anonymous writer 'Stroller' gave a more evocative account of the suburb's density – and endemic poverty. Stroller noted that the suburb had been transformed from open land to Sydney's most crowded suburb in less than 15 years.

"From an almost dense solitude, arose to the amaze of those who looked on, the densest population which characterises Sydney and its suburbs," Stroller noted. "There you see the squalid poverty of the city, for squalid poverty exists within it. There you see babes aye, they are almost babes, picking their steps through the mud, with the fatal jug or the fatal bottle in their hand to the House at the corner. There, also, you will see big burly brawling women, quarrelling with each other in words that sink darkly and gloomily into the heart, sad with miserable poverty, mad with pernicious drink. There, too, sad to say, you will see the man of thews and sinews, ready to work, but oftentimes from the compulsion of circumstances obliged to remain in a state of almost listless idleness."[1]

---

1   Rambles in the Suburbs, *Sydney Mail*, Saturday 4 August 1860, by 'Stroller', page 5

Within 15 years of its settlement, Woolloomooloo had developed into a densely-populated slum, as shown in this photo taken in 1859 by William Hetzer from St Mary's Cathedral (Courtesy of Mitchell Library, State Library of New South Wales)

Stroller's piece also reveals that by 1860, the name Woolloomooloo was now explicitly linked to the valley's dense built-form and to vice, poverty and crime. Consequently, the days of the name Woolloomooloo being used to describe vast swatches of East Sydney were over, and instead the term was only being applied to the valley area between Oxford St and the bay's edge.

The hill above Woolloomooloo – which Stroller describes as having "lordly houses" and "lordly mansions" – was now firmly known as Darlinghurst: the name given to the area by Governor Darling in the 1820s. In fact, Stroller felt that the good citizens of this area now needed to come to the aid of the helpless in the valley below.

"Gentlemen and ladies of Darlinghurst, you have a mission entrusted to your consciences and your practice; protect the poor … reform the vices which exist in the lower part of your beautiful suburb," Stroller wrote.

Just a few short years into its life, the suburb of Woolloomooloo was getting a reputation as a place which needed to be pitied and changed.

CHAPTER 3

"One of the finest streets within the city"

"When opened to its full length and properly formed, Victoria St will be one of the finest streets within the boundaries of the city and, we are satisfied, rapidly be lined with good homes."

The above quote represented the opinion of a group of Victoria St landowners and residents, who petitioned the City of Sydney Council in 1854 to build the street to its full proclaimed length to the edge of Woolloomooloo Bay.

The sentiments reflected the new civic order developing east of Sydney town: while the new suburb of Woolloomooloo was gaining a reputation for squalor and vice, the opposite was true for the street sitting above the valley.

Like many other Sydney streets being developed at the time, Victoria St was predominantly lined with terraces. This reflected the fact that, in the mid-19th century, Sydney was a walking city. It therefore made sense for new housing to have narrow frontages, so that owners and tenants could easily stroll to nearby services, transport and employment.

Some of the street's earliest homes (mainly at its southern end) were modest in size and form, in line with the basic Georgian architectural style common in the first half of the century. For instance, around 1855, a row of three double-storey terraces was constructed at 198–202 Victoria St, near its intersection with William St. These homes have a plain and functional design, built flush to the street and with no verandah or parapet enhancements. While these terraces are anything but eye-catching, one of the homes – number 202 – would be at the very centre of the Victoria St story more than a century later, and now has New South Wales' (NSW) highest level of heritage protection.

From the late 1850s until the 1890s, the construction of new homes in Victoria St (particularly towards its northern end) came at a time of buoyant economic conditions. This meant the street attracted the upper class and respected members of Sydney society, who had the time, money and ego to invest in large homes. Some rose to four storeys in height and featured modern architectural styles intended to publicly signal the owner's good fortune. Homeowners on the western side of Victoria St also enjoyed glorious views over the rapidly developing Woolloomooloo valley and the Sydney town centre.

Terrace homes constructed in Victoria St during this period tended to fall into either the Regency or Italianate styles. The Regency style is generally regarded as being in high fashion between 1830–1860, although in Victoria St it can be seen in homes also built in the 1870s. According to *Terrace Houses in Australia*, the Regency style "aspired to emulate the prevailing architectural taste patronised by royalty and fashionable upper classes in London" and "proved to be an ideal vehicle for the display of new-found wealth and success".[1]

The Regency style did this by introducing classical architectural features, such as columns, French doors, verandahs and iron-lace balustrades, into the basic Georgian terrace form. In Victoria St, the best Regency homes can be found at numbers 55 (alongside the McElhone Stairs), 57–59 (known as Denham Court) and 77–79 (known as Bellevue Lodge).[2]

In the later part of the 19th century, particularly around the 1880s, the Italianate style terrace (also known as the 'boom style' home) became popular. This architectural style – which borrowed design

---

1 *Terrace Houses in Australia*, Lansdowne Publishing, 1999, by Trevor Howells and Colleen Morris, page 28
2 Taken from National Trust listing of the Victoria/Brougham St precinct, 2 May 1973

Left: A group of Georgian-style terraces, including Juanita Nielsen's former home on the right of the photo, at 198-202 Victoria St (Photo: Mark Skelsey)

Right: Regency-style homes at 57-59 Victoria St (Photo: Mark Skelsey)

approaches sometimes found in rural Italian villas – doubled-down on the architectural features of the Regency homes by also introducing elaborate plaster dividing wall and parapet decorations, along with tall windows and more detailed lacework. "Many of the highly ornamental terraces of the boom years of the 1880s were built to display the affluence or social pretensions of their owners," *Terrace Houses of Australia* notes.[3] Terrace homes at 61–69, 119–121 and 80–102 Victoria St are said to be "splendid" examples of this style.[4]

---

3   *Terrace Houses in Australia*, page 60
4   Referred to in National Trust listing of the Victoria/Brougham St precinct

The terraces at 119-121 Victoria St are a good example of the Italianate style (Photo: Mark Skelsey)

The above situation means that Victoria St's terraces have become an open-air museum of changing architectural tastes over a 40-year period, as housing styles moved from the plain-fronted and unspectacular Georgian designs of the first half of the 19th century, to the more decorative styles celebrating the colony's increasing affluence in the second half of the century.

Victoria St's elevated position, along with its fashionable and stylish architecture, also tended to attract citizens marking their mark on 19th-century Sydney society, whether this be in the arts, law or public service.

In 1867, the progressive politician, barrister and judge Sir William Charles Windeyer and his family moved into a substantial Regency-style terrace house at 219 Victoria St. The home contained five bedrooms, a school room, servants' room, laundry, kitchen and drawing and dining rooms – enough space for Windeyer's brood at the time of five girls, which the subsequent arrival of three sons would expand.

Windeyer served various electorates in the NSW Legislative Assembly, and in the 1870s also held the position of Attorney-General

Left: Sir William Charles Windeyer and his family lived at 219 Victoria St, marked in the photo above (Source: Windeyer family photograph collection, courtesy of J.B. Windeyer)
Right: Sir William Charles Windeyer

under Premier Sir Henry Parkes, regarded as a founding father of the Australian Federation.

Windeyer was passionate about creating a free and secular education system, and supported other left-leaning causes such as improving the rights of women, helping the homeless and discharged prisoners, and preserving open space in central Sydney. The present-day users of Clark Island in Sydney Harbour and Observatory Hill can thank Windeyer for his efforts.[5]

In 1879, Windeyer resigned from Parliament and was appointed as a judge in the Supreme Court of New South Wales. In this capacity, and while living at Victoria St, Windeyer oversaw one of colonial Sydney's most scandalous court cases, known as the 'Mount Rennie outrage'.

---

5   See Windeyer's biography in the Dictionary of Sydney at https://adb.anu.edu.au/biography/windeyer-sir-william-charles-1062

Members of the gang accused of the Mount Rennie gang rape, at Darlinghurst Gaol (Courtesy of Mitchell Library, State Library of NSW)

Mount Rennie is a hill in Sydney's Moore Park, near the corner of Cleveland and South Dowling Sts. In 1886, a 16-year-old girl, Mary Jane Hicks, was abducted and taken to the then-isolated location, where she was gang raped by around eight youths, with other youths present.

Windeyer, who saw himself as a protector of women's rights, sentenced nine of the youths to death. A public campaign in favour of the condemned men caused five of the sentences to be commuted to life imprisonment, with the other four youths hanged in 1887.

Exhausted by the Mount Rennie case, the Windeyers auctioned the contents of their Victoria St home and moved out in 1886, before travelling overseas and then returning to a new home in Rushcutters Bay.[6] Their former home on Victoria St was later demolished for the Oriental Hotel, which in turn was demolished for the Holiday Inn that currently sits at this site.

---

6   *William and Mary Windeyer: Law, Politics and Society in Colonial New South Wales*, Australian Scholarly Publishing, 2016, by Dr Leonora Ritter and Jim Windeyer, page 211

Top: 97 Victoria St, the home of NSW Deputy Postmaster-General James Dalgarno, in the 1880s (Courtesy of Mitchell Library, State Library of NSW)

Above: The same terrace in 2024 (Photo: Mark Skelsey)

Another notable 19th-century Victoria St figure was Lucien Henry, the French-born revolutionary and artist who called the street home for 12 years, from 1879 to 1891. Henry's story is worth telling in some detail, given that it forms part of Victoria St's rich tradition of being home to artists and anti-authority activity, while also building the street's spiritual and social connection to France (these themes are further explored in later chapters).

Born in 1850, Henry studied art in Paris but also became heavily involved in the French capital's revolutionary underworld, which was plotting against Emperor Napoleon III. In 1870, Napoleon III made the catastrophic mistake of declaring war on Prussia (present day Germany), only to see his army routed by the Prussians, his Empire collapse, and Paris surrounded and bombed by Prussian forces.

Once the Prussians declared victory and left the country, France descended into civil war. Henry was a regional leader in the Paris' National Guard, which was sympathetic to working class revolutionary causes. The National Guard found it surprisingly easy to run the provisional French Government's forces out of town and form a new revolutionary municipal government, known as the Paris Commune. Henry ordered his men to take the Paris police chief under arrest and was described as a "commanding figure, mounted on a large horse, giving orders in an army greatcoat with a red scarf about his neck".[7]

When the government forces regained control of the city in what is known as the "bloody week", Henry – along with many hundreds of other political prisoners – was deported to New Caledonia. After the prisoners were released from exile in 1879, Henry then chose to settle in Sydney, Australia, of all places.

Henry's decision to move to Sydney can best be explained by the curious and exotic street directory listing from 1879 of one "Madame Juliette Rastoul – professor of the French language" at a Victoria St address. Henry had most likely moved to Sydney for love, but also

---

7 *Visions of a Republic: The Work of Lucien Henry*, Powerhouse Publishing, 2001, by Ann Stephens, page 25

Lucien Henry (France/Australia 1850-96), Self portrait 1880s, oil on canvas 61 x 51 cm, Art Gallery of NSW, gift of Marcel Aurousseau 1983 (Image © Art Gallery of NSW)

potentially for a fresh start. Rastoul had also been expelled from New Caledonia in 1874, and then moved to Sydney where she established herself as a French teacher. With her extensive contacts and reputable profile, Rastoul was able to help Henry establish himself as an artist upon his arrival.

Within six months of his arrival, Henry married Rastoul, who was nine years his senior, and the two appear to be the first tenants in a newly-built terrace at 156 Victoria St. Among the witnesses to Henry's marriage were none other than fellow Victoria St residents Justice Windeyer and his wife Mary.

In Australia, Henry yet again played a pivotal role in a campaign for national reform and change, but this campaign sought to inspire and uplift, in contrast with the subversion and street warfare which were the hallmarks of the Paris Commune.

This reform was the movement towards Australia discarding its colonial status and instead becoming a nation in its own right, which coincided with the years before the centenary of European settlement in 1888. Artists and architects were encouraged to help deliver this new national identity. For instance, as part of these centenary celebrations, influential artist and teacher Julian Ashton argued that artists must "paint the Australia of today" rather than focus on the past.

"Henry's time in Sydney intersected with a rising tide of republican ferment that transformed the debates on nationhood and federation in the 1880s," says author Ann Stephen in *Visions of a Republic*, an illustrated biography of Henry's life. "Henry's radical French origins brought a particularly republican and non-British imagery to colonial culture."[8]

Henry's initial works showed him as an accomplished landscaped painter who was "fascinated by the cliffs and caves around Sydney".[9] He then turned his attention to the forms of Australian flora and fauna as ideal representations of the nation. He painted NSW's waratah flower, not as a botanical specimen, but as an "icon of culture". "Henry was particularly entranced by the waratah which he championed in a number of his own designs and templates for use in architectural and artistic works," historian Mark Dunn writes in the *Dictionary of Sydney*.[10]

Henry's enduring masterpieces, however, were the two decorative stained-glass windows he designed. Commissioned in 1889 to celebrate the colony's centenary, these windows light the stairwells which flank the main hall in Sydney Town Hall.

---

8   *Visions of a Republic*, page 58
9   *Visions of a Republic*, page 62
10 Henry, Lucian, Dictionary of Sydney, 2011

The north window shows a relatively traditional Captain Cook on board his ship with telescope in hand. The more powerful and eye-catching of the two pieces, however, is the representation of NSW in the southern stairwell. This piece depicts the province as a confident young woman, whose haloed head is crowned with the horns and wool of a ram, signifying the colony's agricultural wealth. The woman grasps a miner's lamp in one hand and a seagoing trident the other, while the side panels proclaim 'Advance Australia' and feature mass displays of waratahs, flannel flowers and stenocarpus. Henry's heroine stands on a globe titled 'Oceania', which could be interpreted as a political statement about the potential of the colony to become an independent regional force.

"This dazzling, powerful triptych is more than a celebration of New South Wales: it is a representation of Australia, a political and cultural entity that did not exist at the time. More contentiously, it is also a geo-political statement about 'Australia' as a significant future presence in the Pacific region, one then carved up colonially by Britain, France and Germany," write authors Terry Irving and Rowan Cahill in *Radical Sydney*, which profiles Henry.[11]

Incredibly, a Frenchman who led a revolution in Paris was now helping create Australia's emerging independent national identity.

In 1891, Henry sailed to France, where he published a book on the waratah. Soon after, he faced bankruptcy and divorce proceedings initiated by his wife, and died of tuberculosis in Paris in March 1896. In 2024, Henry's former home was converted from a backpacker hostel and into a single private dwelling.

Of course, Windeyer and Henry were not the only notable citizens to live on Victoria St. The State MP Alexander Stuart resided there for one year in 1880, ahead of him becoming Premier in 1883. Charles Elouis, Deputy Master of the Royal Mint, occupied the striking wide-fronted terrace at 55 Victoria St mentioned earlier in this chapter.

---

11 *Radical Sydney*, NSW Press, 2010, by Terry Irving and Rowan Cahill, page 68

Top Left: The Butler Stairs alongside the newly-built 139 Victoria St, around 1890 (Photographer unknown. Sourced from Caroline Simpson Collection of Museums of History NSW)

Above Left: The same scene today

Right: Lucien Henry's stunning 1889 representation of NSW sits as a decorative window in Sydney Town Hall (Courtesy of City of Sydney Council)

The street was also home to other members of Parliament, master mariners, hoteliers, surgeons, barristers and even a French Consul, as well as a healthy sprinkling of working and middle-class professionals such as gardeners, woodturners, bootmakers and greengrocers.

During the late 19th century, the Victoria St streetscape was also enhanced by the creation of three public staircases linking its heights with the valley below. From south to north, these are the Butler Stairs (1869), the L-shaped Hordern Stairs (1882) and grandest of all, the McElhone Stairs (1904). All three were named after former City of Sydney Council Aldermen.

A correspondent to the *Daily Telegraph* noted in 1881 that Victoria St was "a highly desirable locality" which "if not the rose, it is near it". "The houses therein are mostly good residences of high rentals," the correspondent said, before complaining about noisy children out on the street on a Sunday night.

However, as much as Victoria St had a high status, there was one problem which just wouldn't go away – those wretched goats from Woolloomooloo. In 1889, one E.G. Ward of 111 Victoria St wrote to the Lord Mayor to complain that goats were roaming freely in Woolloomooloo, then wandering into the thoroughfare. "I suppose there is no city in the world which permits such a state of things," Ward sniffed. Some 10 years earlier, another Victoria St resident had gone further and complained that local "larrikins" were deliberately planting the goats in his and other residents' gardens. "Last Sunday week I was victimised, and my flowers and plants were very much injured," he moaned.

The goats were a reminder that, as much as Victoria St stood on the high country, its fate was still linked to the valley below – an issue which would only become more important and divisive in the 20th century.

CHAPTER 4

"A stodgy old maid"

As Sydneysiders flicked through their afternoon newspaper on New Year's Day in 1929, they would have noticed Kings Cross-based writer Gloria Grant taking aim at Victoria St.

"Kings Cross is a modern jade," Grant wrote in the *Evening News*. "She sports jazz quarters, short skirts, and her hat has a coquettish upward tilt that allows a mischievous wink. Her spirit is contagious, like a sparkling cocktail. She is Bohemia itself, and her god is Modernity."[1]

"Darlinghurst Rd and its various environs are graced by handsome blocks of flats – each a votive offering to that same ruling deity. Delightful treasure shops mingle side by side with picturesque tearooms. Cars flash by in an unending stream.

"Yet right within the heart of her lies an anachronism. A feeble gesture to that superb flick of gaiety and defiance.

"Running parallel to Darlinghurst Rd lies Victoria St. Like a grim and somewhat stodgy old maid she disports her meagre length, and halts, with skirts withdrawn, against the outer precincts of Woolloomooloo Bay. She frowns on this spirit of gaiety which surrounds her.

"No trace of modernity shall find its way among those sombre house fronts. Aged, dingy and depressing, they stand defiantly against the sweeping tide of modern flats.

---

[1] Victoria St, *Evening News*, 1 January 1929, by Gloria Grant, page 6

"Occasionally a new house front appears, but it is only a snare and a delusion. Behind it lurks the ancient edifice itself, hiding a laugh behind a cracked and furrowed hand. Not for her the bright lights. At night she lies, impenetrable and dingy, with an occasional glare from a depressing gaslight."

What had happened to poor Victoria St, which had previously been described as one of Sydney's best residential precincts?

In fact, the street's decline had been underway since the 1890s. A combination of general depressed economic conditions, and consumers turning their backs on city terrace housing, had turned Victoria St into a backwater.

Between 1876 and 1890, overseas finance had been abundant and governments were spending the money on public works, such as roads, railways and bridges.[2] This in turn did away with the concept of the walking city, by allowing new spacious suburban housing – sitting on larger blocks of land – to be constructed well away from places of employment and services. Victoria St now had serious competition when it came to quality housing.

In addition to this, outbreaks of the bubonic plague between 1900 and 1922 – mainly confined to crowded slum housing areas in inner Sydney – convinced many Sydneysiders to seek new suburban homes on more spacious blocks.[3]

Furthermore, because of the economic malaise from the 1890s until World War I, it was more difficult to justify the single-family occupation of large terraces. As a result, Victoria St's homes were rapidly being converted into boarding houses or small apartment buildings called 'residential chambers', for working class accommodation.

---

2   The Architectural and Urban Development of Kings Cross, submitted by Zula Nittim, candidate for the degree of Doctor of Philosophy, University of New South Wales (NSW), December 1970, page 96

3   Suburban Development in Sydney: 1850 to 1920, paper submitted for Degree of Master of Arts (Honours), University of NSW, 1989, by Janet Robinson, page 121-22

"There are whole regions now occupied by boarding houses, residential chambers and tenement houses, which were 10 years ago occupied by single private families in one house," noted the *Sydney Mail and New South Wales Advertiser* in 1908.

"Many examples of this exist in Darlinghurst and Potts Point. There are many reasons for it. One is that the growing prosperity of the great city has enabled the rich to build a better and a more modern type of house farther out. The motor car and the tram have modernised transportation.

"The man of moderate income, who formerly occupied a terrace or semi-detached house in inner Sydney, has gone to Strathfield, Burwood or to the heights of the North Shore line."

Or as an advertorial for a North Shore development in the *Sunday Times* in 1929 put it: "Ever since flats and boarding houses have banished private homes from society districts such as Potts Point and portions of Darling Point, wealthy families have been searching for a new and exclusive locality. The pending North Shore Bridge and the excellent motor highways through the northern suburbs have directed attention to Turramurra – the picturesque garden suburb on the line to Hornsby".[4]

The statistics did not lie – the *Sands Directory* showed that in 1882 there were only four boarding houses in Victoria St. By 1920, there were 39 residential chambers and 13 boarding houses, along with two 'flats'.

At the same time, the street had somewhat surprisingly avoided the new flat redevelopment of the booming 1920s, referred to by Gloria Grant, which had involved the mansion estates of Potts Point and Darlinghurst being demolished for apartment buildings. This was probably because the large terraces were on relatively compact parcels of land, making them less attractive for redevelopment, and because their large size meant they could still provide a useful economic return in their existing state simply by being subdivided into small flatettes.

---

4   New Darling Point, *Sunday Times*, 15 September 1929, page 16

The intersection of Victoria St and Darlinghurst Rd, in the 1930s (Courtesy of Mitchell Library, State Library of New South Wales)

However, Victoria St's label as an uninspiring "stodgy old maid" was at least less severe than the public criticism of Woolloomooloo.

In March 1905, some 1,145 people signed a petition calling for the names of Woolloomooloo St and Lane to be changed, with suggested alternative thoroughfare names including Hyde Park, Darley, Rawson and Cathedral. The petition stated the "name Woolloomooloo is unfavourably known through the State and the Commonwealth to the serious injury of those who own property or carry on business therein".

In an editorial, *The Sydney Morning Herald* said it could understand the desire for the name change, given that Woolloomooloo's "narrow little lanes, nestling beneath the cliffs" had become a home for "the criminal, the unfortunate and the very poor ... the old name, with its multitudinous vowels, has become synonymous with evil repute".[5]

---

5   Woolloomooloo, *The Sydney Morning Herald*, 28 January 1905, page 6

In a close decision, the council eventually landed on changing the name of one street from Woolloomooloo to Cathedral, but not before one Alderman warned a move to rename the entire suburb would be next, and another wondered why the council was expunging the name Woolloomooloo from a street but not the suburb.

However, while a potential name change was one thing, there were others who believed total redevelopment was the only answer to this place of "evil repute".

In 1935, architect and publisher Florence Taylor – who at the time had a central role in the State's town planning association – and architect Francis Hood presented a scheme to the City of Sydney titled *An Entrance to the City of Sydney*.

"For the last 20 years, Woolloomooloo has been a problem, it is a blot on the escutcheon of our civilisation," Taylor's report to the council stated. "Respectable poor people, compelled to live in low-lying slum areas where houses should never have been built in the first place, eke out their hopeless existence with the underworld element for company."

"Ramshackle houses, a litter of dilapidated and patched-up fences, rags and clothes lines everywhere ... and this is the city's front door!"[6]

Taylor's bold proposal involved a new east-west street to alleviate traffic congestion, running from Martin Place and across the Domain, along the current Cowper Wharf Rd and then through a Potts Point tunnel to Rushcutters Bay. It also proposed demolishing every existing building and creating a new suburb of streets which followed the hillside contours, and new flat buildings isolated from their neighbours so "air can circulate around them freely".

"The opportunity is ripe to do something in the grand manner and save that part of Sydney ... for all time," said Taylor. "Anything is possible in a place so ready for moulding as is Woolloomooloo Bay. We should not neglect it."

---

6   Woolloomooloo area. Scheme for replanning of, by Mrs Florence M. Taylor, Town Clerk's Correspondence File 3911/35, City of Sydney Council Archives

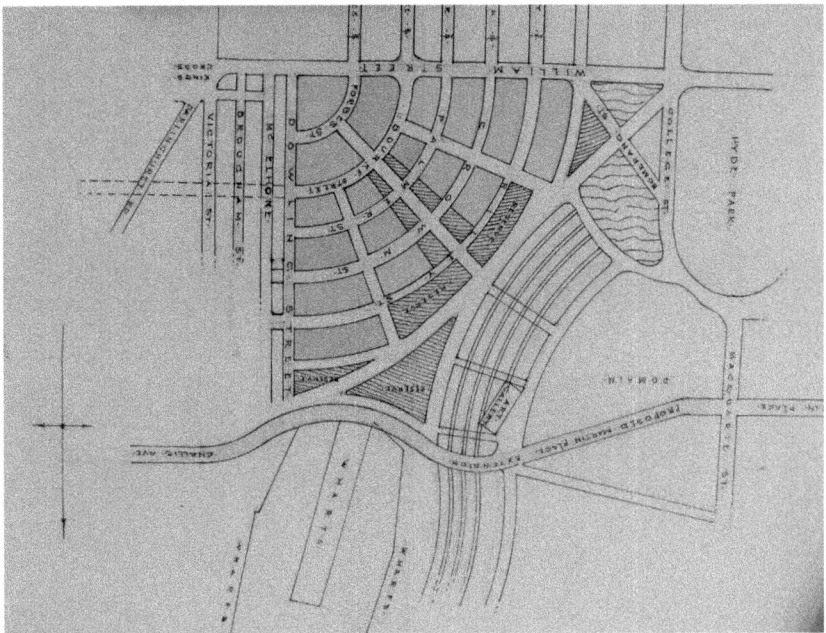

Top: Architect and publisher Florence Taylor's proposed redevelopment of Woolloomooloo

Above: Architect and publisher Florence Taylor's proposed new street layout for Woolloomooloo

A photo of a Woolloomooloo street scene in 1947, taken by Sydney photographer Sam Hood - the picture was captioned "Slum, Woolloomooloo" (Courtesy of Mitchell Library, State Library of NSW)

Not surprisingly, the council blanched at the financial cost of Taylor's extraordinary vision in the middle of the Great Depression.

"Much as the aesthetic and utilitarian interests of the city are its principal considerations, financial exigency compels it to pause, for the time being at any rate, in undertaking new liabilities and obligations," was the reply from town clerk Roy Hendy.

Taylor was not the only high-profile planner proposing to take a wrecking ball to Woolloomooloo. Architect, war hero and City of Sydney Alderman Sir Charles Rosenthal also proposed a scheme.

"The time has arrived when the whole of the Woolloomooloo area should be resumed," *The Sydney Morning Herald* quoted him as saying in 1924.[7] Unlike Taylor, Rosenthal felt as though the site should be

---

7   Woolloomooloo: Site for Public Offices, *The Sydney Morning Herald*, 5 June 1924, page 4

set aside for public offices, including a new town hall, Federal buildings facing Victoria St and State buildings near the Domain.

A third proposal came from John Robert Lee, the State MP for Drummoyne, who argued in 1939 that the entire suburb should be turned into a park and workers' accommodation.

"For a long time I have had in mind that the Government should resume the whole of the low-lying area between William St and the Woolloomooloo wharves, and that this area should be added to the Domain," Mr Lee was quoted as writing. "Under the Government's developmental policy of homes for the working man and the destruction of slums, they could clear this area of a lot of undesirable buildings, and meet the needs of the wharf labourer by building flats similar to Erskineville on the outskirts of the resumed area."[8]

It would be easy to think that the three rejected schemes above were so difficult and fanciful that they would never resurface in the future. But, when it came to Woolloomooloo, Sydney had a deep sense of shame about the urban mess on its front doorstep, and desperately wanted to clean it up. The rejected schemes from the 1920s and 1930s helped build a town planning narrative about what was possible, and therefore laid the groundwork for the future.

A future that required the right politicians, a bull property market and adventurous planners and developers to come together at the same time to transform this much-maligned valley.

---

[8] Woolloomooloo as Park, *The Sydney Morning Herald*, 6 April 1939, page 18

CHAPTER 5

Follow the artists

It was a Saturday night late in September 1960 and painter John Olsen was agitated, disappointed, furious and frustrated. Only six months earlier, Olsen had arrived back in Sydney from a European tour, which included travelling across Spain.

But now the 32-year-old emerging star of Australian art couldn't understand why his new lover didn't want to come to his pokey attic apartment on the fourth floor of a terrace at 109 Victoria St. At the same time, Olsen's marriage was falling apart and he knew divorce was on the cards.

"This small rejection became the final straw," writes Darleen Bungey in a 2014 biography of Olsen.[1] "It must have seemed that too many things in [his lover's] life were more important to her than him. He wasn't accustomed to the feeling.

"His reaction was to find three Masonite panels, prop them up against the wall and paint. He painted all through that night. Recalling the spirit that drove him, he says, 'I felt like a parachutist jumping from an aeroplane. It was just a release, a feeling of defiance'."

The painting, later named *Spanish Encounter*, was painted in a style known as abstract expressionism, which means the viewer can really only guess at its meaning. However, in the painting, it's possible to see the dark earthy colours of Spain, Christian crosses and what seem to

---

1   *John Olsen: An Artist's Life*, HarperCollins, 2014, by Darleen Bungey, page 160

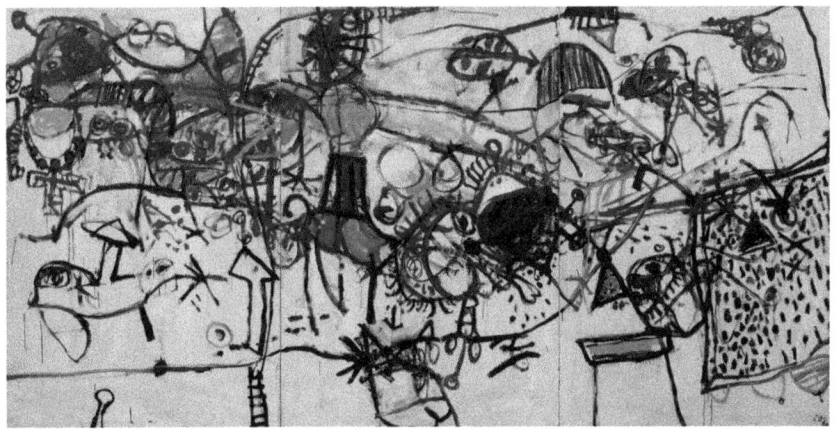

John Olsen (Australia/England/Spain/Portugal 1928-2023), Spanish Encounter, 1960, oil on hardboard, triptych 183 x 366 cm overall, Art Gallery of New South Wales, purchased 1960
(© Art Gallery of New South Wales (NSW), Image © Art Gallery of NSW)

be phallic symbols that yell repressed energy and passion. A ladder and arrow suggest that the lover's visit to the attic was never made. Bungey writes that the painting is a "life surge, an excited rush of passion".[2]

As the dawn approached, Olsen sat back and realised he may have just completed a major work. At the same time, he also reflected that – while the work was impressive – a more immediate problem was that he urgently needed help to move and assemble its three separate panels, so that it could be included in an upcoming exhibition.

He waited until 8am and knocked on the door of William Rose, a fellow abstract painter who lived in the same building. Rose said Olsen told him: "I haven't been to bed all night, give us a cup of coffee … I did a big painting and I think I've got it, could you help me get it down and we'll nail it together".[3] The two men managed to get the still wet boards down the narrow staircase and into Victoria St, then walked them 400m to an art gallery on Macleay St. The artwork then formed part of Olsen's exhibition which started the following Thursday.

---

2   *John Olsen: An Artist's Life*, page 161
3   *John Olsen*, Craftsman House, 1991, by Deborah Hart, page 51

Follow the artists | 35

Above: John Olsen painting in his Victoria St attic in 1963 (Photo: David Beal; Courtesy of Mitchell Library, State Library of NSW). Below: The same attic in 2019 (Photo: Mark Skelsey)

The response to the work was immediate. The Art Gallery of NSW purchased the artwork before the exhibition even opened. Bungey wrote that the critics "spoke with one voice … all found the exhibition distinct and bold, and all agreed that the last-minute addition to the show was the standout".[4] Another biographer, Deborah Hart, said the painting "is widely considered to be a masterpiece both in Olsen's own output and the history of Australian art".[5]

Spanish Encounter would be one of the highlights of Victoria St's brief but important period as the centre of the Kings Cross art colony.

At the time, Victoria St could hardly have been regarded as a romantic or artistic destination. In a book which covers the 1950s and 1960s, former shopkeeper and resident, E. Campbell Bone (known as Cam Bone) documented life in the street.

"Victoria St had had its day," Bone wrote. "It was now a shabby backstreet full of ordinary working-class people struggling to make ends meet.

"If any talent existed behind the solid walls of the old buildings there was no apparent evidence of it. But surely, I thought, not all had lost the urge to do something worthwhile. There had to be some who dreamed. Then again, they could be like me. Stuck with it, the dream I mean.

"Daily we came in contact with petty thieves, alcoholics, wife bashers, prostitutes, homosexuals and smoothed-tongued confidence men. The last mentioned pests, imagining that we, kind motherly ladies, would fall for their hard luck stories and stake them a few free groceries or a couple of packets of cigarettes, almost always went away with a flea in their ear.

"Not all our customers were undesirables. Just like any other suburb there were couples with children from babies to teenagers. They were in crowded rooms and built-in balconies, not always from choice but until

---

4   *John Olsen: An Artist's Life*, page 162
5   *John Olsen*, Craftsman House, page 51

the housing situation eased and they could move to where there was fresh air and plenty of space for the children to play and grow up."[6]

This environment provided the affordable housing needed by struggling artists, close to the vibrant retail and nightlife strip of Darlinghurst Rd. However, the artists also saw beauty and character in the area which others couldn't: the views across the rusty roofs and ramshackle yards of Woolloomooloo and to the city, the colour and movement of passenger and military ships from Woolloomooloo Bay and Garden Island, the stubborn majesty of its tired terrace homes and dappled light flowing through the street's rows of plane trees.

As Australian painter Tim Storrier stated in 2018, in conjunction with an exhibition on an art colony at Sydney's Lavender Bay, "If you go to any city ... find out where the artists are moving, because they always have a good eye for value and beauty".[7]

To be fair, artists had seen beauty in the area for some time.

In 1885, influential Sydney artist and teacher Julian Ashton had painted the Hordern Stairs, which had only been constructed three years earlier. In 1945, Swiss-born figurative painter Sali Herman controversially won the Wynne Prize after painting the McElhone Stairs, which were just around the corner from his flat on Wylde St. He followed this in 1946 with *Autumn in Victoria St*, which features the top of the McElhone Stairs and Charles Elouis' former terrace at 55 Victoria St.

In the mid-to-late 1950s, Gladys Owen twice painted a picturesque row of terraces at 119–139 Victoria St, Darlinghurst, known informally as the Pigeon Terraces, perhaps named so because they look like little bird-houses. Designed by the prolific architect and developer Thomas Rowe, these terraces – with their distinctive triangular dormer windows – have a modest two-storey presence to Victoria St. However, the three-

---

6   Knock Around the Cross, produced in co-operation with City of Sydney Library, 1995, by E. Campbell Bone, pages 101 and 180
7   This a quote in conjunction with Bohemian Sydney: Artists of Lavender Bay, Museum of Sydney exhibition in 2018

Left: Julian Ashton's 1885 painting of the Hordern Stairs (Reproduced with permission of the National Gallery of Australia, Canberra). Right: The same scene today (Photo: Mark Skelsey)

storey rear of the terraces sit in an elevated and dominated position on the Victoria St escarpment, making them impossible to miss when looking east from the Sydney Central Business District (CBD) or up from the Woolloomooloo valley.

The focus by Owen and Herman on so-called 'slum areas' was questioned, if not criticised.

"Mrs Owen does not make a great case for art or for the preservation of 'national' monuments," said *The Sydney Morning Herald*'s review of her 1954 exhibition at David Jones. "Indeed, many of the buildings she paints in watercolour have outlived their usefulness for anyone bar the painter in search of the picturesque."[8]

---

8   Landmarks of Old Sydney, *The Sydney Morning Herald*, 18 October 1954, page 2

In addition to this, when Herman won the Wynne Prize for the McElhone Stairs, the *Bulletin* called the work a "melancholy account of one of metropolitan Sydney's slummiest aspects".[9]

Herman was among the first to embrace Victoria St. In 1953, sick of painting in his dark flat on Wylde St, he set up a studio in 34 Victoria St – a 1900 terrace with grand views out to Woolloomooloo Bay and the CBD skyline.[10] "[Herman's] late wife, Paulette, loved the house and always wanted her husband to buy it," a note in a National Trust file on Victoria St reports. In 1964, the same terrace was purchased as a home by *Art and Australia* editor Mervyn Horton, who renovated the property and then held parties there which often appeared in newspaper social pages.

From the mid-1950s onwards, Victoria St increasingly became home to abstract artists, such as Olsen. In 1954, William Rose – known for his abstract paintings with geometric forms – and his wife Sharn moved into 109 Victoria St. For a period of around six months, Rose worked as a rigger for the Navy Department during the day and painted at night.[11] In her aforementioned book, E. Campbell Bone described Rose as a "half-starved looking artist", who for a brief period took over the running of her shop.[12]

Meanwhile, in 1955, Yugoslav emigrant Stan Rapotec (an abstract painter with focus on religious forms) established a single room studio in a since-demolished home at 44 Victoria St. Soon after, Rapotec took over the entire home and shared it with other artists, including Romanian-born abstract painter Leonard Hessing, art critic and author Robert Hughes, and abstract painter and teacher John Passmore. Rapotec also recalls that he lured famous Australian figurative rural landscape painter Russell Drysdale to the area and that figurative painter

---

9   *Sali Herman*, Collins, 1971, by Daniel Thomas, page 20
10 *Sali Herman*, page 25
11 *The Most Noble Art of Them All, The Select Writings of Laurie Thomas*, University of Queensland Press, 1976, page 160
12 *Knock Around the Cross*, pages 180 and 192

Charles Doutney, who won the 1952 Sulman Prize for his Darlinghurst Rd streetscape, lived in a nearby flat.[13]

However, the dominant abstract artist was Olsen – charismatic, articulate, handsome, and full of cosmopolitan zeal and energy. During 1956, Olsen briefly took over the attic apartment at 109 Victoria St that had previously been occupied by Peter Upward – another abstract painter known for his calligraphic style – who had departed for Melbourne. Olsen then travelled to Europe, before returning for a second stint at the same location in Victoria St in early 1960.[14]

At a time when the Sydney art world was much smaller, and artists were seen as oddities or even outcasts, the Victoria St artists embraced each other. In an interview given in 2011, Olsen said: "It was a real community, we were very close, hung out, ate together, went to pubs and restaurants in Victoria St. Chewed the fat. [Victoria St's] Piccadilly Hotel was one place, and there was a German Restaurant [as well] … it was a lively time".[15]

In her 1992 analysis of the Victoria St art colony for *Art and Australia*, author Christine France noted that "[Victoria St] allowed younger artists to benefit from the experience and advice of older, more established artists such as Drysdale and Passmore … they in turn enjoyed the company and working atmosphere in what can be an isolated and lonely profession. It allowed for a fervent exchange of ideas and enthusiasm".[16]

Importantly, as would soon become clear, the street's setting also provided rich and inspirational fodder for the artists themselves.

In 1956, discussions between the Victoria St artists led to the staging of the exhibition 'Direction 1' at the Sydney CBD's Macquarie Galleries, which introduced abstract art to a stunned Sydney society.

---

13 Sourced from Abstraction in Victoria St, *Art and Australia* Quarterly Journal, Winter 1992, page 470, and interview between James Gleeson and Stanilaus Rapotec, National Library of Australia, 22 October 1979
14 *Abstraction in Victoria St*, page 468
15 John Olsen, Artist, Red Globe Light Liquor Green blog, 2011, by Darian Zam
16 *Abstraction in Victoria St*, page 476

While the show was regarded as a commercial failure, it did announce to the world that not all art needed to be a faithful reflection of the physical environment.

The 'Direction 1' artists were inspired by Victoria St's rare dress circle position overlooking a busy city and teeming harbour, and its location alongside Kings Cross – at the time Sydney's only genuine cosmopolitan precinct. France notes that "the exhibition of abstract works was intended as a statement of change", but furthermore it was largely based on the area around Victoria St. "The physical relationship of the artists' work to Victoria St can be seen in a number of [the exhibited] abstract works," she writes. "For instance, the water's edge, the giant Garden Island cranes and city views are echoed in Olsen's *View of Western World No. 1*, which was based on the giant crane at Woolloomooloo."[17]

Olsen continued to reference Victoria St and its surrounds in his work. In 1960, the same year he painted *Spanish Encounter*, Olsen also delivered his interpretation of the street outside the front of his home in *People Who Live in Victoria St*.

In explaining the piece, Olsen says it was borne from the view that artists no longer needed to limit themselves to painting from a fixed point, and that it was now possible to move around and "inhabit the landscape" in the one work. As such, the painting – prepared in Olsen's attic flat – is an abstract, stylised journey of the artist walking down and admiring his home street.

Olsen helpfully explained in detail what the piece represented.

"I tipple down the stairway – it's morning in Victoria St and even with my good intentions I stop when I arrive at the street," he wrote. "I stop, walk back two paces for the sun is making the most gorgeous green through the plane trees and I find myself rolling with the sky – I am a little stunned by this and walk a little crooked on the footpath.

---

17 *Abstraction in Victoria St*, page 473

"A mongrel dog barks at me and my route becomes quicker. I meet a friend – stop, pace back and forward – and he gets excited and moves his hands a lot – goodbye – shaking hands I must hurry, I want to cross the street – taxis floating past and one stops in front of me and conks me on the mousetrap; where I had in my mind to walk in a straight line, I have to walk around the cab in an angular fashion."[18]

Other paintings by Olsen from the period also called out the local area, including 1963's *Half Past Six at the Fitzroy*, where the drinkers' faces at the famous Woolloomooloo pub can be spotted, along with 1963's *Five Bells*, which embraces Sydney Harbour, and 1964's more abstract *McElhone Steps*.

Speaking of this period, biographer Deborah Hart wrote: "[Olsen] was struck by the brightness of the light, the chaotic activity of street life, the fluxing tides and the voluptuous topography of the harbour connecting with the landforms and people".[19]

While the Victoria St artists felt alive with the excitement, innovation and giddy pace of change, another more conservative artists' group in Melbourne did not share the same view. As such, the Victoria St art colony ended up playing a central role as the Australian art community descended into civil war.

In August 1959, a group of Melbourne artists – headed by the conservative art historian Bernard Smith – published a sensational document known as the *Antipodean Manifesto* in the catalogue accompanying their new exhibition. The artists – who called themselves the Antipodeans – believed in figurative art, which is defined as art which "retains strong references to the real world and particularly to the human figure".[20] These artists had seen how abstract art – which made no commitment to the "real world" – was receiving critical and popular acclaim in New York and London. "The mood and critical attitude of the time was to downgrade [our] type of painting and I can remember

---

18 *John Olsen: An Artist's Life*, page 163
19 *John Olsen*, page 49
20 Sourced from description of figurative art at London's Tate Gallery website

feeling very high-minded with a passionate crusader spirit," one of the Antipodean group members David Boyd later said.[21] The rapid shift towards abstract art in Sydney, as illustrated among the Victoria St artists, and the traditional rivalry between the Sydney and Melbourne, was also a factor behind the document's drafting.[22]

The manifesto sought to vandalise abstract art.

"Today, we believe, like many others, that the existence of painting as an independent art is in danger," the manifesto stated. "Today … action painters, geometric abstractionists, abstract expressionists and their innumerable band of camp followers threaten to benumb the intellect and wit of art with their bland and pretentious mysteries.

"And yet, wherever we look, New York, Paris, London, San Francisco or Sydney, we see young artists dazzled by luxurious pageantry and colour of non-figuration. It has become necessary for us to point out … that the great Tachiste Emperor has no clothes – nor has he a body. He is only a blot – a most colourful, elegant and shapely blot.

"Art is, for the artist, his speech, his way of communication. And the image, the recognisable shape, the meaningful symbol, is the basic unit of his language. Lines, shapes and colours, though they may be beautiful and expressive, are by no means images."[23]

While the statement did not explicitly name the Victoria St abstract artists, they knew they were under attack and needed to respond. Two abstract artists, painter Peter Upward and sculptor Clement Meadmore, defected from Melbourne to Potts Point, and helped the Victoria St group organise an exhibition in Melbourne in August 1961, known as the 'Sydney 9'. The young art critic Robert Hughes was also drafted for the Melbourne trip, to defend the exhibits.

---

21 *A Quiet Revolution: The Rise of Australian Art 1946-1968*, Text Publishing, 1995, by Christopher Heathcote, page 114

22 *Documents that Shaped Australia: Records of a Nation's Heritage*, Murdoch Books, 2010, by John Thompson, page 284

23 *Documents that Shaped Australia: Records of a Nation's Heritage*, pages 285-286

This exhibition had all the hallmarks of an invasion party. According to Robert Hughes, Stan Rapotec hired a helicopter to transport the group from the airport and stepped from the craft carrying an abstract painting, like a general visiting a new battle zone. Later, at a dinner, one of the Melbourne painters challenged Olsen to a fight. "Olsen drew a line on the floor and dared the artist to step across it," Hughes recalls. At the same event, another Melbourne artist reportedly confronted one of the Sydney abstract artists and said they were trying to take "bread from our mouths". The Sydney artists then attempted to drive around Melbourne's suburbs and throw stones at the houses of the Antipodean artists, but instead simply became lost.[24]

The schism did have one very tangible benefit: the resultant publicity helped drive demand for work by a number of the Victoria St artists. By late 1960, the term 'Victoria St Group' was being used to describe the abstract artists who lived in the Kings Cross area.[25] Ironically, soon after, and thanks to the 'arts boom' of the early 1960s, these same artists had the means to move out of Victoria St and purchase homes in more fashionable suburbs. Olsen moved to Paddington and then Watson's Bay, Herman to Avalon and Russell Drysdale to Killcare Heights on the NSW Central Coast.

In interviews years later, the Victoria St artists spoke with reverence about the period.

"It was a fascinating period I believe in, let's call it [the] history of art in Sydney, and that period of early 1960s was quite important, I should say," said Rapotec. "A very lively one, and a lot of jolly good exhibitions went on." In 1970, art critic Laurie Smith wrote "ten years ago ... [Victoria St] was the artistic centre of Sydney ... this has changed as artists have drifted away to other parts and each has gone his own road".[26] Olsen himself said that "Victoria St was the hub of Sydney's art world, what a time it was. We were young and wanted to change

---

24 *A Quiet Revolution*, page 137
25 *Abstraction in Victoria St*, page 473
26 *The Most Noble Art of Them All*, page 105

everything. I painted some of my best pictures there".[27] And Robert Hughes is quoted as saying "everything I know about painting I learned in John Olsen's old Victoria St studio in Kings Cross".[28]

The Victoria St art colony represented a coming of age for Australian art. Thanks to the colony, existing art orthodoxies were challenged and dismissed, and artists turned from being viewed as recluses and misfits to instead being seen as rock stars of Australia's emerging cultural economy of the 1960s.

However, irrespective of the street's influence on Australia's art trajectory, the period also had another critical impact on Sydney's urban planning. While they may have only lived in Victoria St and surrounds for a short period, the artists developed a deep and enduring sense of affection for the area. This was the precinct that had sustained them with affordable housing, provided them with stimulating intellectual discussions in late-night cafes and restaurants, and had inspired their early work with its beauty and eagle's nest location overlooking a dynamic urban and maritime scene. While Victoria St had previously been identified as something approaching a slum, a group of fresh thinkers now celebrated its character and rhythm.

This meant that, when the physical fabric of Victoria St came under attack just some 10 years later, the artists would help lead the alliance to fight for its future.

---

27 *John Olsen*, page 50
28 *John Olsen: An Artist's Life*, cover

Victoria St in 1968 (Photo courtesy of Wilford Peloquin)

PART 2
RIPE FOR REDEVELOPMENT

CHAPTER 6

Business comes first

As far as Pat Morton was concerned, governments needed to be in the business of helping business. Morton's philosophy was influenced by the fact that, at the age of just 14, he joined a company which sold and manufactured motor parts. He would later become secretary, manager and director of the same company.

Given that three of his uncles had been members of parliament (MPs), it was almost inevitable that Morton would pursue a political career alongside his business interests. He was elected to Mosman Council in 1945, before becoming the New South Wales (NSW) MP for Mosman just two years later after he defeated the sitting independent.

In 1955, when he became leader of the Liberal Party and therefore also the State Opposition, Morton made it clear that helping enterprise was his cause. "I intend to approach the government of NSW in the same way as I would approach a business problem. If we sell to the people the philosophy of free enterprise – and I'm sure we can – we will overcome all our problems."[1]

Morton's period in Opposition however did not go as planned, with him losing two elections to the incumbent Labor party. Morton had angered some of his colleagues by extending his business interests, at a time when they wanted him to solely focus on being Opposition Leader

---

1   New State Political Leader Comes of Political Family, *The Sydney Morning Herald*, 21 September 1955, page 2

and winning government. In 1959, he was sacked from his leadership roles and replaced by Robin (later Robert) Askin, the MP for Collaroy and another strong believer in free enterprise.

Using the presidential-style campaign slogan "with Askin you'll get action", Askin and his Liberal and National party coalition finally took control of the NSW Government in 1965, ending the Labor party's 24-year run in power. Askin gave Morton the Local Government and Highways portfolio, which meant the Mosman-based MP now had control of the local council and planning system of Australia's largest State.

It was a critical time for the State's planning and development. Australia and Sydney were in the middle of the long post-war economic boom. During the 1960s in particular, Australia enjoyed ideal economic conditions, including an unemployment rate of under 4 per cent, inflation averaging 2.5 per cent and an average gross domestic product growth of more than 5 per cent.[2] What's more, from around 1950 onwards, the percentage of Australia's jobs in Australia's services industry began to climb, initially at the expense of jobs in the nation's agricultural industry and then manufacturing.[3]

This economic transformation led to a surge in office construction in Sydney's Central Business District (CBD), which was assisted by the decision in 1952 to remove the State's 45m building height cap. The growing army of service industry workers – in areas such as public administration, education and financial services – along with the move towards computers in the workplace, required larger amounts of office space.

From the mid-1950s, new office construction was carried out by redeveloping old warehouses or older office buildings. However, at the time of Morton's appointment, the best sites had already been picked off and there was a looming shortage in new office development sites in the Sydney CBD. This meant that developers were starting to look towards

---

2 Australia's Century Since Federation at a Glance, Australian Treasury, 2019
3 Structural Change in the Australian Economy, Reserve Bank of Australia Bulletin, September Quarter 2010, by Ellis Connolly and Christine Lewis

Aerial view of the Woolloomooloo valley in 1976, looking back to the Sydney CBD (Courtesy City of Sydney Archives)

the residential areas adjoining the CBD.[4] Or as former secretary of the Builders Labourers' Federation (BLF) Joe Owens would put it in the late 1970s: "The CBD of Sydney rapidly became exploited … so [developers] began to look at surrounding areas, which had traditionally been low-income residential areas and some of them very historic".[5]

That meant looking at Woolloomooloo, immediately to the east of the CBD, and The Rocks, which was immediately to the north.

In Sydney's first comprehensive plan scheme, the County of Cumberland plan which was released in 1951, both of these areas had been set aside as 'County Centre' – effectively saying they were potential future extensions of the CBD. In the case of Woolloomooloo, the 'County Centre' boundary incorporated the western side of Victoria St, in a decision which would have major implications for the street later in the 1960s. In the same document, The Rocks and Woolloomooloo had also been nominated as "areas which require immediate redevelopment", in a map focussing on housing age and condition.

---

4   City of Sydney Strategic Plan, City of Sydney Council, 1971, pages 39-40
5   Quotes taken from film documentary Woolloomooloo: A Redevelopment 1969-1977, 1978, directed by Pat Fiske, Denise White and Peter Gailey

While both these areas were indeed historic and working class, during the 1950s and 1960s there was little popular appetite for the preservation of these areas and indeed strong support for Morton's notion that free enterprise – in the form of private property development – should play the key role transforming them. Despite its working-class readership, the *Daily Mirror* was particularly alarmed by the continuing decline in the population of inner-Sydney areas and was a veracious advocate for their redevelopment.

"For some time, the *Daily Mirror* has been stressing the seriousness of the threatened decay in inner-Sydney city areas," a 1959 *Daily Mirror* editorial titled "City Blight" said.[6] "Slums have spread. Dwellings built in the last century continue to be used although they are falling into disrepair. The population of the inner-Sydney districts continues to decline.

"The *Mirror* will continue to press for vigorous and early action to save Sydney from the insidious growth of the blight that kills the heart of all cities unless it is halted."

Some work had already been undertaken to redevelop The Rocks, a precinct in the shadows of the Sydney Harbour Bridge which contained Sydney's most historic buildings and where the government itself was the predominant landowner.

In 1961, the former Labor government had launched an ideas quest, which envisaged the area being redeveloped into predominantly residential uses, supported by shops and offices, but only after the developer had been able to provide alternative accommodation for the existing tenants.[7] In 1963, construction company James Wallace was selected for the redevelopment, with a scheme to demolish all buildings and instead construct four large commercial buildings, a 100-bedroom hotel and 13 residential buildings.

---

6   City Blight, *Daily Mirror*, 18 September 1959, page 6
7   Information sourced from 1961 document issued by NSW Government to invite proposals on The Rocks redevelopment

But as was often the case, the new Liberal-National government saw things differently after coming to power. Askin and Morton broke off negotiations with James Wallace, claiming it had not furnished the necessary financial guarantees, and sent The Rocks redevelopment project back to the drawing board.

Then there was Woolloomooloo.

Woolloomooloo was arguably a more difficult area to plan. Firstly, irrespective of the 'County Centre' zoning, the Labor-dominated City of Sydney Council had always been reluctant to support the concept of commercial and industrial development in the valley, fearing this would antagonise the local residents who represented its voter base.[8] This meant that, over the course of the 1950s and 1960s, no clear plan emerged for the area's future, with schemes supporting increased commercial or industrial development often abandoned or back-tracked.

Secondly, unlike The Rocks, the NSW Government was only one of several large landowners in Woolloomooloo and therefore was in a less dominant position to determine the area's outcome. For instance, the Australian Government owned an entire block of land, including housing, where it proposed to build new stores for the Garden Island navy base. All up, private owners controlled about half of the land, the City of Sydney 40 per cent, and the rest was shared between the State and Australian Governments.

Given the confusion and disunity, the economic conditions and Woolloomooloo's history of attracting grand redevelopment visions, it wasn't surprising that the area attracted a major offshore unsolicited development proposal.

In January 1965, in the final months of Labor's control of the NSW Government, a British company known as Haleybridge announced a proposed $160 million plan to redevelop approximately 30 hectares of Woolloomooloo, including Victoria St. The scheme proposed around 3,000 dwellings, in high density commercial and residential buildings,

---

[8] For a detailed analysis of planning for Woolloomooloo during the 1960s, see the Civic Design Society report "People, Plans and Profits in Woolloomooloo", September 1973

The Haleybridge scheme for Woolloomooloo, 1965

new parklands fronting the Domain, and a neighbourhood shopping centre and school. The Labor government had been aware of this scheme in 1964, before its public release, and in response had decided to set aside the Woolloomooloo area for "comprehensive redevelopment".[9]

However, there was a fatal flaw in the Haleybridge scheme: the company didn't own the land. What's more, in its report to the NSW Government on the scheme, the company said it would need the government's help to compulsorily resume some of the land, and then pass this land on to the company to redevelop.[10]

The residents of Woolloomooloo, so often brow beaten in the past by the 'slum' label, found a voice. Residents and small businesses quite rightly feared being involuntarily turfed out of their own homes so someone else could make a profit, and then being unable to afford moving back into the area. The newly-formed Woolloomooloo Progress Association fired off letters complaining that "we fear that existing homes may be resumed to make way for high-cost buildings out of

---

9   Report on the City of Sydney Planning Scheme as submitted to the minister, State Planning Authority of NSW, 1964

10 Woolloomooloo: A Report on Comprehensive Redevelopment Proposals, Tait, Wilson, Reay and Nathaniel Lichfield, 1964, page 12

reach of most of the people in the area".[11] Some of the residents erected protest signs on their front verandahs – such as "The Rocks, 'Loo, Next It's You" – only to be threatened with fines by the council for alleged illegal development. It appeared as though public participation in planning issues was still a foreign concept for the council.

The Haleybridge scheme remained unresolved at the time of the 1965 State election. As with The Rocks redevelopment, when the Liberal and National parties came to power in this election and looked at the British scheme, they saw things differently.

In September 1966, the NSW Government told Haleybridge it wouldn't agree to such a scheme unless it had been put out to public tender. For a conservative-led government, with a strong belief in the rights of individual property owners, the thought of allowing a private company to forcibly acquire another person's land, and then profit from this, was too much to bear. Haleybridge's grand unsolicited proposal was dead.

The decision had some significant ramifications. Firstly, the failure of the British scheme – and the ongoing 'comprehensive redevelopment' rezoning – seemed to indicate it might finally be time to create a government-backed plan for the area. Secondly, it put Morton – the champion of free enterprise – in the position of being able to plan Woolloomooloo from scratch. And thirdly, it meant a view now emerged within the government that the planning system should do everything possible to encourage property developers to redevelop large sections of the area, meaning it would be easier for these developers to purchase land. This was seen as a more palatable option than forced acquisitions.

For the previous half century, Woolloomooloo and Victoria St had been undesirable and decaying locales. Now, the area's residents were about to experience the pain and tumult which came from a government inviting big business into the area.

---

11 Watch on the Loo, Residents of Woolloomooloo Group, 1983, by Honora Wilkinson

CHAPTER 7

"Fairylands and Hollywood"

In late 1968, Juanita Nielsen received a $50,000 gift from her father and found herself in the unexpected position of being able to buy a house. There was no question about where she would move.

"I first lived here in Victoria St when I was a kid, during the Second World War, and I'd come from the country, and it was fairylands and Hollywood and everything that means anything to a kid," Nielsen told the ABC during an interview in 1974. "There were literally tens of thousands, perhaps hundreds of thousands of people; it was reputed to be the most densely settled white area in the world, there were always people at every hour of the day and night.

"You could get a meal 24-hours a day; it was full of coffee shops, places where people would meet, and everybody knew everybody else which was remarkable in such a large population.

"I've come back to the Cross over the years; I was living abroad for a very long time, and when I came back to settle in Australia there was no question I would live anywhere else and I bought the house which I am now living in, in Victoria St."[1]

Nielsen was a distinctive figure around Kings Cross. She was 1.74m tall – five foot and seven inches in the old parlance – and would accentuate her already impressive natural height by wearing towering

---

1   Australian Broadcasting Commission interview with journalist Juanita Nielsen, 1974, item ID 13473524, National Archives of Australia

beehive hairpieces long after these were fashionable. Her complexion was fair, some would say like a 'china doll', and she wore expensive clothes with colours and combinations which would stand out from the crowd. To top it off, Nielsen spoke with a soft but firm and cultured accent which was a sign of both her privileged Sydney North Shore upbringing and her confident outlook on life.

The house at 202 Victoria St was tiny, just 3.5m wide and 18m long. It was also just 200m from the original 'Kings Cross' intersection of Victoria St, Darlinghurst Rd and William St – a place which in the 1960s had developed into a riot of neon advertising signs, late-night restaurants and strip shows, and a constant buzz of pedestrians and cars. Nielsen renovated the terrace to her own style, including installing a

Nielsen lived on the doorstop of the original 'Kings Cross', photographed here with its riot of neon advertising signs in 1970 (Source: National Archives of Australia)

bar and church pew in the front room, and Spanish ceramic tiles in the small rear courtyard.

Nielsen had received the $50,000 gift from her father Neil Smith as something of a peace offering, after a difficult time within the family over the future of the Mark Foy's retail empire. Smith and Nielsen's aunts Tibby and Joan had a 14 per cent stake in the Foy's empire, which dated back to 1909. The company's flagship Piazza store covered most of one city block with frontages to Liverpool, Castlereagh and Elizabeth Sts, in the southern section of the Sydney Central Business District. However, by the late 1960s, this store was experiencing difficult trading conditions and the company had received a takeover offer.

Nielsen opposed the offer, fearing what it would mean for the company's employees who had worked there for up to 50 years, and mounted a resistance movement trying to rally smaller shareholders against the takeover proposal. At the time, Nielsen was working at the main Piazza store in its trendy 'Gear Box' boutique, after convincing management it needed to target the teenage market.

Nielsen's campaign was ultimately unsuccessful, with the takeover approved after her father decided to sell his crucial shareholding. Despite the corporate shenanigans, the Piazza store only traded under the Mark Foy's name until 1980, before it closed down for good in 1982. The building is now used as a major courthouse.

Soon after the takeover matter was settled, Nielsen bumped into photographer David Farrell as they were going into the office of the *Mosman Daily*, on Sydney's Lower North Shore. The two had met briefly some time earlier, when Farrell had taken photos of Nielsen modelling clothes from the 'Gear Box' boutique.

Nielsen told Farrell she'd left Mark Foy's to become the owner of a small Kings Cross newspaper called *NOW*, that she was producing out of her Victoria St terrace. Nielsen asked if Farrell wanted to take photos for *NOW* and he accepted. Soon after, the two were not just workmates but also lovers, with Victoria St the centre of their lives.

"We were making money, we were having a ball, were in love, we'd been around Europe, we drove around Australia for umpteen months

Juanita Nielsen on the 'Nowmobile' outside 202 Victoria St

and had a fantastic time," Farrell said.[2] "The paper was not making billions, but it was in profit, and [Juanita] did the writing and I did the photographs and layout."

In a sign of the carefree nature of the times, Nielsen purchased a cut-price second-hand car and branded it as the 'Nowmobile' for a Sydney festival. "We had it painted up, she stood on top and waved, I

---

2   From interview with author

Nielsen walking her cat, Charlie, down Victoria St, for a 1971 edition of NOW

think we got rid of it after that … it was pretty useless," Farrell recalled with a laugh.

The two also regularly went out around Kings Cross and surrounds, as part of paid reviews. At the time, all editorial in *NOW* was advertiser funded. Nielsen also regularly appeared in photos, including to model clothes for advertisers. "The Cross at that time was made up of a lot of the old denizens, people who lived there for years, and the arty farty people who met in the coffee shops, who talked about philosophy in the middle of the night," Farrell recalled.

"We liked the atmosphere and it was fairly cheap; there were ordinary people around who had an interesting focus on life. We liked all that, it was people being themselves. You could go out at 2am and they would be there by candlelight and discussing poetry. You had a few strip clubs but not that huge.

"As for Victoria St, it was like a gracious lady that had seen better times, but still wore the lace very well. A bit like someone you've met and you can see she has had good times, and behaved perfectly, but doesn't have the bucks she used to have, but she still had class about her. The street's plane trees were critical, we loved the plane trees."

Whether they realised it or not, Nielsen and Farrell were part of the growing number of homebuyers who were looking at the inner-Sydney area in a new light. These buyers saw inner Sydney as more than just a place for affordable housing, but also an attractive urban lifestyle with easy access to transport and employment.

What Nielsen and Farrell didn't understand however was that, at the time they were embracing each other and the Kings Cross and Victoria St lifestyle in 1968 and 1969, forces were at work to take all of this from them. In fact, as its profits began to sag in the mid-1960s, Mark Foy's had decided to rent out the fourth floor of its Piazza building to the New South Wales Government's chief town planning agency, the State Planning Authority. In the same building where Nielsen had worked and fought to save the company, planners were at work to destroy everything she and Farrell cherished.

CHAPTER 8
The planner who was "not fond of research"

Despite having a surname with Czech origins, Peter Kacirek was described by a colleague as being "thoroughly English in every way".[1] Kacirek was born in Salisbury – a cathedral city in the south of England – and after studying civic design, had risen up the ranks to become deputy chief planner for the United Kingdom's Ministry of Town and Country Planning.

However, at the age of 50 and after a long career in the English town planning bureaucracy, Kacirek was looking for a change. In September 1964, the tall, well-dressed Englishman wrote to State Planning Authority (SPA) chairman Nigel Ashton, stating that he was looking at bringing his wife and family out to Australia. He said this was "mainly for the summer climate, but partly because the idea of being involved in planning and development work in a rapidly growing country intrigued [him]".[2] Kacirek and Ashton's mutual connection was Nathaniel Lichfield, the English town planner behind the ill-fated Haleybridge scheme for Woolloomooloo.

Ashton jumped at the opportunity, offering Kacirek a role as a special planner. The United Kingdom was regarded as the birthplace of

---

1   From letter from English town planner Nathaniel Lichfield to State Planning Authority chairman Nigel Ashton, 15 October 1964, in Nigel Ashton papers in State Library of NSW
2   Letter from Kacirek to Ashton, 7 September 1964, in Nigel Ashton papers

the modern town planning profession, therefore having such a senior British planner ready to move to Australia was very exciting. "It is unlikely that the SPA will receive an application from employment by anyone with a greater experience in planning in the broad sense," Ashton said in a minute to the authority's board.

However, as part of the referee reports collected to accompany the recruitment, there were some red flags. While saying he would be a "first class officer" in the SPA, Lichfield opined that Kacirek "is not particularly fond of research and tends to be somewhat tedious in his verbal and written communication". Yet despite this, Lichfield had a "supreme confidence in [Kacirek's] abilities". It was a warning sign that perhaps should have been heeded.

Meanwhile an academic, who was also interviewed as part of Kacirek's recruitment process, stated that he was "very puzzled as to why [Kacirek] should have given up a very senior and important post in the United Kingdom". The same academic stated that Kacirek was a "steady and reliable person" who had a "sound knowledge of planning".

Nevertheless, Kacirek and his family did relocate to Australia and, after some career movements, the Englishman was appointed to the position of Deputy Chief Planner at the SPA in mid-1966, starting the role in early 1967. This meant he was in the box seat when it came to planning the new Woolloomooloo.

CHAPTER 9
All the pain and no gain for Woolloomooloo

"With Askin you'll get action". So often, political slogans are meaningless and quickly forgotten after the election. But in the case of the Askin Government, it stayed true to its word, at least in the case of inner Sydney. It was just the case that not everyone agreed it was the sort of "action" that governments should be undertaking, and it seemed like the residents of Woolloomooloo and Kings Cross would bear the brunt.

For more than a hundred years, a railway had been proposed to connect the Sydney Central Business District (CBD) with its eastern suburbs. Funding had been announced in 1915, 1927 and 1928, but there hadn't been any actual construction. Actual tunnelling commenced in 1951, only to be shut down a year later. Media stories referred to the project being a perpetual "mirage".[1] Now the Askin Government was going to deliver this project when its predecessors had failed to do so. In March 1967, it announced that construction would resume and the railway would be operational within 10 years, with new stations at Martin Place and at Victoria St, Kings Cross (just a few metres from the home Nielsen would purchase the following year).[2]

---

1 The Mirage of the E.S.R., *The Sydney Morning Herald*, 1 October 1960, by Bruce Davis, page 16
2 E. Suburbs Line to Take in Bondi Junction, *The Sydney Morning Herald*, 1 March 1967, by John O'Hara, page 1

Woolloomooloo would experience much of the pain from the project, but none of the gain. In early 1968, demolition of the first of 100 homes began in the suburb – most of them old terrace houses – to clear space for the footings of a sweeping 425m long viaduct sitting up to 10m off the ground. Aerial photos gave the impression that a

Woolloomooloo viaduct under construction in the 1970s (Courtesy of City of Sydney archives)

The construction of the Woolloomooloo viaduct cut the suburb in half like a "tornado"

tornado had descended on the suburb, clearing all homes in its path. Not only would the viaduct divide the suburb, be visually obtrusive and create noise, there wouldn't even be a Woolloomooloo station. Trains would merely sail across the top of the suburb, between the Martin Place and Kings Cross stations.

Another "mirage" project was the Kings Cross road tunnel. While the elevated intersection of Victoria, Darlinghurst and William Sts may have been an exciting riot of neon lights and activity after dark, it had also long been considered a traffic nightmare as it had to carry an intolerable load of vehicles moving between the Sydney CBD and eastern suburbs. However, like the Eastern Suburbs Railway, for decades no-one had been able to decide on, or fund, the required tunnel to get traffic off the streets. In 1941, the New South Wales (NSW) Government approved a tunnel running deep under the Kings Cross hill, which would have had the handy wartime advantage of also doubling as an air raid shelter. However, in times of wartime austerity, the government was denied the necessary loan approvals to make the project happen.

The Askin Government, however, solved the problem with the sort of effective but brutal solution which had become its trademark. In February 1969, Pat Morton – in charge of the Local Government and Highways portfolio – announced a shallow 240m long tunnel plan that would require the resumption of 119 properties, housing around 600 tenants. Acquisition notices would be issued within the coming weeks, with affordable homes right at the very centre of Kings Cross being cleared out. Ever the pro-business politician, Morton also managed to design the tunnel so it would incorporate "complementary development" on its roof, in the form of high-rise buildings. The Labor Opposition, and around 200 residents who marched on Parliament in late February, said they favoured a deeper tunnel which wouldn't involve resumptions. They were ignored and the mass demolition soon began.[3]

Together with the construction of the Kingsgate tower development, the tunnel's construction meant the top of William St was transformed, virtually overnight, from an exciting buzz of neon signs, historic shop facades and traffic chaos into an orderly and bland tunnel opening, high-rise tower and single fluorescent Coca-Cola sign.

---

3   Cross Marchers Miss Morton, *The Sydney Morning Herald*, 26 February 1969, by David Wyatt, page 5

AREAS DEMOLISHED FOR KINGS CROSS ROAD TUNNEL AND KINGSGATE TOWER DEVELOPMENT

Harvard Flats on Kings Cross Rd

Terrace in Craigend St

Advertising signs and buildings on Victoria / Darlinghurst St

Artist's impression of development on top of the Kings Cross road tunnel at the time its construction was announced (Image sourced from City of Sydney Council Town Clerk's Correspondence File 1580/64)

70 | Ripe for redevelopment

However, the government's most contentious move came in September 1967, when Morton introduced legislation to sack the elected City of Sydney Aldermen and replace them with appointed Commissioners, while at the same time reducing the size of the council to make it more likely to appoint a pro-business political party.

In the second reading speech was worded like a political hatchet job, Morton said the council should be dismissed and restructured because it had failed to deliver major capital works, had a bloated and expensive bureaucracy, and wasn't allowing some Aldermen from minority parties to sit on external committees. He also accused the council of allowing central Sydney to stagnate over a period of 20 years. "I do seriously question whether [the council area's] advancement has been in any way what it should have been in this miraculous era of progress," he stated.[4] Harold Coates, the NSW Local Government Association president and independent State MP, supported the bill as he said it would allow the redevelopment of inner-Sydney areas. "I believe Labor in the city council has a vested interest in maintaining, for political purposes, the depressed residential areas surrounding the city proper," he said.[5]

Irrespective of whether there was merit in sacking the council, Morton had engineered an outcome where inner-Sydney residents were now left without any elected representatives to fight for their cause, at a time when their area was facing upheaval due to major infrastructure projects. The three appointed Commissioners were Vernon Treatt, a former State Liberal leader, John Shaw, a former Commissioner for Main Roads, and William Pettingell, managing director of the Australian Gas Light Company.

They were an odd bunch. In an interview for a book published in 1992, former council deputy chief building surveyor Frank Hanson noted that, in his opinion, Treatt was so old that "if he wasn't senile, he was approaching that stage", Pettingell had "taken the appointment

---

4   NSW Legislative Assembly Hansard, 19 September 1967, page 1339
5   M.L.A. Explains Why He Favours Changes, *The Sydney Morning Herald*, 22 September 1967, by John O'Hara, page 1

under duress" and had a "minimum of time" and Shaw was "reputed to be a difficult person".[6] For the same book, chief council planner John Doran went further, saying that Shaw "was what would be called in the old days a martinet" – in other words "a person who demands complete obedience; a strict disciplinarian".[7]

Just how much of a "martinet" became clear very early on, when Shaw banned council employees from using the front steps and door of Sydney's Town Hall to access their workplace. This decision was apparently taken because some junior staff had committed the previously unknown and unspeakable offence of walking up the front steps while eating "dribbly" pies.[8] He then went on to ban staff from having tea breaks at their desks, forcing them to sneak into cupboards and lockers to enjoy a sip and biscuit.[9]

The three Commissioners then illustrated their commitment to secrecy by banning the media from attending and hearing their deliberations at committee meetings (the elected council had previously allowed this). At their first meeting, which lasted just three minutes, the Commissioners then adopted the decisions of these meetings without discussion, and even unsuccessfully tried to ban photographers from attending. Short meetings would be a hallmark of the trio during their two-year reign. "If you got there after the bell stopped reverberating you missed the meeting, because that's about how long it took," Doran later recalled. "They'd ring the bell, adopt a prayer and close the meeting and walk out. Anything over thirty seconds was a long meeting."[10]

The most critical decision, however, came in March 1968, when Treatt announced to the media that a joint committee would be formed with the State Planning Authority (SPA) to "deal with redevelopment"

---

6   *Planning Sydney*, published by City of Sydney Council, Paul Ashton, 1992, page 100
7   *Planning Sydney*, page 80
8   Pie-eaters Must Use Side Door, *The Sydney Morning Herald*, 22 November 1967, page 1
9   Running Things to a T, *The Sydney Morning Herald*, 23 November 1967, page 9
10 *Planning Sydney*, page 80

in Woolloomooloo.[11] Initial details were scarce, but a letter to Treatt from the SPA's chairman Nigel Ashton from February shows it had been agreed the two bodies would work together to develop a "detailed plan of development" for Woolloomooloo.[12]

Morton, of course, was the force behind the plan. In July 1967, just before he sacked the council, Morton travelled around the city council area with SPA deputy chairman John Wickham and Kacirek, to examine contentious sites. One site included 'Victoria St, Woolloomooloo area', to which Wickham noted that "the Minister asked that the Authority press on with the completion of a scheme for redevelopment in the Woolloomooloo area".[13]

In the space of around 18 months, between mid-1967 and early 1969, everything had changed for the residents of Woolloomooloo and Victoria St. During this period, this affordable backwater had lost its local elected representatives, was in the process of losing hundreds of homes for transport projects and was about to lose many more for a redevelopment scheme ushered in by unelected Commissioners and a pro-business Minister.

---

11 Bid to Make New Buildings Blend into the City, *The Sydney Morning Herald*, 13 March 1968, page 16
12 Letter from State Planning Authority chair Nigel Ashton to City Chief Commissioner Vernon Treatt, 8 February 1968
13 Inspection of sites regarding which a number of objections to the City of Sydney planning scheme were lodged, internal memo by State Planning Authority Deputy Chairman John Wickham, 10 July 1967

CHAPTER 10
A suburb "ripe" for change and development

After years of campaigning for the redevelopment of inner-Sydney areas, the *Daily Mirror* couldn't contain itself. It was August 1969 and the City of Sydney Council, along with the New South Wales (NSW) Government, had released a plan to transform the Woolloomooloo area. The plan would see the area demolished and redeveloped in its entirety, with office and residential towers to be constructed for around 35,000 workers and 9,000–10,000 residents. In fact, once this ambitious redevelopment was complete, only the historic hillside sandstone staircases, "various" cast iron fences and bollards, lamp posts, "a range of" local house decorations, and commemorative plaques and stones would be left to remind people of the 'old Woolloomooloo'.[1]

"It's our city … imagine catching the 5.20 copter home," said the *Daily Mirror's* front page headline. The story showed an artist's impression of the Woolloomooloo plan but then went on to fantasise about what life would be like when the plan came to reality.

"The high-rise hotels, apartment and office blocks will claw at the clouds," the story said. "Helicopters might flutter overhead, carrying a handful of wealthy commuters. Peak-hour monorails will speed passengers along 10 feet off the ground."

---

1   Woolloomooloo Redevelopment Study, undertaken for City of Sydney Council by State Planning Authority, June 1969, page 8

Daily Mirror front page, 20 August 1969

The story even predicted what sort of clothes people would wear in the future Woolloomooloo, with quotes from fashion personality Maggie Tabberer who channelled the annual Rio Carnival and predicted that women in the year 2000 would wear form-fitting clothes, incredible head gear and bright make-up and body paint.

The resourcing of the plan had started just 16 months earlier, at the first meeting of the joint steering committee. Peter Kacirek was the officer in charge of leading the plan's development, while the State Planning Authority's (SPA) chair Nigel Ashton and the new City Commissioner John Shaw were the other leading figures.

In later years, bureaucrats and lawyers would pore over these meeting minutes and the accompanying Woolloomooloo file, trying to understand what went wrong with the development plan. Certainly, the available records in the council and NSW archives offer up some intriguing hints as to how the calamity unfolded.

For starters, there was the issue of how long it would take to produce the plan. There seemed to be an urgency to get the plan complete, with Ashton saying "we should proceed on the basis of pushing it forward as fast as we can", which he estimated would be six months.[2] It's possible the rush was influenced by the fact that the Commissioners would only be in power for a limited period before elections for Aldermen would again be held, and Ashton and his Minister wanted the plan finished prior to then.

Then there was the question as to whether expert consultants were needed. Despite the complex task involved in redeveloping an entire suburb, Kacirek – whose job referee had said he was "not fond of research" – announced that "at this particular stage I do not myself see any question arising of outside consultants". Another SPA staff member suggested that at least a traffic or retail consultant be hired, but no-one seemed to respond to the idea. The plan for Woolloomooloo was to be developed without expert assistance.

There was also the matter of what consultation was required. As word got around about the committee's work, it was inundated with requests from property owners, real estate agents, prospective property owners and developers who wanted to attend its meetings to push their projects. Kacirek wrote a memo to the committee members, stating that it might be a good idea to meet with these people, to "assist public relations" and "in order to enable them to feel satisfied that the authorities concerned … have been prepared to take note of views".[3]

---

2 Detailed minutes of first meeting of Woolloomooloo Steering Committee, 11 April 1968, page 3

3 Deputy Chief Planner's Report, Consultation with Land Owners and Developers, presented to Woolloomooloo Steering Committee, 23 July 1968

Meeting with developers, who were seeking support for their plans, became a regular part of the committee's and project team's work.

There were several problems with this approach.

One problem was that, in talking to developers, the NSW Government planners went way beyond listening to their views, or giving preliminary advice, and in fact started becoming a cheer squad for their plans or encouraged them to expand their ideas.

In a March 1969 memo to his chair Ashton, Kacirek said he had met a major international developer earlier in the year and "encouraged him to think seriously about development in the Woolloomooloo area in a fairly big way". "It is very heartening to see now that the [developer] is prepared to spend up to $45 million on land and a further $100 million on redevelopment works in the Woolloomooloo area, provided there is a reasonable assurance that an adequate start can be made on redevelopment within a reasonable period of time," he wrote. Meanwhile, in May 1969, Ashton met with Australian developer Mainline and told the developer a site it was looking at was "a good site, that the Authority was looking at it as one which should be developed comprehensively". Ashton then passed on the likely development yield for the site.

Earlier, in January 1968, a Sydney developer had met with Kacirek and stated that it was planning to establish a consortium with American companies and then build a "Hong Kong-style" hotel and shopping centre tower in Woolloomooloo for international tourists, linked by a privately-funded train line spur to the airport in Mascot. Apartments were to be built around the tower to provide a "visually protective barrier" between the tower and the existing "sub-standard" accommodation in the basin. Kacirek said the development proposal was "similar in many respects … to the Authority's own proposals".[4]

These discussions were in turn feeding a land speculation boom in the area, before the plan had even been released. In May 1969, the *Sun-*

---

4   Woolloomooloo Redevelopment, State Planning Authority minute paper, dated 10 January 1968

Herald reported that "wealthy speculators, anticipating that the new scheme will permit high-rise development, have already moved into Woolloomooloo, sending property values beyond imagination". The paper reported that three terraces which had sold for $21,000 the year before were now on the market for $125,000.[5]

An additional and even more serious problem was that, while the SPA representatives were stoking a development frenzy, they were not adequately consulting with the government organisations responsible for delivering the services for these proposed new developments. As was later confirmed in a 1981 NSW Supreme Court ruling, the Department of Main Roads and Commissioner of Railways were not consulted about the proposed level of development in the valley, or asked whether they could realistically provide the road and railway network needed to transport the tens of thousands of additional people who'd be coming in and out of the area each day.

The decision to not adequately consult these two authorities is all the more incredible given Kacirek and his team were given multiple internal warnings that they were on the wrong path on this issue. In November 1968, the SPA's transport expert John Caldwell raised concerns that Woolloomooloo had very poor road and railway access, and that this would need to be improved if the area was to be redeveloped. "An examination of the public transport facilities indicates that at the present time this area is not particularly accessible, except from the harbourside suburbs," Caldwell warned.[6] In February 1969, Caldwell wrote directly to Kacirek and argued in favour of significant transport upgrades. "Having regard to the limitations of the present transport arrangements, the proposed Eastern Suburbs Railway will play a vital role in providing improved access to Woolloomooloo. In order to get the maximum benefit from the railway, provision should be made [for a station at Woolloomooloo]. Ideally the entrances and exits should be

---

5   Rush for Land in City Area: Prices Rocket, *Sun-Herald*, by Adrian McGregor, page 23
6   Sydney Region Outline Plan: Public Transport to Woolloomooloo, memo from John Caldwell, 20 November 1968

closely integrated with the planned redevelopment so that the station becomes the focal point of passenger movement in the area."

Caldwell's advice was not heeded.

In May 1969, without any certainty about whether a railway station would be provided at Woolloomooloo, the steering committee pressed the button on the crucial issue of development density controls. Also known as floor space ratios, these controls allow developers to build a certain amount of building floor space, depending on how much land they control. For instance, if the ratio was 1:1, it would mean the developer could build a single storey across the entire site, or two storeys on half of the site.

What's more, the density limits were organised so that the greater the land area controlled by the developer, the larger the floor space ratio, therefore increasing the likelihood that the maximum development yield could be achieved. The maximum floor space ratio approved was 10:1, or 12:1 with the Minister's support.

This policy approach was designed to make it easier for developers to acquire land, by putting them at a distinct advantage over owners of smaller land parcels who could not access these incentives. This was also the SPA's attempt to avoid the need for government land resumptions, which had been such a problem with the Haleybridge scheme announced in 1965. At the same time, however, the approach created an in-built incentive for developers to try to assemble huge commercial office tower precincts, which was of significant concern when the transport problem had not been solved.

This floor space ratio was accompanied by a vague and high-level analysis of the types of development which would be supported within the different parts of Woolloomooloo.

For instance, in Victoria St and Kings Cross, the 19th-century terraces which overlooked Woolloomooloo in the northern part of Victoria St were set aside for significant residential redevelopment, with the same developer incentives in place as in the valley below to encourage site amalgamation. There were also no requirements to preserve these terraces in any redevelopment applications. This was surprising, given that in July 1968 Kacirek had commented in an internal memo that this may have been advisable.[7] This decision would also effectively split Victoria St in two, with the western side now earmarked for soaring skyscraper redevelopment, while on the eastern side the existing low-scale terraces would be likely to remain in place due to far lower building height controls.

Meanwhile, as Juanita Nielsen would soon discover, the southern end of Victoria St was also a new development hotspot. Towers were proposed on both sides of Victoria St over the top of the future Kings Cross station, linked by a wide above-ground pedestrian and shopping plaza which would effectively plunge part of the street into permanent shade. A tower was also proposed over the top of the Kings Cross road tunnel.

Down in Woolloomooloo Bay, the 1915 finger wharf – the largest timber-piled wharf in the world – was earmarked for demolition, to be replaced by a new ocean passenger terminal with commercial and residential space and "substantial carparking facilities" set against the north-eastern corner of the bay.

The overall impact was that this sleepy valley of terrace homes, factories, corner shops and pubs was being tagged for similar density levels which could be found in the skyscraper-packed Sydney Central Business District just to the west.

The plan was now complete. Ashton wrote a chair's minute to his board, recommending the plan's report be forwarded to the city council. "The study is the largest and most complex urban renewal study so far undertaken in Australia to my knowledge," he wrote. "[Woolloomooloo's] strategic position immediately adjacent to the heart of the city offers the opportunity to integrate the presently separated business and entertainment areas of the metropolitan area." Ashton said the Woolloomooloo area had a "ripeness" for "change and development" and "there is now a very considerable interest on the part of developers, and a real prospect of early and substantial action".

---

7   Deputy Chief Planner's report for Woolloomooloo Steering Committee, 26 July 1968

"Ripe for redevelopment": View of the Woolloomooloo valley in 1970 (Photo courtesy of Wilford Peloquin)

While the plan's key policy approach was now resolved, there were still a few late surprises in store as part of its actual release.

One of these surprises related to who should take credit for the plan. The plan's steering committee had been chaired by the SPA's Ashton and the plan itself had clearly been developed by the Ashton's planning staff led by Kacirek, with input from the council. Now, with the plan's release just weeks away, Morton was pressuring his bureaucracy to distance itself from the document.

Ashton and his deputy chair John Wickham were sent down to Sydney Town Hall to ask the council for payment for preparing the plan. A memo by Ashton said this move was designed to show that the SPA was acting as a consultant for the council and therefore "establish clearly, should the matter be raised, that the scheme for Woolloomooloo was not the Authority's scheme but is the scheme prepared for the city council".[8] While Chief Commissioner Treatt expressed surprise at this

---

8   Woolloomooloo Study, memo by State Planning Authority Chair Nigel Ashton, 9 July 1969

request, saying the issue of payment had not been raised before, the city's ratepayers ultimately coughed up $25,000 for the plan.

At the same time, again because of pressure from Morton, the exhibition material needed to be delayed and re-printed to state that "the study is prepared on behalf of the City of Sydney by the professional planning organisation of the SPA" and the "SPA as such has not considered the merits of the proposal".

This was clearly an example of further political shenanigans by Morton. With the reign of the Commissioners due to come to an end and council elections scheduled for late September 1969, Morton was desperately trying to keep the Askin Government's name out of the election debate by creating the deliberately misleading impression that the City Commissioners had been the force behind the plan, and the SPA had a technical advisory role only.[9] Morton's intervention, however, now meant the supreme town planning body in the State – which ordinarily is responsible for reviewing the work of the council – was being presented as a technical consultant to the council. It was a very odd state of affairs and would end up causing considerable confusion as to who was ultimately responsible for the plan's implementation.

The more serious issue, however, related to public consultation once the plan was released. In his chairman's minute in May 1969, Ashton had flagged a potential three-month exhibition period, during which people could make submissions on a draft plan. He suggested that Morton would then consider these submissions, before approving the plan and incorporating it into the City of Sydney planning scheme.

However, when Treatt presented a minute to the council meeting on 11 August 1969, he recommended that people be given just two weeks to examine what had been described as the most complex urban renewal study in the nation's history. He also recommended that the

---

9   Peter Kacirek refers to this in a memo to State Planning Authority Deputy Chairman John Wickham, titled "Woolloomooloo Redevelopment Plan" on August 20, 1969, when he states "about this time, the question of elections for the new city council arose ... the Minister felt it then desirable that the State Planning Authority as such should not be directly involved".

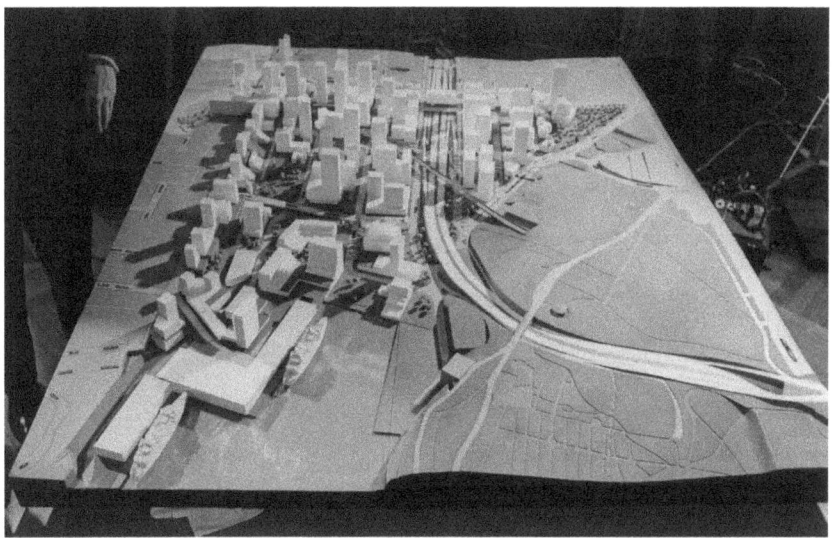

The model unveiled during the 1969 Woolloomooloo redevelopment plan "exhibition" (Source: City of Sydney Archives)

council "accept [the plan] as its plan for the redevelopment of the Woolloomooloo area", which seemed to indicate that if anyone did bother to make a submission, it wouldn't even be considered.

This recommendation also appeared to be designed to ensure the plan – which from the start had been something of a rush job – would be finalised before the council election. Kacirek, however, thought the two-week exhibition period was far too short, and would get an "unfavourable reaction". The council extended it by a further two weeks, with the publicly stated reason being "intense public interest".[10]

Following political games, rushed and sloppy research, ignored warnings and inadequate or one-sided consultation, the Woolloomooloo plan was now out in the world.

---

10   Exhibition of Plan Extended, *The Sydney Morning Herald*, 29 August 1969, by Ian Frykberg, page 10

CHAPTER 11
"The rest of the development industry has always followed me"

Risk-taker. Entrepreneur. Opportunist. Even visionary. During his long and colourful life, Sid Londish attracted many labels.

In 1924, Londish was born in the then multicultural melting pot of Tientsin in China, to an English-Australian father who was trying to build a typewriter manufacturing factory and a Russian mother who had escaped the Bolshevik Revolution. His parents brought him to Australia when he was just 11 months old. During his childhood, Londish briefly lived in Woolloomooloo, in a flat above an engineering business that his father Joseph operated.

In an interview for this book, Londish said he had jumped into the real estate game after changes to purchaser depreciation allowances by former Prime Minister Robert Menzies had rendered the family's engineering businesses unprofitable.

"We're out of business. Everybody [was] cancelling orders," Londish recalls. "My father said to me, 'Have you realised what we've done?' I said, 'Yes, we've lost everything.' He said, 'No, that's not what I'm talking about … the factory has saved us, so why aren't we building factories?' And that started me in real estate."[1]

---

1   Interview with author

Londish recalls subdividing land to build 27 factories in Botany. Then, in the late 1950s and 1960s as Australia continued its car-dependent suburban growth, Londish was one of the first to recognise the huge potential of drive-in shopping centres.

He built new low-scale shopping centres in Sydney suburbs including St Ives, Rockdale, Hillsdale, Miranda and Hornsby.

"The rest of the developing industry has always followed me," Londish said. "They haven't been the originators."

Londish's risk-taking nature also extended to inventing, however with mixed success. In 1946, after a difficult night babysitting his nephew, and during the immediate post-war period of material rationing, Londish invented a nappy which used far less material than traditional nappies. "I called it the snappy nappy that kept baby happy," Londish said, although noting that his father didn't support him commercialising the idea. "He said, 'I couldn't have my son associated with bloody nappies'," Londish recalls.

Londish also developed a commercial wool press and self-opening farm gate, neither of which were commercial successes. His final invention was a septic tank toilet – nicknamed the 'nutcracker' – with a lid which snapped shut after use and was designed to stop troublesome redback spiders getting into places they shouldn't be. "I sold these in the thousands ... I [then] sold out of the business," Londish said.

However, Londish really sensed opportunity when he saw the State Planning Authority's (SPA) scheme for Woolloomooloo, and in particular the floor space ratios that could be achieved by assembling large parcels of land. Londish already owned some property in Woolloomooloo, including his own development company office, and like other developers had met directly with the scheme's steering committee before its release.

"When the plan was released, I could not believe the conditions that were being offered ... the offer to consolidate large sites," Londish said. "The massive gain that would be got from being able to accumulate and the price you could afford to pay to consolidate large sites. The incentive was overwhelming."

Londish said he was buying "everything and anything that was available" so he could consolidate land in large chunks. Londish waited until the scheme's release before buying up land, but this wasn't the case with other real estate speculators who made extraordinary profits from either gambling on the scheme's outcomes or by leveraging inside knowledge as a result of the SPA's decision to brief landowners and developers.

For instance, in April 1969, a well-known Sydney development company purchased four homes in one street for $180,000 and in May 1969, it purchased a further home in the same street for $30,000.[2] This was a substantial purchase some three months before the Woolloomooloo scheme was released. The final purchase did come, however, after the company's managing director met with the SPA's chair Nigel Ashton in early May to discuss the Woolloomooloo planning scheme. At this meeting, the managing director admitted his company had "bought a good deal of land in the area". He also lobbied for the New South Wales (NSW) Government to acquire private land for developers, so they could complete development sites in the event that the developers were being "held to ransom or held up unduly" by holdout owners. There is no record of Ashton's response to this highly controversial suggestion.[3]

In July 1970, well after the Woolloomooloo plan was released, Londish then paid this development company some $638,812 for the entire site – or nearly three times the price from just the year before. This was not the only site bought and sold by this particular development company in the Woolloomooloo and Victoria St area for fantastic profits, with purchases made from as early as February 1969.

Between November 1969 and October 1971, Londish had spent $25 million – the equivalent of approximately $280 million today – buying up 3.4 hectares of land, or around 20 per cent of all privately

---

2   This information is sourced from an analysis of sales document conducted in the mid-1970s to inform land acquisition costs, it is unknown who conducted the analysis but it is located in the council Woolloomooloo plan file

3   Sourced from minute paper by Nigel Ashton, 12 May 1969

owned land in the area covered by the government's scheme. This made Londish the biggest single private landowner in Woolloomooloo.[4]

Londish's splurge was funded by debt, in the middle of what is still regarded as one of the city's greatest property booms. "Sydney had never experienced a property boom on the scale of that between 1968 and 1974," says author Maurice Daly in *Sydney Boom, Sydney Bust*.[5] "It involved a frenzy of buying, selling and building which reshaped the central business district, greatly increased the supply of industrial and retailing space, and accelerated the expansion of the city's fringe. It was an extraordinary event for Sydney, and for Australia."

Sydney's development industry in the early 1970s was awash with foreign money, much of this coming from the City of London. In addition to this, during the 1960s, unregulated finance companies went from being simple lenders for household items and cars to taking part in joint ventures for complex development projects.[6] Ian Kiernan, an early 1970s Woolloomooloo developer who was later known for founding the anti-littering movement Clean Up Australia, provides the most revealing description of the times in his 1995 book *Coming Clean*. "Almost every day I fielded phone calls from finance companies who would ask 'What have you got coming up? Put up a deal to us.' Some went even further, offering 110 per cent mortgages which meant you could call this a bonus and have some cash for the next deal."[7]

In Londish's case, he was able to turn to an unusual source for funds: a bank controlled by the Russian Communist Party. The Moscow Narodny Bank (in other words, the Moscow People's Bank) had been created in London in 1915, with the aim to encourage east-west trade. In the early 1970s, it had opened a branch office in Singapore. Despite the bank's links to a regime that disavowed capitalism, it worked in the international arena and, therefore, was not bound by domestic Russian

---

4   From a 1972 brochure produced by Gateway Developments Pty Ltd
5   *Sydney Boom*, Sydney Bust, Allen & Unwin, 1982, by M.T. Daly, page 1
6   *Sydney Boom*, Sydney Bust, page 6
7   *Coming Clean*, by Ian Kiernan and Phil Jarratt, MacMillan, 1995, page 75

politics. Like any other bank, it was on the lookout for money-making ventures. Through a business partner, Londish was introduced to the bank's Singaporean branch manager.

"[The manager] was a capitalist. He had a big job, he was making quite big money [and] he was drinking his champagne every night," Londish said. "There was nothing poor about him or [his] missus. And his vision was that he fell in love with this scheme. He was terribly supportive of it and offered me the money. I could get up to $400 million if I needed it."

Just as Ian Kiernan was able to get "bonus" money on his loans, Londish was also able to come to an unusual arrangement with his financier. Because of the sky-high valuation of the property, thanks to the extraordinary floor space ratio incentives offered at Woolloomooloo, Londish wasn't even initially required to pay interest on the money he was borrowing to buy the land.

Londish wasn't the only developer buying up big. Another was Frank Theeman, a publicity-seeking migrant success story who liked to host lavish parties, but also had a dark connection with the Kings Cross underworld.

In 1913, Theeman was born to Jewish parents in Austria. Like so many other European Jewish families, the onset of World War II led to misery and despair. After annexing Austria, the Nazis seized the family's textile business and temporarily interned Theeman in a concentration camp. He was able to leave the camp by agreeing to immediately emigrate overseas. During the boat trip leaving Austria in 1939, Theeman was famously lent 1,000 pounds by an Australian businessman and racehorse owner, which the then penniless emigrant used to set up a hosiery business when he arrived 'down under'.

Starting with six sewing machines sent from Vienna, Theeman built the business – named Osti Holdings Ltd – into one of the three largest of its kind in Australia. It was the first Australian manufacturer to produce and treat nylon fabric, and turn it into clothing.

Theeman was not afraid to flaunt his wealth and his views on life in general. In 1967, he purchased the entire top floor of one of the new

Theeman moved into one of the high-rise apartment towers which sprung up on Darling Point in the late 1960s (Source: Mark Skelsey)

soaring apartment towers being built at the northern tip of Darling Point, just east of Potts Point. Showing no propensity for modesty, Theeman told the *Sun-Herald* that "I have been told my penthouse is the biggest in the Southern Hemisphere with its seven bedrooms and five bathrooms". He also added: "I had a bigger home in Killara but it was taking my wife an hour to drive into town through the traffic".[8]

In 1968, Theeman also gave an awkward interview with *The Sydney Morning Herald*, where he outlined his views on women. Theeman said he was annoyed by women who were not punctual or who didn't look after their appearance. "Physically, I like a woman to be as trim and slim as possible with a good shape, whether that woman might be 25 or 45," Theeman was quoted as saying. He also went on to say that he had an intense dislike for women "who do not look after their smell". "A dab of eau de cologne takes such little trouble. To me, a fragrant smell has

---

8   $134,000 Paid for Sydney Penthouse, *Sun-Herald*, by Graham Gambie, 12 March 1967, page 8

Theeman's uninspiring eight-storey development at 339-343 Oxford St, Paddington (Photo: Mark Skelsey)

much more appeal than an attractive face and figure," he said.[9] Even accounting for accepted social attitudes to women in the late 1960s, it was fairly stomach-churning stuff.

In 1970, Theeman's wealth would only increase after he sold his interests in Osti Holdings Ltd to Dunlop Australia Ltd for $3.5 million. The sale left Theeman in a cashed-up position to take on a new business interest: real estate.[10]

Theeman had already been dabbling in real estate for some time. For instance, in the early 1960s, he constructed a particularly bland eight-storey apartment building at 339–343 Oxford St, Paddington, which

---

9   Punctuality is a Must with Him, *Sun-Herald*, 15 December 1968, page 115
10 Frank William Theeman, Dictionary of Sydney, 2012

is still in place. In the approval process for this building, Theeman used his consultants to aggressively pursue the city council for a speedy decision, and complained bitterly that the council had made his project non-viable by limiting its height and requiring a basement carpark.[11] This was a harbinger of his similarly aggressive planning tactics to come.

Like Londish, Theeman saw great opportunity in the incredible planning incentives offered by the Woolloomooloo scheme. According to author Peter Rees, it was likely that Theeman was advised to move into Victoria St by Sir Paul Strasser, a fellow Jewish emigrant and success story, who ran a large development company called Parkes Development. Rees also reports that Theeman was "restless and looking for new challenges".[12]

Between March 1970 and June 1971, Theeman's development company – Victoria Point Pty Ltd – undertook a major buy-up of 42 properties, taking control of a 1.2 hectare site with two street frontages running from 55–115 Victoria St and 2–30 Brougham St. An undated and unauthored analysis of development site land sales – which appears in official council and NSW Government Woolloomooloo planning files – says Theeman spent $5.5 million acquiring the properties. According to a 1976 newspaper report, Theeman required a loan of $4.536 million to purchase the properties, which means his personal investment was at least $1 million.[13] What's more, Theeman also personally guaranteed the entire loan, which means his house and personal assets were on the line if the whole deal went wrong.[14]

Theeman had little affection for the Victoria St terraces. "As the houses in Victoria St were old-fashioned and dilapidated, it obviously was and is a street which needs reconstruction," he said some years later.

---

11 Taken from a review of City of Sydney file 3963/62 related to application by F.W. Theeman for 339-343 Oxford St, Paddington

12 *Killing Juanita: A True Story of Murder and Corruption*, Allen & Unwin, 2004, by Peter Rees, page 48

13 Peter Rees on page 48 of Killing Juanita has a different estimate of the purchase cost, saying it was $7 million and Theeman's personal investment was $1.6 million

14 Victoria Street is Financially Quiet These Days, *Nation Review*, 23-29 January 1976, by Malcolm Turnbull, page 369

"Old-fashioned housing sooner or later needs to be replaced, and I saw in it something like Sutton Place in New York, which is a tree-lined district very close to the heart of the city. So I wanted to make it more habitable."[15]

Theeman wasn't just splashing out on land for a property development – he also was spending up big building his own home. Theeman moved out of the Darling Point penthouse and purchased a new home and land with spectacular harbour views, on Rose Bay Avenue in Bellevue Hill. Woollahra Council records show he then spent $150,000 (about $1.7 million today) altering and expanding the house into what one media report described as a "fairytale Mediterranean villa".[16] The home included Moorish-inspired external archways, grand decorative brass entrance doors leading to a foyer which – like the dining room – had Italian-marble lined flooring, and a swimming pool outside. In 1971, the house won the *Sun-Herald*'s House of the Year award, in the award's most expensive construction value category, and was said to be the "largest, most expensive and most spectacular house" in the award's history.[17]

Theeman wasted little time using the home as a backdrop for exorbitant parties. In November 1971, he invited 300 guests for a Spanish-themed party, complete with Flamenco dancers, a mock sabre battle between two men in 17th-century costume and "groaning tables laden with oysters and suckling pigs", topped with ice swans. It was, according to the mesmerised *Sun-Herald* social correspondent, a party of "rare splendour".[18]

However, while Theeman may have projected a public image of a successful businessman, respectable family man and social A-lister,

---

15   Quote from Theeman interview broadcast in film documentary Woolloomooloo: A Redevelopment 1969-1977, 1978
16   A Dramatic Contrast of Material Textures, *The Sydney Morning Herald*, 16 April 1971, by Pat Morath, page 12
17   Spectacular House on Bellevue Hill, *Sun-Herald*, 12 September 1971, by Jock Reid, page 67
18   Night of Flamencos and Caballeros, *Sun-Herald*, 28 November 1971, by Leslie Walford, page 166

Frank Theeman photographed in the 1970s (Photo courtesy of News Ltd/Newspix)

he also had a key connection with a Kings Cross underworld figure. Theeman was close to a club manager named James McCartney Anderson, more widely known as 'Big Jim' Anderson. Born in Scotland, the imposing 1.8m tall Anderson had arrived in Australia in the late 1950s and earned a living from organising entertainment for, and managing, nightclubs. By 1971, Anderson was also working for Abe Saffron, a now well-known Kings Cross businessman with the nickname 'Mr Sin'.[19]

---

19 *Killing Juanita*, page 98

After meeting through a family connection, Theeman said he saw Anderson either each month, or once every two months, from 1971 through to 1975.[20] The connection was even more surprising, given that, in 1970, Anderson had made the news after being charged with murdering Sydney underworld hardman, Donny 'The Glove' Smith, at the Venus Room, a Kings Cross club Anderson managed on behalf of Saffron. It's been reported that Anderson had, for some time, been resisting Smith's attempts to take over prostitution operations at the club.[21] Smith arrived at the club with a gun, however, Anderson had been tipped-off about the visit by police, and was laying in wait with a gun of his own. The bloody confrontation ended with Smith dead on the footpath outside the club, and Anderson allegedly telling police "I'm sorry about any trouble, but this (expletive) had to die".

Anderson was later committed for trial on the lesser charge of manslaughter, after the magistrate commented that it was likely he was acting in self-defence.[22] The charge was eventually dropped. An unsuccessful attempt had also been made in 1971 to extradite Anderson to Singapore on counterfeit currency charges.[23]

The scene was now set for the transformation of Woolloomooloo and Victoria St.

Two larger-than-life Sydney developers – Londish and Theeman – had undertaken a debt-fuelled land buying spree, with the expectation they would be able to turn streets of low-rise terraces and cottages into a new Manhattan. What the two men didn't realise, however, was that at the precise time they were putting their finances and futures on the line, the Woolloomooloo planning scheme was in trouble.

An early red flag was that the fact that, on 11 November 1969, the Metropolitan Water Sewerage and Drainage Board lobbed a letter to the council, expressing surprise that it hadn't been consulted about the

---

20 The National Crime Authority and James McCartney Anderson, A Report by the Parliamentary Joint Committee on the National Crime Authority, March 1994, page 197
21 *Killing Juantia*, page 35
22 Man for Trial in Restaurant Death, *The Sydney Morning Herald*, 12 August 1970, page 9
23 The National Crime Authority and James McCartney Anderson, A Report by the Parliamentary Joint Committee on the National Crime Authority, March 1994, page 11

Even as it was becoming clear the Woolloomooloo scheme was flawed, the City of Sydney Council booked this promotional ad in The Sydney Morning Herald in July 1970, backing the scheme and the redevelopment of the inner city

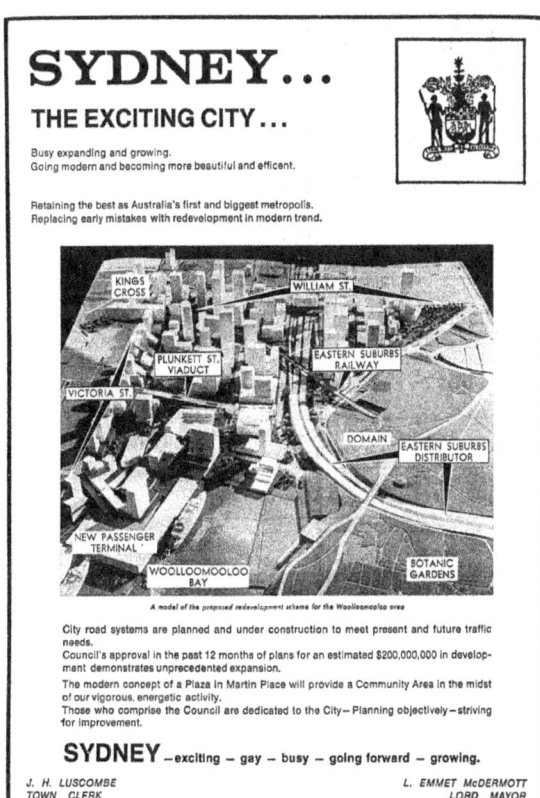

plans and stating it was "concerned at the implications of the proposals, should they come to fruition, as regards their effect on water, sewerage and drainage services".[24] In other words, the consultation on the plan had been so shoddy that no-one thought to talk to the organisation responsible for supplying drinking water, sewerage services and stormwater drainage to an extension of the Sydney Central Business District (CBD). The council didn't seem to know what to do with this letter and simply ignored it, forcing the Water Board to send a follow-up inquiry in February 1970.

Next up was the Royal Australian Navy, which feared that the redevelopment would restrict traffic access to its Garden Island facility,

---

24 Letter from Metropolitan Water Sewerage and Drainage Board Deputy Secretary to Town Clerk of City of Sydney Council, 13 November 1969

and in turn compromise an essential plank of Australia's east coast military defence system.

On 17 November 1969, the Royal Australian Institute of Architects (RAIA) also savaged the plan, stating that Woolloomooloo was the wrong place to extend Sydney's CBD and that the lack of a railway station would cause "significant inconvenience". It also deplored the plan to demolish the existing finger wharf and replace it with an "industrial wharf" with "undefined function" which would "destroy the visually interesting juxtaposition of ships, cliff faces and housing, which give the area its present character and identity".[25]

Meanwhile, in early December, the City of Sydney Council's solicitor warned that the scheme itself may have been legally invalid, because it hadn't been prepared in line with State planning law, which included seeking formal feedback from landowners and then considering that feedback. "Considerable legal doubt must exist as to the legality of the procedure which has been adopted with respect to the preparation of the Woolloomooloo area redevelopment scheme," the solicitor's report said.[26]

Other political changes were also working against the plan. In late September 1969, council elections were held and the conservative Civic Reform party swept to power. In reply to the RAIA, the new Lord Mayor Emmet McDermott showed signs of backing away from the plan, curiously stating the council was aware that it had "certain deficiencies" and noting that it was intending to embark on a new strategy for the entire council area.

While big money was flowing into Woolloomooloo and Victoria St, the planning scheme on which it was based was starting to fall apart. While no-one knew it at the time, this was an impossible situation which would ultimately lead to financial failure, street warfare, anarchy, a kidnapping ... and murder.

---

[25] Letter from Royal Australian Institute of Architects President Richard Norman Johnson to Lord Mayor, 17 November 1969

[26] Report of City of Sydney Solicitor to City Development Committee, dated 5 December 1969

CHAPTER 12

Transforming an "ugly step-daughter"

Robert Askin was not happy. In October 1971, the New South Wales (NSW) Premier had fronted the media to launch a spectacular $400 million scheme by developer Sid Londish to transform the Woolloomooloo basin into a sea of office and residential towers. It was touted as the largest redevelopment scheme in Australia and Askin backed it to the hilt, stating "we are now turning the clock forward and taking a peep at Sydney of the future".[1] He also dismissed any potential blowback by saying "as always when you are dealing with progress and development you get a few critics".[2]

Now, some six months later, Londish was in Askin's office complaining that the Premier's own planning bureaucrats were refusing to back the scheme. Askin wrote to his Local Government Minister, Pat Morton, to complain about the situation.

"You may recall that some months ago, I unveiled a model of the [Londish] redevelopment scheme down at the Astor building when a number of City Council Aldermen were present and also officials of the State Planning Authority," Askin wrote. "While I can claim no knowledge of detail, the general project seemed to have a lot of merit

---

1 Premier Hails $400 million Peep at Future, The Australian, 16 October 1971, page number unknown
2 Foreign Cash for Big Plan, *The Sydney Morning Herald*, 16 October, by Ian Frykberg, page 2

Premier Robert Askin (centre) at the launch of the Woolloomooloo Gateway scheme in 1971

and as you know the government's general policy is to help genuine developers who will replace antiquated housing and structures with modern buildings.

"I gather from what Mr Londish said that the City Council favours his scheme at least in principle but apparently there are some hold-ups with the State Planning Authority. I think in these matters it needs to be realised that, irrespective of the final outcome which must of course be based on merit, the time factor is a very costly ingredient so far as private enterprise is concerned with various projects."[3]

When it arrived at the State Planning Authority (SPA) office, the letter caused sheer panic. "Very urgent ... please see me", SPA chair Nigel Ashton scribbled across the letter in a note to one of his planning staff.

Askin's letter shone a light on the predicament faced by the SPA: having lit a development wildfire in Woolloomooloo, it was now trying to douse the flames.

Known as the Woolloomooloo Redevelopment Project, this ambitious and futuristic scheme reflected Londish's belief in himself as a visionary, leader and risk-taker. It was proposed to include nine office blocks up to 40 storeys high, around 2,000 hotel and motel rooms, a seven-storey retail centre, 18,000 square metres of convention and exhibition space and two cinemas. One of its public plazas would be modelled on Denmark's historic Tivoli Gardens pleasure grounds and would include taverns, restaurants, a porpoise pool, ice skating rink, gardens and fountains. In addition, the project would be centred around an artificial lake set six levels above the ground, including restaurants both around and under the lake. The clincher would be a futuristic monorail system, connecting the project to Kings Cross and the Sydney Central Business District.

"For 178 years, Woolloomooloo has existed without any particular identity – ignored like an ugly step-daughter," the scheme's

---

3   Letter from Premier Robert Askin to Local Government Minister Pat Morton, 11 April 1972

Artist's impression showing how Sid Londish envisaged the redeveloped Woolloomooloo and Darlinghurst areas, with his development shown in green

promotional brochure said. "Even in the early days, no-one planned for the development of Woolloomooloo as a suburb. It grew up like an undisciplined child. Trapped by its step-daughter past, Woolloomooloo's potential for years went unrecognised, until the State Planning Authority announced its masterplan for the area. This redevelopment project has accepted the challenge laid down by the Authority – to make Woolloomooloo a dynamic, vital extension of Sydney, while at the same time, giving it something it had always enjoyed – its own inherent identity."[4]

However, there was a major problem with the redevelopment scheme, and Londish knew it.

---

[4] Woolloomooloo Redevelopment Project promotional brochure, Gateway Developments Pty Ltd, 1971

To move the people in and out of this new mini-city, a new Woolloomooloo railway station was required, but despite Londish's best endeavours, there had been no government decision to construct such a facility.

All up, Londish's scheme would house 21,500 office workers, by developing to the absolute maximum floor space ratio allowable under the Woolloomooloo planning scheme. Londish's consultants calculated that, if the same level of development was replicated across Woolloomooloo, the valley would have 80,000 workers. This was more than two times the 35,000 workers envisaged in the Woolloomooloo planning scheme.

As we now know, the SPA had failed to heed warnings that adding even 35,000 workers to the valley would require a new railway station. Once a developer had shown that the SPA's workforce forecasts were wildly inaccurate, it revealed that the potential transport disaster in the valley could be even worse than originally feared.

The concept of a Woolloomooloo station had been batted around between developers, the SPA and the NSW Department of Railways for several years. Everyone seemed to agree that, if such a station was to be built, it would be located on the railway viaduct being built over Woolloomooloo, at the point where this intersected with a proposed new expressway. However, there's where the unanimity started and finished, with railway chiefs dead against the idea and the planners and developers in favour.

In December 1969, well after the Woolloomooloo planning scheme had been released, the SPA – at the request of Ashton – had written a strange letter to the Department of Railways. The letter requested that "the way be kept open to build a station … should the situation at some future time demand the provision of such a facility". It was a bit like requesting a gate to be built well after the horse had bolted. The Secretary for Railways didn't respond until November 1970, and in this response stated that the station would be too difficult to build and too close to Kings Cross and Martin Place stations. Or, in the words of an earlier 1967 Department of Railways memo rebutting the station idea,

A booklet produced for the Gateway scheme was extremely disparaging about the Woolloomooloo area which existed at the time, showing photos of rundown buildings

the Eastern Suburbs Railway would become "little better than a tram system".[5]

In the same month, Londish approached NSW Transport Minister Milton Morris to lobby for a railway station, and offered $800,000 to help pay for it. After having the matter examined by an inter-

---

5   Memo from Secretary of Railways to Under Secretary of Transport, 4 September 1967, in response to representations from Local Government Minister Morton for a railway station at Woolloomooloo, in Department of Government Transport file 74/T98/2221

departmental committee, Morris prepared a minute for a Cabinet meeting planned for 29 June 1971 which recommended that – despite Treasury opposition – the station be built. It looked as though Londish's wish was going to come true, and in turn the Woolloomooloo planning scheme would become a reality.

Then, for Londish, disaster struck.

After coming to office in 1969, the City of Sydney Council's newly-elected Civic Reform Aldermen flagged they would create the city's first long-term strategic plan. According to Sydney's leading planning historian Robert Freestone, the plan was needed because "Central Sydney in the late 1960s was in trouble … suburban development had a negative impact on business, particularly retail, theatres and cultural institutions … [and] an increasingly vertiginous skyline of uninspiring high-rise buildings obliterated the past and towered over narrow, traffic-choked streets".[6] Unlike the SPA's scheme, the council's strategic plan had the benefit of extensive expert advice, along with stakeholder input. All up, it was supported by nearly 40 subject area specialist consultants, and reflected the input of hundreds of stakeholders, including unions, charities, companies and government departments.

The plan, when released in July 1971, skewered the Woolloomooloo scheme in no uncertain terms. It declared that the SPA's scheme was a flawed document which had "unfortunately failed to appreciate the relationship between suggested floor space ratios, potential workforce, and transportation capacities". The report said that, if the scheme was implemented, the valley's workforce could be well over 100,000, which "would require the enlargement of currently envisaged transport facilities".[7] The plan also recommended that Sydney's future office space growth be concentrated in a central spine between Circular Quay and Central Sydney, where existing railway stations were in place to serve future workers, rather than to the east to Woolloomooloo. "For

---

[6] Jubilee Celebration for Sydney's First Foray into 'People' Planning, *The Sydney Morning Herald*, 7 August 2021, by Robert Freestone, page 23

[7] City of Sydney Strategic Plan, released 20 July 1971, page 89

the future economic wellbeing of the City as a whole, the valley of the 'Loo … should be re-established as much as possible in predominantly residential uses," the plan said.

Woolloomooloo had arrived at the crossroads. There were now two official plans – one developed by the NSW Government and the other by the council – in place for the same area, with contradictory policies. The council's new plan supported Woolloomooloo remaining as it was – eliminating the need for a railway station.

Internal NSW Government documents show that, after Transport Minister Morris became aware of the upcoming release of the council's plan, he withdrew the Cabinet minute. Only one copy of the draft Cabinet minute was left in the files, with all others destroyed. From this point forward, NSW transport authorities would cite the council's strategic plan as a reason not to build a railway station, whenever the matter was raised.

Londish was now in a pickle. In July 1971, he wrote to inner-Sydney Liberal MP John Barraclough[8] stating that "our plans for the area are now at a very advanced stage and cannot proceed without knowing whether a station will be located in the area or not".[9]

Despite the impasse, Londish decided to press the button on the scheme's launch, after managing to convince Premier Askin to attend. He spent $6,000 building a model, and then hired the Astor Motel in Woolloomooloo for a launch event.

Asked why Askin attended the launch, despite the transport problem, Londish said: "He wanted to get the kudos from the scheme – he saw a lot of mileage politically for himself. And he started to support me on the scheme".

"It was the biggest real estate scheme Australia had ever seen," Londish said. "In today's terms it would probably be close to twenty

---

8   Barraclough's seat of Bligh adjoined Woolloomooloo
9   Letter from Sid Londish to John Barraclough, 22 July 1971, in Department of Government Transport file 74/T98/2221

billion dollars. It was going to change everything in Australia. And it was going to bring life back to the city."

However, while the Premier may have been willing to back the scheme, it had caused panic and division among bureaucrats. Within the SPA, Kacirek had initially given in-principle support for the Londish scheme in July 1971, saying it was in line with the "base principles and structure of the Woolloomooloo plan", although he expressed concern about the amount of office space. However, one of his planners, Grahame Crockett, disagreed. "A development proposal of this scale ... irrespective of whether a railway station is included ... will be likely to cause serious congestion and operate economically contrary to the main city core ... the development in its present form is unsatisfactory."

After two inter-departmental investigations, the SPA was forced into the humiliating position of being forced to drastically scale down Londish's plans, and in doing work against its own scheme. In a decision communicated to Londish in June 1972, it removed around 100,000 square metres of office floor space from his scheme, and cut his proposed workforce from 21,500 to just 10,000. Where the SPA had promised developers an impressive 10:1 floor space ratio, Londish was now being told he could only claim 4:1 for office space. His plans for a large regional retail centre were also in tatters, with the SPA stating this now needed to be a local centre. For Londish, it seemed that having the Premier onside was not enough to save his grand vision.

The debacle also was a factor in ending the political career of Pat Morton, who announced in June 1972 he was resigning from State Parliament. In something of a political obituary, *The Sydney Morning Herald's* State Political Reporter John O'Hara wrote that Morton's "free enterprise" philosophy had become "outdated by events" and many of his policies were now "near collapse". The story cited Morton's stalled redevelopment plans for Woolloomooloo and The Rocks, and increasing opposition to the construction of new freeways.[10]

---

10 A Free Enterpriser Bows Out, The Sydney Morning Herald, 16 June 1972, by John O'Hara, page 7

Morton's departure was yet another sign that Londish's highly ambitious project was in trouble. Londish had outlaid some $25 million to purchase land and was losing around $6,000 a day in interest payments, while his vision was now in tatters.

Not surprisingly, and as shown in a meeting with City of Sydney Aldermen in March 1972, Londish was in a gloomy frame of mind. "I'm in the hot seat," he told the Aldermen. "I have to pay out [a partner] soon and I can't raise the money because the land has no value on it. It was a mistake to have tried to go for the big scheme."

Two of the Aldermen interjected, saying "it was not a mistake", but the Civic Reform Alderman Andrew Briger said "you are a pioneer and pioneers are usually penalised". The Deputy Lord Mayor Nicholas Shehadie then made a curious comment, which could be read as either holding up Londish as a hero, or as a hopeless victim. "Sid," Shehadie said, "we'll bury you there."

PART 3
URBAN WARFARE

CHAPTER 13

From a "black night" to a green ban future

Even after accounting for the physical rough and tumble of Sydney's industrial relations scene in the 1960s and 1970s, this was a melee for the ages.

On the evening of 20 May 1971, union delegates had assembled at the historic sandstone Sydney Trades Hall in Goulburn St for the weekly meeting of the supreme body of the State's trade union movement, the Labor Council of New South Wales (NSW). After the draft minutes of the previous week's meeting were read, there was some heckling (including claims of a "sell out") from a group of around 15 rank-and-file union members who had trespassed into the area set aside for union delegates. A delegate who turned and complained to the group about their behaviour was reportedly "punched full in the face". Within a matter of seconds, the meeting then turned into what one witness described as an "all out blue".

Over the next 15 minutes, dozens of attendees traded blows and threw chairs, loudspeakers and microphones at each other, with some men kicked as they tried to defend themselves on the floor. A group of visiting trade union officials from the United States also were threatened. "It raged all over the hall, and savagery was used by both sides," one eyewitness said. At the end of fracas, a one-legged 55-year-old union delegate from the Rubber Workers' Union was found lying unconscious and bloodied on the floor, after being "kicked insensible".

The man was later taken to hospital, where he received four stitches for chin lacerations.

As the dust settled, the council's secretary Ralph Marsh had no doubt who was to blame. He moved to defer the meeting and then to suspend the NSW Builders Labourers' Federation from the Labor Council, until a full investigation was undertaken. The next day's issue of *The Sydney Morning Herald* delivered its verdict with a front page story which stated "The builders' labourers carried their campaign of violence into the NSW Labor Council last night, breaking up the council's weekly meeting".[1]

What had gone wrong?

Since the 1870s, the NSW Builders Labourers' Federation (best known by the acronym BLF) had represented unskilled and some semi-skilled labourers on building sites, including dogmen (who placed hooks on to, and sometimes rode, construction material loads being transported by crane around sites), scaffolders (responsible for erecting scaffolding), powder monkeys (responsible for explosives) and hoist drivers. Labourers were central to bringing old buildings down and putting new ones up, working alongside tradespeople (such as plumbers, carpenters and electricians) and machine drivers, who were represented by other unions.

Under the leadership of Jack Mundey since 1968, the BLF had become one of the most militant unions in NSW. Mundey was born in North Queensland and, in the early 1950s, had come to Sydney at the age of 19 to play rugby league for Parramatta and to work as a builders' labourer.

Mundey gained national attention in 1970 after confirming in an interview that, during a recent strike, his union deliberately set out to damage private property. Mundey said this action was taken if the union believed that the property had been built by 'scabs', or in other words workers who refused to obey the union's strike action. "Deliberate damage to property was the most controversial aspect of

---

1   Strike is Over but Violence Renewed, *The Sydney Morning Herald*, 21 May 1971, by Fred Wells, pages 1 and 10

the strike," he said. "It was also the one that worried the employers the most of all. We did not set out on a wanton destruction campaign, but attacked only buildings where employers were attempting to use scab labour to break the strike. This had a devastating effect on employers, government and police alike."[2] He then added: "Future action of this type will be most successful if hundreds and thousands of strikers are involved, so making it difficult for full police and government defence of employers' property".

Needless to say, the tabloid press had a field day, with a *Sunday Telegraph* headline screaming "Reds Ordered: Destroy" and the paper's editorial calling on Mundey to be prosecuted.[3] Then Attorney-General Thomas Hughes was so concerned by the comments he asked the Solicitor-General to examine whether Mundey should be prosecuted for sedition – an offence which dates back many hundreds of years, and in its widest sense means to use speech to challenge established order. Hughes received advice that this was impossible, as the relevant Commonwealth legislation had specifically excluded industrial relations actions from being considered as sedition.[4]

In early May 1971, around 38,000 workers from the BLF and nine other unions had brought the State's building industry to a halt by going on strike, seeking a $6 a week wage increase and full pay after being injured at work. Three weeks into the strike, the State's Industrial Commission said it would be willing to make a decision on the accident pay issue, but only if the workers called off the strike.

Mass meetings of building workers were held across NSW to consider the offer. Around 4pm on 20 May, approximately 1,300 workers met at the Wentworth Park greyhound track in Sydney and voted (by a narrow margin) to stay on strike, but were overruled by their colleagues around the State, who voted overwhelmingly to go back to work.

---

2   Towards a New Militancy, *Australian Left Review*, August-September 1970, page 6
3   Reds Ordered: Destroy, *Sunday Telegraph*, 16 August 1970, by Alan Reid, page 2
4   Sourced from file entitled Jack Mundey and the *Australian Left Review*: Question of prosecution for sedition, correspondence file 1970/2998, Attorney-General's Department, National Archives of Australia

This set the scene for the appalling brawl later that night. A group of builders' labourers – who were unhappy with the work return decision – left Wentworth Park and then spent the next four hours enjoying the hospitality of the Sussex Hotel in Sussex St, before being overheard talking about wanting to start a fight as they walked into the Labor Council meeting. After entering the meeting, they then decided to sit near and heckle (of all people) the Police Association delegates, before the meeting erupted.

Mundey himself said he knew nothing of the group's plans and only arrived on the scene as the brawl was in full fly. He was then accused by the Labor Council's right-wing leadership of deliberately arriving late to avoid suspicion and being the secret mastermind of the whole shameful event, given his comments on violence and property damage only the year before. "Mr Mundey does not come to the council with clean hands," the council's assistant secretary John Ducker said. "If we cop this sort of thing tonight, who will be next?"

It was one thing for Mundey to be attacked by the government and right-wing tabloid press; it was quite another to be labelled as a pariah by his trade union colleagues, irrespective of where they sat on the political spectrum.

The next morning, Mundey gathered with his executive team, who decided to hold a commission of inquiry into the issue. This would involve a group of 15 union member representatives from major building sites and the executive passing judgement on whether nine of the BLF members said to be involved in the brawl should be suspended from the union, for obstructing the work of the BLF delegates to the Labor Council.

At this inquiry, held on 26 May, a chastened Mundey said the melee could have contributed to the union's downfall. "It will go down as a black night indeed in the union's history," he said. "It seemed earlier this week that we wouldn't see the week out after all the attacks made on us. We had it on good authority that the employers were moving for deregistration of our union." The nine members were found guilty

BLF president Bob Pringle (left) and secretary Jack Mundey (right) at a May Day march in 1973 (Courtesy of Mitchell Library, State Library of NSW and SEARCH Foundation)

and suspended by the inquiry.[5] This decision was narrowly supported by a full branch meeting but later overturned by Mundey's political opponents, who held sway at the union's Federal level.[6]

It was in the aftermath of this dark chapter that a surprise gift emerged for the Mundey's BLF – one that would bring the union praise from community and social activists, and badly-needed positive press. The gift would also align with Mundey's stated philosophy that the union should have a broader social improvement objective, beyond just arguing for better pay and conditions.

A few days after the Labor Council brawl, it was reported that a developer was proposing to build 25 homes on 2.6 hectares of bushland

---

5   Details of the Labor Council brawl issue are taken from a Sydney Morning Herald front page story published on 21 May 1971 by industrial reporter Fred Wells, and the minutes of the NSW BLF executive, branch and commission of inquiry from 21-25 May, sourced from Noel Butlin Archives at the Australian National University

6   *Green Bans and Beyond*, Angus and Robertson, 1981, by Jack Mundey, page 71

called Kelly's Bush, near Sydney Harbour. The State Planning Authority was proposing to acquire the other 2.3 hectares for harbour foreshore open space. Three women from Hunter's Hill had already secured a ban on the development from the Federated Engine Drivers and Firemen's Association (FEDFA), which would not allow its workers to drive bulldozers and graders to clear the land. Would the BLF now support the FEDFA and commit to not building the homes, the women asked?

At a BLF executive meeting on 8 June 1971, the union decided to back the women. The minutes of this meeting have a casual, low-key tone and provide little insight that this decision would be the start of the BLF's storied green ban era, which would halt Sydney's most destructive development, and spark a new environmental and conservation movement.

The minutes report the union's president Bob Pringle saying that Kelly's Bush was in a "middle class area" and "residents claim it is the only bushland on the Parramatta River". "Suggest we make a decision not to work on the project and make a press release at the appropriate time," the minutes note Pringle as saying, with the executive agreeing to "support the issue".

On 17 June 1971, in a small back page story, *The Sydney Morning Herald* reported on the fact that unions had banned work on Kelly's Bush.[7] A day later, in the same paper, a similarly-sized small back page story reported that developer Frank Theeman had lodged plans for a soaring skyscraper development which would replace terrace homes in Victoria St, Potts Point.

These two matters – the green ban issue and Theeman's development – had now entered the public realm on adjacent days in June 1971, although neither issue appeared to have really captured public imagination. It would take two more years before these two forces would become entangled and lead to front page stories about bloodshed and violence.

---

7   Unions Act on Kelly's Bush, *The Sydney Morning Herald*, 17 June 1971, page 10

CHAPTER 14

"If ever I saw an example of visual pollution, this is it"

By the late 1960s, there was broad consensus that Sydney's greatest natural asset – its sprawling, sumptuous harbour – was in deep trouble.

For many decades, planning for the ridges, valleys and flats around this grand waterway had either been non-existent, or incompetent. This had resulted in light and heavy industry, and defence establishments, lining and excluding the public from much of the harbour's foreshores, even though many of these installations didn't specifically need to be next to the water. When foreshore land was redeveloped, the resulting apartment buildings were only required to comply with generic site coverage codes, which took no heed of the foreshore or landscape. This resulted in structures which towered over the water's edge, blocked views from the street and continued to exclude the general public from their beloved waterway.

"In many parts of Sydney's waterfront suburbs, it is almost possible to believe that Sydney Harbour does not exist," *The Sydney Morning Herald* reported in 1969.[1] "In most of Kirribilli and Darling Point, in large areas of Elizabeth Bay, McMahon's Point and Cremorne, even for residents and strollers within a few hundred yards of the shore, little trace of the water can be seen – except that is, through a tangle of

---

1   Sydney as It Is ... and as It Could Be, *The Sydney Morning Herald*, 15 February 1969, by Evan Williams, page 4

In the 1960s there was a backlash against tower blocks, such as this Neutral Bay example, along the edges of Sydney Harbour

concrete and hoardings, misaligned rooftops, high-rise apartments … and parking areas crowded with cars."

The piece went on to criticise the "obliterating jungle of multi-storey units and commercial blocks that give the foreshores their air of spectacular ugliness and confusion".

The State Planning Authority's (SPA) chair Nigel Ashton, and his Minister, Pat Morton, were also acutely aware of the problem, both from a personal and professional perspective. Ashton lived at Greenwich, looking out over the Lane Cove River, but also on the other side of the road from the Gore Cove petroleum storage terminal. Morton was the State MP for the harbourside seat of Mosman. Both men lived and breathed the harbour on a daily basis and therefore quite understandably had a keen interest to improve planning for the waterway.

As a result, in 1967, the SPA released a detailed study of the harbour foreshores, which sought to understand the problem and point to potential solutions.[2] It recommended that high-density development

---

2   Sydney Harbour Foreshore Study, State Planning Authority, December 1967

should be confined to the ridges of the harbour's peninsulas, with only low-density development allowed on the peninsula slopes and alongside the water, as well as trying to preserve views either through or around buildings from harbourside streets.

A prudent, intelligent developer of land anywhere near Sydney Harbour would have realised that change was in the air, and that the old ways of doing things would no longer cut it. Frank Theeman was not this type of developer.

The Woolloomooloo planning scheme had specifically set aside Theeman's site, which overlooked Woolloomooloo Bay, for high-density residential development. Theeman was now going to test just how much development was possible.

In February 1971, he lodged an application with the SPA seeking to build three soaring 45-storey apartment towers above Victoria St, along with a 15-storey office building. Under these structures, Theeman was also planning to excavate the 18m height difference between the Victoria and Brougham St frontages of the site to build 64 stepped terrace apartments, an 850-space public carpark and 1,300 further private carparking spaces.

The future apartment residents would have access to around 4,000 square metres of private garden space, along with swimming pools located on the top of each of the towers.

All up, Theeman's application was seeking to construct new building floor space equivalent to 10 times the total site area – a ratio usually only applicable in the Sydney Central Business District (CBD). This meant he was trying to replicate a CBD-scale outcome after demolishing existing terrace homes, and on a site which was located across the road from terraces which would remain in place.

It was, arguably, a level of character change unprecedented in Sydney's history. Theeman argued that, given the land was zoned for CBD purposes when he purchased it, he was entitled to this level of development. This was despite the fact that the 1969 Woolloomooloo scheme, which in itself sought to turbo-charge new development, envisaged 30 per cent less floor space than Theeman's proposal.

Theeman's envisioned towers loomed large over the nearby Woolloomooloo Bay finger wharf and dominated the harbour foreshore, and in doing so went against the prevailing view that such towers should be set well away from the waterfront. In fact, the towers were so high that they would even dominate the view from Elizabeth Bay – the next bay to the west and divided from Victoria St by the Potts Point ridge.

Theeman was trying to replicate the high-rise towers already constructed during the 1960s on the end of Darling Point – the next peninsula to the east and where he had until recently owned an apartment. Theeman's architects produced an aerial photo for the SPA, which sought to show how his towers would reflect the built-form already in place at Darling Point. In addition, Theeman was calling his project Victoria Point, because it had the same waterside high-rise concept as Darling Point.

The City of Sydney's Aldermen were highly supportive of this proposal, mainly because the council would be getting a new public carpark as part of the deal. This was despite the fact that the council's principal architect found it difficult to support the scheme, stating only in a report that "the three circular towers are more acceptable than the smoke-belching stacks of the White Bay power station" and that "the impression gained from the plans is that the site is over-developed" but this could be mitigated by good design and building materials. This was faint praise indeed.

Theeman's plans were, however, deeply unpopular in the SPA, which needed to concur with the council's recommendation before construction could begin. Around the same time as Theeman lodged his application, the SPA was firming in its view that high-rise towers on the foreshore – as had happened at Darling Point – were exactly the sort of development which should be avoided.

"The advent of high-rise residential development on the foreshore slopes has posed a difficult problem and been the source of considerable public opposition," a 1971 paper to the SPA board stated.[3] "These

---

3   Chief Planner's Report to State Planning Authority board, 22 January 1971

Top: This artist's impression produced by the State Planning Authority shows how Theeman's three proposed towers were so tall that would be visible from Elizabeth Bay, on the other side of the Potts Point ridge

Above: The same view in 2024 (Photo: Mark Skelsey)

Top: Another artist's impression produced by the SPA, which shows how Theeman's towers would appear from Woolloomooloo Bay

Above: The same view towards the Woolloomooloo Bay finger wharf in 2024 (Photo: Mark Skelsey)

aspects have been most severe in the municipalities of Woollahra, Mosman and North Sydney and to a lesser extent Leichhardt, Drummoyne and Hunter's Hill."

In January 1972, after receiving a report from Ashton that Theeman's proposal should be rejected, Morton commissioned the New South Wales (NSW) Government Architect's office to provide confidential advice on the scheme.

Unfortunately, we don't know who specifically wrote the response from that office, as the letter is unsigned, but we do know the response was colourful and damning, and also seemed to mock the ridiculous "power station" comment from the council architect.

"If ever I saw an example of visual pollution, this is it," the NSW Government Architect response said. "The three proposed towers look like some kind of monstrous power station of inhuman scale. Visually the towers are about twice as high as they should be. As they are shown they make nonsense of the present (quite sensible) height restrictions in the Kings Cross area.

"I do not want to appear emotional about this but I do sincerely think that the ruthless exploitation of our wonderful city in the pursuit of the quick dollar will have to stop before our city is ruined beyond repair ... with all the character and personality that made it Sydney, just a memory."[4]

Theeman, and the council, knew they were in trouble and played their final card – lobbying Premier Askin to over-rule Morton and Ashton. Theeman sent a copy of his plans to Askin, while Deputy Lord Mayor Nicholas Shehadie also made his views known to the Premier. After being alerted to this, Morton wrote to Askin, saying he would keep him abreast of the situation.

---

4 Unsigned memo dated 24 January 1972, under letterhead of NSW Department of Public Works. In this quote, the NSW Government Architect's office uses the word "ere" instead of "before". Given the word "ere" has fallen out of use, the word "before" has been used in its place, as it has the same meaning

Top: The white silhouette tower image on the top left corner of this photo illustrates Theeman's proposed new towers under his 1971 plan – as is made clear from the image, the heights of the towers would be equivalent to the Sydney CBD

Above: The first Victoria Point scheme was compared to the chimneys of the White Bay Power Station, seen here in 2013 (Photo: Mark Skelsey)

This would have been an extraordinarily stressful time for Ashton. We know that, around the same time, Premier Askin was raising questions about why the SPA was not approving the Londish scheme for the Woolloomooloo valley, which Askin had launched. Now, the city council and another developer were challenging Ashton's decision, this time on the Woolloomooloo valley's eastern ridge, and again going all the way to the Premier.

The tension was palpable, even in internal memos. On 17 April 1972, Ashton wrote an angry memo to his Deputy Chair John Wickham, stating "if the council gets away with this proposition then the planning for Sydney could be placed in an untenable situation".[5] In June 1972, Ashton then lashed out at Theeman's architect, telling him that "any major firm of architects should know the very tall buildings proposed on this conspicuous site would be contrary to policy together with excessive density, and his client should have been so advised".[6]

Ultimately, yet again Askin – despite his later reputation as a 'development at all costs' Premier – did not intervene, and Ashton and the SPA prevailed in its view that Theeman's application should be refused.

While Sydney may have been saved from a new and hideous harbourside eyesore, the SPA's decision yet again showed that its Woolloomooloo scheme was deeply flawed, by encouraging levels of development which were ultimately not sustainable. It also fuelled Theeman's quite understandable belief and resentment that the SPA's planners had lured him into making a major investment in Woolloomooloo, and then failed to deliver on their promises.

However, if Theeman thought the SPA's refusal would be his only setback, he'd have been mistaken. The refusal was, in fact, the start of a long, frustrating and expensive journey.

---

5   Memo from State Planning Authority Chair Nigel Ashton to Deputy Chair John Wickham, 17 April 1972, in file 181 J5/1/7 NSW Government Archives

6   Note to file by State Planning Authority chair Nigel Ashton, 8 June 1972, in file 181 J5/1/7 in Department of Planning functional files in NSW Government Archives

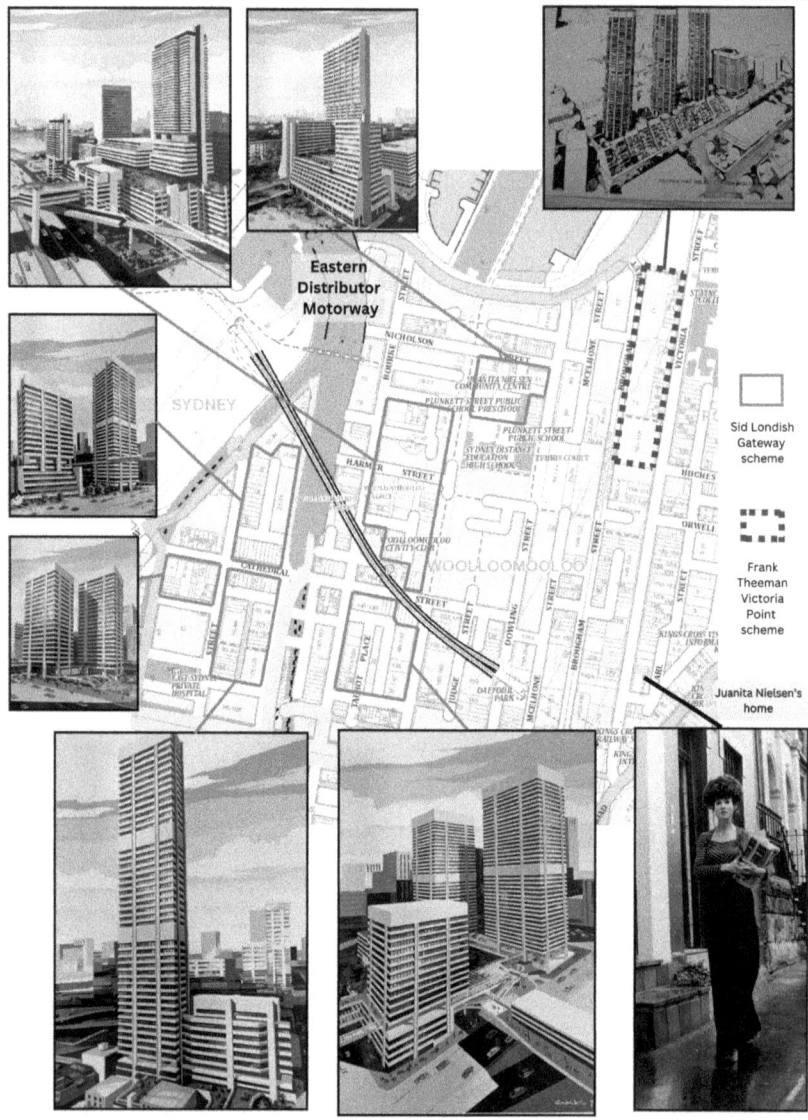

CHAPTER 15

Naughty nuns outside court

On any given morning, the entry foyer of Sydney's historic sandstone Central Local Court is usually a hive of activity as lawyers and their clients await their day in court for low-level crimes such as assault, drug dealing, drink driving and property damage.

However, on a chilly morning in August 1970, the foyer had an entirely different feel.

About 50 people were holding a protest, including a group of young women dressed in nun's habits and someone in a gorilla outfit.

One nun in particular attracted attention. She had a habit with a bib which could be raised to reveal the ribald slogan "I have been fucked by God's steel prick". Then, to top it off, the nun – like her colleagues – was handing out flyers to passers-by with the words to a provocative poem entitled *Cunt is a Christian word*.

This was Wendy Bacon, a 23-year-old University of New South Wales (NSW) sociology student.

Bacon had grown up in Melbourne, in a family which could have been mistaken as traditional, god-fearing and conservative but in fact, behind the scenes, tended to be against censorship, was ambivalent about religion and was supportive of leftist causes.

For instance, Bacon recalls that her father, Francis, a doctor, admitted to Australian Security Intelligence Organisation (ASIO) officers in the

Wendy Bacon (at right) dressed as a nun and holding an "offensive" poem with fellow protesters at Central Local Court in August 1970 (Photo originally published in Tribune, courtesy of Mitchell Library, State Library of NSW and SEARCH Foundation)

1950s that he had bought the Communist party newspaper every week from a patient.

"I think [my father] was probably someone who came from a mildly progressive background, went in the Second World War, probably met people who were Communist in the army, and was influenced by them … and he came back like a lot of people with more progressive ideas," Bacon said in an interview for this book.

"And there was one big story in my family about my great great grandmother. The thing that was always said about her, that we were meant to admire, is that a convict came to her house in the bush and she hid him in the cupboard [from soldiers looking for the convict]. So that was regarded as a really, really good act. So she was presented in an extremely favourable light by my grandmother.

"I think we were getting messages that you stood up for justice. Even though we were in this sort of Presbyterian environment, at home it was: you actually do research, you investigate things, you think for yourself. That was the definite message."

Bacon brought this mindset to Sydney, after following her boyfriend to the city in 1966. She initially enrolled in a master's qualifying course in politics at the University of Sydney, before being lured to the University of NSW to study an honours degree in sociology, before being given a scholarship a year later to undertake a post-graduate Doctor of Philosophy (PhD) in sociology.

Bacon says her PhD topic was "the social theory of anarchism" but admits with a laugh that she never completed her studies because "I got too involved in the practical application" of the subject matter. What this means is that Bacon threw herself into fighting for anti-authority causes, including campaigning against the Vietnam War, racism and censorship, and for indigenous land rights and abortion rights. Along with fellow students Val Hodgson and Allan Rees, Bacon was also part of an editorial team which took control of the university's student newspaper *Tharunka* in 1970. This activity meant that – like her father – she came under scrutiny by ASIO officers, who spied on her movements and tapped her phone.

Bacon became involved in the Sydney Libertarians group which espoused anarchist ideals and was part of the Sydney Push – a loosely-formed intellectual sub-culture group which had existed since the 1940s. "For me the Sydney Libertarians were very influential intellectually because I think I was a person who was very drawn to progressive movements but I really was non-authoritarian," Bacon said. "I really was not someone who was going to rush off and join the Communist party." Bacon estimated that, at the time of her involvement in the Sydney Push, it had about 250 members and was made up of people who "drank in the same pub on Friday night, in fact the pub almost every day of the week" and also held "great parties".

By February 1971, the official newspaper of the Communist party of Australia stated that Bacon was "one of the most courageous left activists in Sydney".

"Few among those on the left who adopt a slighting attitude to her campaigning on the censorship issue can match Wendy Bacon's record

Wendy Bacon at the 1970 Vietnam Moratorium march, waving a red and black anarchist flag (Photo credit: Allan Rees)

of fearless activism and initiative in a variety of progressive causes," the paper stated.[1]

Bacon and the other protestors were at court to support three people and a printer which had been charged for publishing "indecent material" in *Tharunka* – namely the above-mentioned poem which Bacon and the other nuns had also paraded outside court. The nun habits reflected the fact that the poem took a shot at the nuns' celibacy requirement, which it was claimed meant they were actually getting screwed by God. "Soon you will realise … that you have been getting fucked all along … for there is no cock as big and rough … as the one your church has thrust in you … God's great steel penis," the poem stated.

Not surprisingly, given the conservative social standards of the early 1970s, Bacon's antics in the court foyer meant she was charged with

---

1   The Case of Wendy Bacon, *Tribune*, 10 February 1971, page 1

making an obscene exhibition (namely the nun's habit with the ribald slogan) and distributing an indecent publication (namely the flyer with the poem). Over the next 18 months, Bacon became a household name due to the fact she spent an inordinate amount of time in court fighting obscenity issues, and because of her ability to shock and offend Sydney society.

Within a few months of her nun's habit outrage, Bacon and fellow Sydney Push agitator John Cox were charged for distributing copies of another allegedly obscene student underground publication – this time known as *Thorunka* – at Brookvale and Paddington. The prosecution focussed on what it regarded as the most offensive aspect of this publication, namely a range of well-known cartoon characters engaged in sex acts.

Both matters wound their way through the courts, with Bacon in February 1971 receiving a $100 fine and a three-year good behaviour bond for the nun's habit offence, but only after spending a week in jail on remand after being found guilty. She then spent more time on remand in 1972 during the trial for the distribution of *Thorunka*, before again being found guilty and fined $200. Bacon and Cox appealed the decision. "Of course I get sick of appearing in court, but I'm involved in the whole issue of obscenity," Bacon told the *Bulletin* in 1972.[2]

Bacon also took time to attend the "Red and Black" anarchist conference at East Minto in south-western Sydney in July 1971, where the undercover ASIO agent in attendance described her as having a "loud mouth". The same agent also wrote a memo complaining about the food – "we had frankfurts camouflaged in three different ways over the weekend" – and noted that while the conference had lively intellectual discussions, its "principal aim … was to have a 'good weekend' … sex and drugs were blatantly displayed and there were rumours of quite a bit of 'swopping' going on."[3]

---

2   The Right to be Obscene, *The Bulletin*, by Elizabeth Wynhausen, 28 October 1972, page number unknown
3   From Wendy Bacon ASIO file B/77/46, National Archives of Australia

Bacon and her supporters stated that their campaigning was not just about arguing in favour of artistic expression, or removing unnecessary barriers to publishing information, but was also about fighting and undermining the very concept of authority and established society. Bacon wrote that her activity "does lie in a revolutionary tradition … on the one hand an attack on existing society, on the other an attempt to 'build a new society from within the shell of the old'". She also wrote how working on one of the publications was a "liberating experience" which "does present the possibility of something less oppressive, of a less authoritarian way of organising our lives".[4] Her University of NSW student colleague Val Hodgson, was clear in explaining the motives. "Our efforts have been misconstrued by the general public … to be a challenge against censorship laws … we see *Thorunka* as a means of direct action, it is a challenge to the authority of all laws," Hodgson said.[5]

In February 1973, Bacon and Cox were successful – due to technical legal reasons – in overturning their conviction for distributing *Thorunka*. Bacon's long time in the spotlight for censorship issues had come to an end.

However, it would take only a few weeks for a new issue to emerge, this one with far more at stake than publishing ribald locker room poems or outrageous cartoons.

Bacon had moved to a home at Caldwell St, Darlinghurst, with some fellow Push members. Bacon recalls that one day in April 1973, the home had an important phone call – from a fellow Push member called Arthur King.

---

4   *Uni Sex*. Eclipse Paperbacks, 1972, pages 64 and 65
5   *Uni Sex*, page 37

CHAPTER 16
Inner Sydney - "a region in transition"

After being chastened by the rejection of his 1971 plan to build 45-storey towers, Frank Theeman decided to turn to a rising star of the architecture world.

Aged 39, Ken Woolley was rapidly gaining a reputation for high-quality work which was bucking the architectural norms of his times.

In the 1950s and 1960s, Sydney's most iconic new buildings were towers set among open space – designed in the modernist architectural style – which had little consideration for the landscape or existing built forms around them. Architect Harry Seidler's isolated and much-maligned Blues Point Tower, and his 10-storey cliffside apartment building at Kimberley St, Vaucluse, are classic examples of this approach.

Woolley didn't subscribe to this view. He took a keen interest in the topography and climate of his building sites, and then used this knowledge to design buildings which attempted to respond to, and complement, their surroundings.[1] "Every one of the buildings Ken's released [that] I can think of, relates beautifully to its context," said Peter Webber, a former New South Wales (NSW) Planning and Environment Commissioner, in an interview for this book.

Woolley had received critical acclaim for implementing his more sensitive and considered approach at a project known as 'The

---

1   Vale Ken Woolley, *Architecture, Au*, 14 December 2015, by Tone Wheeler

Woolley's Penthouses development hugs a foreshore slope, helping it blend into the landscape, unlike the tower form at the right of the photo which was built in the late 1950s (Photo: Mark Skelsey)

Penthouses' at Darling Point. This project embedded new housing apartments tightly against a slope leading to the harbour foreshore. By doing this, the project was unobtrusive, both when viewed from the harbour below it and also from the top of the ridge behind it.

In 1969, the project won the Wilkinson Award for the best new residential project in NSW, with *The Sydney Morning Herald* noting that the clever use of the slope meant that "no part of the building is more than two storeys high, although there are six levels". "This makes an ideal foreshore development, since people further up the hillside can look over the top [of the project] and the building appears much less bulky than a home unit block," the paper went on to say.

Theeman knew that if his proposal for Victoria St was to be approved, his development would need to be more sympathy with the landscape. As such, in late 1972, Theeman signed up Woolley to prepare revised plans for his Victoria Point site.

"I had the impression I had come into [the project] as a kind of name that was going to take a fresh approach ... that would do what was currently avant-garde or world's best practice thing on that site," Woolley said, in an interview for this book.

Woolley found Theeman to be the perfect client. "What was good about Theeman was that he listened to the people who put pressure on him ... and he gave it that kind of authority. He basically wanted to do a very good housing development at a big scale.

"He was almost the ideal client ... [he had] no professional advisors or project managers, he relied on his architect, he took advice, he paid his bills [and was] very nice to work with."

However, while Theeman had potentially solved a planning and architecture problem through Woolley's appointment, the delay caused by the refusal of his first set of plans meant he was now facing another more serious problem.

Since the early to mid-1960s, a complex and connected range of economic and social forces had increasingly been leading to conflict between developers and residents. By early 1973, as Theeman prepared to release Woolley's plans, this conflict had arguably climaxed.

The state of the inner-Sydney region's economy was a significant factor behind this conflict. Across the 1960s, there had been a decrease in the number of 'secondary' jobs – such as in factories and warehouses – and an increase in 'tertiary' jobs – such as in finance, property, public authority and professional services.[2] This reflected the fact Sydney was stealing Melbourne's mantle as Australia's commerce capital.

"Since the Second World War, shifts in both political and economic geography have favoured Sydney as a central location for business and commerce," the City of Sydney Council's 1971 Strategic Plan reported.[3] "Australian political, trade and investment links have been expanding with North America and with Asia, while links with the United Kingdom have tended to be less and less dominant. In this context, location in Sydney is proving to be more convenient

---

2   City of Sydney Strategic Plan, City of Sydney, 1971, page 34
3   City of Sydney Strategic Plan, page 30

to a greater proportion of the new firms being formed, and to an increasing proportion of the Australasian head offices of multinational corporations. Sydney's climate and topography have probably also influenced the making of many decisions to locate in Sydney."

Inner-Sydney's education institutions, meanwhile, were undergoing rapid growth, in part to help service this new knowledge-based economy. The proportion of Australian university students aged between 17 and 22 increased from 4.2 to 9.5 per cent between 1955 and 1975, with around one in five people in this age group receiving tertiary education if vocational education colleges were added.[4]

This change meant many Sydneysiders were viewing inner Sydney in a new light. Since the 1890s, inner Sydney had been hollowed out as young people and families left – or chose not to occupy – the inner suburbs, instead preferring new suburban areas. This trend was now being reversed, as academics, professionals and students (such as Wendy Bacon) began to increasingly value the proximity that inner-Sydney suburbs provided to this changing economic and educational environment.

In 1981, in a thesis for a Bachelor of Town Planning degree, inner-Sydney resident Peter Gray studied this gentrification trend over the 1950s, 1960s and 1970s.

"The concentration of a high proportion of Sydney's financial, commercial and administrative activities in the city centre has created intense land use competition and pressure for change in the inner area," Gray wrote. "The consequently high numbers of white collar jobs in the city centre have increased the attractiveness of an inner area residential location for some of these white collar workers, particularly the higher status ones in the pre-family stage, that is young marrieds and singles, without children."[5]

---

[4] *Australian Liberals and the Moral Middle Class*, Cambridge University Press, by Judith Brett, page 141

[5] Whose Housing? The Housing Problems of Inner Area Lower Income Earners: The Political Economy of Gentrification and the Declining Supply of Low Cost Housing in Inner Sydney, by Peter Gray, Bachelor of Town Planning, University of NSW, 1981, pages 11 and 12

Gray said these gentrifiers were also rejecting the long commuting times which came with Sydney's ever expanding growth boundary, along with the dullness of these areas.

"Initial impetus for the gentrification process came from small numbers of non-conformist middle class groups (artists, architects, academics) who were attracted to what were more conventionally called slums," Gray said.[6] "This group was rejecting the apparent conformity of low-density, middle-class suburbs, and at the time was attracted by the architectural potential of the older inner-city houses and the more heterogeneous or cosmopolitan nature of the area."

The fact that many of these gentrifiers were childless couples also meant they were less concerned with the small private open space areas of the traditional terrace or semi-detached home found in inner Sydney.

However, when they arrived in inner Sydney, these new professional, middle-class home owners found the government policy environment was not to their satisfaction.

The owners soon realised that, since the mid-1950s, State Governments – both Labor and Liberal – had introduced policies and legislation which had encouraged the redevelopment of the inner city.

For instance, after World War II, architects and developers – particularly of commercial office towers – had increasingly pressured the NSW Government to abandon its 150-foot (46 metres) maximum building height limit, which had been in place in Sydney since 1912. The then Labor NSW Government agreed to do this, subject to some conditions, arguing that the resulting higher towers would more likely be surrounded by "light and air", rather than being crammed alongside each other due to the lower height limit.[7] The deletion of the maximum building height finally allowed developers – both office and residential – to more easily take advantage of Sydney's glorious harbour views, but also increased the chances that new projects would steal the sunlight or privacy of neighbours.

---

6   Whose Housing? by Peter Gray, page 43
7   Second reading speech by C. Kelly, Chief Secretary, for the Height of Buildings (Amendment) Bill 1957, NSW Legislative Assembly, 12 March 1957, page 3965

In 1961, the Labor Government followed this by introducing a new land title framework for apartments, which would again help the development industry. The new strata title legislation created a separate legal land title for the air space in each apartment, thereby making it easier for banks to loan money to purchasers, and in turn making it easier for developments to construct new unit blocks.

Finally, across the 1950s and 1960s, the Labor and Liberal NSW Governments progressively watered down the existing laws which had been put in place to control rent increases and restrict evictions before and during World War II. These laws had effectively guaranteed lifetime affordable accommodation for many long-time inner-city tenants, but at the same time had dampened interest in property investment and contributed to the rundown nature of many inner-Sydney homes and streets. In 1954, all new buildings were exempted from the legislation, while in 1956 residential premises could be uncoupled from the legislation when vacated.

Further reforms in the late 1960s relaxed 1930s-era restrictions on rent increases.[8] These reforms, again, made it easier to justify new development projects in inner Sydney.

The problem was that, while measures had been taken to make it easier for new development to happen, there had been no real changes to help plan for this development, particularly during the boom economic conditions of the late 1960s and early 1970s.

In the mid-1970s, the US-based Conservation Foundation sent a young American lawyer, Richard J. Roddewig, to Australia to study the country's environmental policies and planning procedures. Roddewig's resulting book provides what is arguably the best analysis of the failures of the State's planning system during this period.

Roddewig found that, during the critical late 1960s and early 1970s period, residents had no real opportunity to influence planning decision-making, an example of which was the lack of consultation

---

8 Protected Tenancies: History and Proposals for Reform, NSW Parliamentary Research Service, by Edwina Schneller, March 2013

in the development of the Woolloomooloo scheme. Roddewig found residents only had the opportunity to object to new council-led planning schemes, but had no ability to contribute in a positive way to the creation of these schemes. He also found that, in most cases, residents had no right to be notified of new development proposals, which meant the first time they found out about new developments was when construction began.[9] What's more, unlike in other Australian States, NSW residents had no right to challenge the merits of an approved project in the courts. Roddewig concluded that, given this, it was no surprise that residents formed themselves into groups and turned to unions to impose construction bans on projects.[10]

"When the citizen action movement found that the traditional methods of political persuasion were fruitless, it looked elsewhere than to the law. It found a more effective means, not in the courts but in the halls of trade unions," Roddewig said.

An anecdote from Woollahra Council here is informative. In the mid-1960s, the council refused to let neighbours know about, or even see, plans for new Darling Point skyscrapers, before a decision was made on these plans. The council's Town Clerk stated the council had no authority to release these plans, and at any rate such consultation was not required because the council's decisions needed to be interpreted as the "will of the people".[11] Nevertheless, community members were sometimes leaked plans by accommodating Aldermen, and then charged into council meetings to object. "I am sick of these last-minute objections," Woollahra's Mayor A.C. Murchison told one meeting.[12] In 1970, the NSW Government introduced new legislation to require councils to seek feedback from adjoining landowners on new residential flat building proposals, but not for many other types of applications.

---

9   The exception being legislation moved in 1970 to require the notification, including to adjoining residents, of development applications for new residential apartment buildings
10 *Green Bans: The Birth of Australian Environmental Politics: A Study in Public Opinion and Participation*, published with the Conservation Foundation (Washington) by Hale & Iremonger, 1978, by Richard J. Roddewig, pages 52-64
11 Building Plans Private Says Town Clerk, *Wentworth Courier*, 27 April 1966, page number not known
12 Huge Property Developments at Woollahra, *Wentworth Courier*, 7 June 1967, page 1

Adding to this problem was that the planning system provided no detailed guidelines about what sort of development could be constructed. Most local planning schemes, if they were even in place, tended to divide streets and suburbs into different potential land-use zones – including industrial, lower density residential, higher density residential and open space. There were typically no building height limits and no requirements to consider the privacy or over-shadowing impacts on neighbours or open space.

According to Peter Webber, the planning system at the time was primitive. "I mean, there were zoning of areas so that what you could build in various areas was within a zone, but there was literally no control on what you could build. So it was, by today's standards, a very primitive sort of era [in which] people began to get more and more upset and more concerned."

At the same time, these new gentrifiers found that the planning system not only didn't allow them to participate in decision-making, but also didn't share their newfound fondness for the historic streetscapes and buildings which dotted inner Sydney.

In the 1940s and 1950s, town planners – with the express support of sections of the media – regarded many parts of inner Sydney as slums which were worthy of demolition and reconstruction into concrete blocks of flats. According to author Brian Turner, this reflected the fact that, in these decades, inner-Sydney's housing held "memories of hard times, in squalid, over-crowded conditions" while in the post-war years, Sydneysiders also wanted a "fresh start" in housing styles, rather than look to the past.[13]

However, by the 1960s, the tide was turning and more people were developing a deep affection for the housing types previously regarded as slums. "In the early 1960s, young couples who had perhaps grown up in and were disillusioned with the sprawling new suburbs, began to buy terrace houses in Sydney's Paddington and Balmain," Turner

---

13 *The Australian Terrace House*, Angus & Robertson, by Brian Turner, 1995, page 86

writes. "To their delight, they found most of these houses, now almost a century old, to be remarkably sound in structure. Removal of the years of accumulated paint often exposed superb cedar joinery and elegant marble fireplace surrounds, which, like the houses themselves, had survived through a process of protective neglect. All in all, the effect was stunning."[14] Turner notes that terrace owners then went on to form location associations to "protect and improve the Victorian character of their streetscapes as a whole".[15]

Long-time Sydney restoration architect Clive Lucas had a ring-side seat as this trend was underway. In the early 1970s, Lucas was an eager young member of the National Trust, an organisation established in 1945 in NSW to preserve built and natural heritage.

He was among a group of volunteers who walked Sydney's streets and NSW country areas during weekends, deciding whether buildings and areas were worthy of preservation. The Trust's preservation list had no power under law but did have the potential to influence property owners and government agencies, and had the added bonus of actually documenting some buildings which were later doomed for demolition.

In an interview for this book, Lucas said that the Trust's 1945 founders were only interested in pre-Victorian buildings – colonial-era places such as the city's Hyde Park Barracks (1819) or Parramatta's Elizabeth Farm (1793). However, he said that by the 1960s and 1970s, he was able to influence the Trust to also show an interest in Victorian-era architecture, built between 1837 and 1901.

Lucas said another important change was recognising the need to protect streetscapes and precincts, rather than just individual buildings.

"All the [Trust's] early listings were individual buildings, we listed a house and we might have listed a terrace of three houses. But we hadn't really thought of listing a whole street or a whole area," Lucas said. "And [it] suddenly became a new idea that the Trust would start to

---

14 *The Australian Terrace House*, page 84-85
15 *The Australian Terrace House*, page 88

think of, instead of just keeping one house in that street think that the whole thing, and some of those houses weren't as good as others, but the general combination of it all built up into something quite good."

The problem was that, despite this increased interest in heritage protection, again the legislative framework was lacking.

During the first half of the 1970s, there was – at best – an ad hoc approach to heritage protection. The State Planning Authority and its predecessor – Cumberland County Council – had proclaimed 15 historic buildings, which meant it had an obligation to purchase the buildings and they couldn't be demolished. Some councils had also introduced their own heritage policies, such as the City of Sydney which had implemented a preservation zone over Paddington, and the Hunter's Hill Council which had listed 200 buildings that required development consent for demolition. But, in general, the State did not have an over-arching framework to allow councils, communities and the NSW Government to plan for heritage issues.[16]

A final – and potentially the most significant – issue for many of inner-Sydney's gentrifiers, was the plan to demolish large sections of suburbs for new freeways. This meant homes would either be resumed for roadways, or residents would have the discomfort of living near one of these major roads. New expressways were proposed to snake through suburbs such as Pyrmont, Ultimo, Glebe, Chippendale, Woolloomooloo and Redfern, all designed to siphon traffic in and out of the Sydney Central Business District (CBD). Of course, as we know, work was also underway on the Eastern Suburbs Railway and the Kings Cross road tunnel, both of which involved the demolition of hundreds of homes.

Given all these factors, the gentrifiers formed themselves into resident action groups, including an umbrella body broadly representing all of these groups. In February 1971, a University of NSW social work tutor, Murray Geddes, helped bring together 10 such groups to form

---

16 Based on internal State Planning Authority report 'Preservation and Restoration of Historic Buildings' by State Planning Authority town planner Gabrielle Kibble, February 1973

November 1972 advertisement published in The Australian newspaper supporting by union green bans, endorsed by resident action groups

the Coalition of Resident Action Groups (CRAG). By 1973, CRAG's membership had ballooned to around 100 groups.[17]

The losers from this entire scenario were, of course, existing lower-income residents of the inner-Sydney area. For the previous seven decades, this group had had the region largely to themselves, living in rundown but character-filled historic housing close to workplaces in factories, warehouses and docks. Now, the tide had turned, and if it wasn't the gentrifiers, then it could be property investors, developers, speculators or the demolition of homes for expressways which would see them slowly and silently forced out.

"It can be said that the inner-city region is a region in transition, with many of the traditional low-income groups being bidded out

---

17 Sourced from letter from Wollstonecraft resident Joan Heggie to John Gorton MHR, 26 November 1973, located in CRAG file State Library

of housing stock," said a 1974 submission from the Inner Sydney Interim Regional Council for Social Development.[18] "If you are poor and manage to escape an expanding CBD or the Department of Main Roads, you will just as likely fall prey to middle-income couples or groups of students, who can bid you out of the housing rental market or increase prices so that you cannot meet the rates.

"If these trends continue, it is not unrealistic to imagine the inner-city region in a few years' time as being mainly composed of middle-income rehabilitated housing, with pockets of low-income earners in Glebe, Woolloomooloo and Waterloo, and mainly white collar employment."

The one piece of good news for inner-Sydney's lower income families and residents was that, by the late 1960s, more people were willing to challenge authority, including advocating for the rights of the poor. This meant that, while lower income groups remained powerless and without government support, they were often not alone in their struggle, even if this meant support from the students who were part of the problem in pushing them out of town.

The reason for the rise in anti-authority behaviour in the late 1960s and early 1970s is, somewhat ironically, itself subject to debate and disagreement.

In a 2019 analysis of the period, author, lawyer and academic Russell Marks states that the protest uprising can be linked to an increasingly affluent middle class – which had benefited from the extended post-war boom years – having a new-found independence to think for itself, rather than rely on institutions such as unions, political party, family or the church. "The growing sense of control over their own lives and futures, accelerated the notion that individuals had a responsibility to their own consciences, rather than to an external structure of authority," Marks argued.[19]

---

[18] Submission from Inner Sydney Resident Action Group and Inner Sydney Interim Regional Council for Social Development, to the Commission on Human Relations, page 1

[19] The Far Left in Australia Since 1945, a series of essays published by Routledge, 2019, including '1968 in Australia' by Russell Marks, page 136

Political academic Judith Brett links the times to a dramatic increase in tertiary education levels and white collar employment. "The new, educated middle class, many of them employed in the public sector, depended for their social power on the control of knowledge rather than on their capital or character," Brett wrote. "They were impatient with the slowness of political change as the 1950s gave way to the new ideas and movements of the 1960s."[20]

In an interview with this author, sociologist Andrew Jakubowicz agrees that the improved educational level of the population was a factor, but says the radicalising effect of the Vietnam War cannot be understated. "[The war] meant that there were literally thousands and thousands of young people, not only young people, their parents had been involved in protest movements ... and knew about organising and recognised the value of people coming together," he said.

Irrespective of the reasons, change – and appetite for change – was in the air.

It was in this fractious environment that on 3 April 1973, Theeman ordered the eviction of around 400 low-income tenants from the terraces on his Victoria Point development site. Just three days' later, Woolley lodged his first application for the Victoria Point site.

Woolley's scheme accommodated some 416 apartments and 232 hotel units, in a building that rose 36m from Victoria St at its northern end and 70m at the south. A unique feature of the project was that it would include an internal shopping street – described as being like an "English village narrow street" – which would be penetrated by shafts of light and enjoy harbour views. "That would have been one of the major buildings in the world of its type ... no doubt about that," Woolley told this author. Peter Webber concurred, stating that "if Ken's original scheme had been built, it would have been very beautiful".

While an imposing structure, which demolished all terraces at the site, Woolley's scheme at least made some attempt to integrate with

---

[20] *Australian Liberals and the Moral Middle Class: from Alfred Deakin to John Howard*, Cambridge University Press, by Judith Brett, 2003, page 141

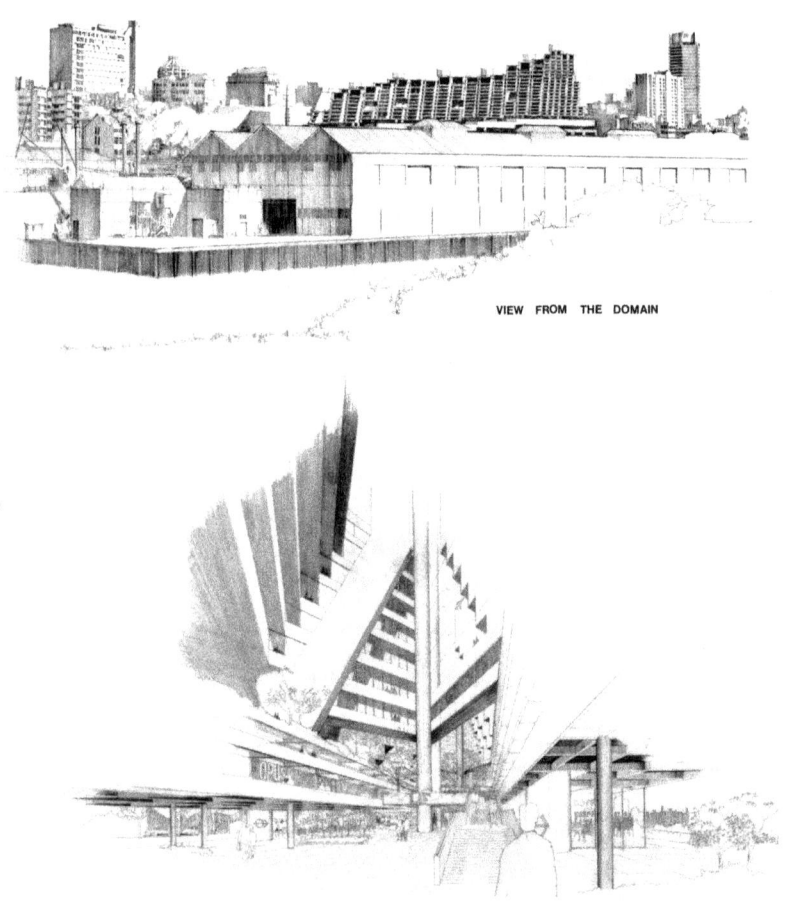

Top: Architect Ken Woolley's March 1973 scheme for the Victoria Point site, visible behind the wharf - it was never built or approved

Above: Woolley's scheme would have included an internal street

the surrounding area, by leaning back from the site edges and also providing local shopping and office facilities for nearby residents.

The problem for Theeman, and Woolley, was that activists such as Arthur King almost immediately swung into action to fight the plans, trying to preserve affordable housing and the terraces. Naively, these activists thought they were fighting yet another property developer, who may be open to reason and compromise. In fact, they were fighting deeper and more malevolent forces.

CHAPTER 17

An unwanted South Coast holiday

Gagged, blind-folded and held captive in the back of a strange car, Arthur King realised he needed to think quickly to preserve his life. Only minutes before, two thugs had abducted King from his bedsit apartment at Victoria St, Potts Point, and dragged him bare-footed into a large Chrysler sedan.

As the car sped through Sydney's suburbs in the pre-dawn light to an unknown destination, King decided on a two-pronged survival plan. Firstly, he would create some sort of rapport with the two men, to deter them from harming him.

"There was a time when I stopped being a piece of meat and became a human being," King said in an interview for this book. "I was on the floor of this car, we were going out of town and they stopped somewhere. I was a smoker then, so I said 'Give us a package of smokes, Camel Plains', they said 'Where do you think you are, the Hilton?' and I said 'If you are going to buy a packet of smokes, may as well be the one I like'. One of the guys at least laughed at that, for one of them I was no longer a piece of meat but a person, and that may have helped."

At the stop, King was slipped some sleeping pills and bundled into the car's boot, before being driven to a New South Wales (NSW) South Coast motel. On arrival, he was hustled into the motel with a knife at his neck, and a warning that a false move would see him "drown in [his] own blood".

This is where the second tranche of King's survival strategy kicked in. He realised that to survive, it was imperative that he didn't see his captors, given this would mean they'd have no option but to murder him. For this reason, whenever King felt like his blindfold was coming loose, he'd asked the thugs to tighten it for him.

King then spent two nights in the motel with the thugs. Asked what he talked about with them during that period, King said: "Well they weren't exactly chatty … mainly you are thinking about what you can possibly do to change the situation". King however considered that his life was very much under threat and therefore avoided taking any risks. The thugs told him their instructions were to "keep him out of the way for a few days".

After his captors made some phone calls, King was given more sleeping pills, bundled into the boot once again and driven back to Sydney. When King later awoke, he could see Long Bay Jail and the suburbs of Dover Heights and Rose Bay, through small gaps in both his blindfold and the car boot. After a further phone call from a public booth at Rose Bay, one of the captors told King that there had been some "trouble in the organisation about this whole business". King was told he would be released if he left his flat in Victoria St within two days and didn't tell anyone what had happened over the weekend. King readily agreed.

After the car parked outside the Venus Room nightclub in Kings Cross, the abductors suggested King make up a story to explain his absence to his fellow residents. The story landed upon was one where King had decided to travel to a relative in northern NSW, but had suffered a migraine along the way and stayed at Port Stephens. It was a highly implausible story, given King had left all his shoes and his car behind in Victoria St.

With this, the pair of thugs drove King to a laneway near Darlinghurst's St Vincent's Hospital, and allowed him to leave the car on the condition that he walk away with his back to them while wearing sunglasses. As King reached the hospital, he saw a heavily built man standing on a street corner. He later recognised the man as Frank

Theeman's apparent friend and associate, and Kings Cross identity, Jim Anderson.

King arrived back at Victoria St but refused to answer questions about his disappearance. After having his first shower in three days and making a tape recording of his experience, King left Victoria St, never to take part in the action group or the Victoria St struggle again.

"I was just scared," King told this author. "I could see I was not just fighting a few crims … the crims have [also] got the coppers on their side … that makes a difference to how much you are going to resist."

The only silver lining of the whole terrifying episode was that King soon realised the criminal forces who had kidnapped him had made a tactical mistake. "[It was a] pretty stupid thing to do … it brought the whole movement together," King said.

CHAPTER 18

"None of us were really the sort of people who were going to back off"

Roelof Smilde had been introduced to horse racing through a most unlikely path: his maths teacher. During the late 1940s, when Smilde was in his final year at North Sydney Boys High School, the teacher organised a class trip to a Saturday afternoon Randwick race meeting, in the belief that it would teach the students about probabilities and odds.

"I had no idea this thing went on every Saturday afternoon. I remember the last race in particular," Smilde later recalled. "There were about 20 runners. And the betting on it was frantic, everybody was trying to win more or get their losses back. And as the horses got to the turn, the roar of the crowd got louder and louder. And I was standing in the crowd, with all the buzz going on around me. And I was looking at the leaders of the race, naturally assuming they would be in the front at the end as well. But I looked around me and all of the people around me were looking at the tail of the field.

"And then the two horses … running last and second last around the turn and really wide on the track … come swooping down the outside. And they were the two favourites and the crowd knew that's how they ran.

"I was captured. I just got swept up. And the thunder, as they came down the straight and this long stretch, brilliant green and the

Roelof Smilde (left) and fellow activist Sasha Soldatow talk to media at the Victoria St site in 1973 (Photo: Allan Rees)

thundering hooves and the roar of the crowd. And there was something like 25,000 people there, at an ordinary Saturday meeting."[1]

Smilde was spellbound. From that moment, he became infatuated with horse racing and betting, spending more time checking the form and attending the track. It also happened to be the case that this lifestyle closely aligned with Smilde's unconventional political and personal beliefs.

Smilde was born in the Dutch countryside, near a village called Hattem. However, at the age of five, his father had a severe religious conversion and family life changed forever. "It became demanded practice that each one of us in turn would have to read out a bit of the Bible, at every dinner time … and we went to church twice on Sundays, and that was miles walking too," Smilde said. "Everything public was miles away."

---

1   Taken from interview with Roelof Smilde by Martin Thomas, between 2015 and 2016, available in National Library of Australia

Prior to the onset of World War II, when Smilde was still a young boy, the family decided to flee Europe and move to Australia. The international shift, however, didn't change his father's strict religious rule. Smilde deeply resented this, and by the age of 14 had become a "thorough atheist". It was the start of his anti-authority journey.

Smilde was a strong high school student and sportsman, which led to him receiving a bursary to study at the University of Sydney. There, he became involved in a campus group called the Free Thought Society. "It quickly developed to a position where the whole group of us became very anti-authoritarian in our outlook," Smilde said. "As a result of the sort of influences and new ideas that I encountered at Sydney University, I carried that through the rest of my life. I didn't have any ambition, and I didn't want to be professional at anything. That became the whole political outlook as well as a psychological outlook."

By the mid-1960s, Smilde had become a professional gambler. Betting allowed Smilde to use his above average intelligence to beat the bookies and earn enough income to survive without needing to work full-time, which in turn was completely in line with his anarchist approach. "The basic plan was to win enough at the races to be able to give up work, and enjoy yourself and enjoy your practices," Smilde said. "And when the races failed, you had to go out and get another job. We were ready to work for one week, or one month. Freedom, independence [and] excitement all go together in an anarchistic way of life."

Smilde became a leading figure in the Sydney Push, where he regularly met Arthur King and Wendy Bacon. For much of his time in the Push, Smilde had believed in the principle of "permanent protest" – which means that groups and individuals who disagree with society don't actually attempt to overthrow or challenge that society, because they don't want to end up in power. "We developed the view that while we would like to change the nature of society, we didn't expect that the revolution would ever do that," Smilde said. "A revolution might be successful in overthrowing a regime, but it's hardly ever the case that a revolution establishes the sort of society that was in the mind of people when they were being revolutionary. It nearly always leads to the establishment of another ruling class, another despotic regime."

However, Smilde began to reassess this theoretical viewpoint after receiving a call from a friend in 1973. The friend said Arthur King had not kept his regular appointment to meet him at the Saturday Randwick meeting, and he suspected he had gone missing.

Along with Bacon, Smilde became part of the team desperately trying to ascertain King's whereabouts, including calling police stations and hospitals, and spreading the word about his disappearance. For instance, Smilde discovered that King's car was still sitting in the street, and that all his shoes were still in the apartment. He sensed that something was terribly wrong.

One of those alerted to the disappearance was Jack Mundey from the Builders Labourers' Federation (BLF). Soon after the Victoria St tenants' eviction, Mundey and the BLF had placed a green ban stopping redevelopment in the street. This was the twenty-eighth such ban imposed by the union since its ban on Kelly's Bush in mid-1971. The union was regularly in the news, and popular among resident action groups, because of its edicts stopping unpopular projects such as The Rocks redevelopment, a new Opera House carpark, the demolition of the Theatre Royal in King St and a new sports complex in Centennial Park. In his interviews responding to the King disappearance, Mundey linked King's disappearance to his advocacy against development and warned of serious retribution by his union if developers were found to be involved.

Then everything changed again when King made a surprise return on Monday morning, accompanied by his story about his shoeless and carless trip to northern NSW. Smilde said that because the police had accepted this implausible story, the "journalists turned on us and said the whole thing had been a stunt".

However, Smilde – with his deep mistrust of the police and all forms of establishment and authority – smelt a rat and decided to keep fighting. The concern about King's potential abduction, along with the eviction of low-income tenants, meant that Smilde – and fellow Push members – began to abandon their "permanent protest" stance and became deeply embedded in a struggle.

"I got involved [in Victoria St] because I was outraged by what had happened to Arthur," Smilde said. "Instead of the Victoria St Action Group falling apart and losing its force, the action group got 10 times stronger after Arthur was dealt with. I was going down there every day … we were trying to persuade them [the residents] to stay on.

"The main thing was the right of ordinary people on low incomes to live near the city. You know, that was number one. Number two was the threat to the environment.

"People said Victoria St was a slum. That's not right at all. There were some really grand buildings at Victoria St. They'd been turned into little units and flats and corridors, which happens near the city. The buildings themselves were marvellous. The important thing to do was to restore those buildings and maintain them."

Wendy Bacon recalls a meeting held among the protest leaders, to decide whether to press on with the campaign in the wake of King's departure. "There was some disagreement [at the meeting]," Bacon said.[2] "Not like, heavy arguments, but just some people saying, look, this really is too dangerous, this is not our problem … people could get killed, and other people saying well look, we're really involved now, there's all these tenants. And also, none of us were really the sort of people who were going to back off."

Rather than kill off the Victoria St resident protest movement, as had been intended, the abduction of Arthur King had instead inflamed the situation. In fact, the abduction had awoken an activist sleeping giant, in the form of the Sydney Push. It was now only a matter of time before Victoria St would descend into complete anarchy.

---

[2] Interview with author

CHAPTER 19

Strangers in the street

In the second half of April 1973, the remaining tenants left in the Victoria St terraces began to notice a curious but unsettling sight – well-built men ambling up and down the street carrying crow-bars and pick-handles. Some tenants were told that these men had been hired to protect their safety, but it soon became clear that this was not the case.

The alleged activities of these men first came to light in a *This Day Tonight* story which aired on ABC TV on 15 April 1973. The story showed images of the houses looking vandalised and rundown, including windows broken and boarded-up, doors hanging off hinges and building debris left scattered in front yards.

One of the tenants told the ABC's reporter: "This is the sort of tactics they have been up to, breaking in the doors. My door was broken in this weekend, after the services were cut off. Nothing was taken, which makes me feel it certainly wasn't vandals or thieves, I think the conclusion is obvious". Asked whether he believed the men were trying to force him out, the tenant said "yes". A development company representative denied tenants were being harassed, and claimed property damage was because of "thieves".

However, the complaints kept coming. On 30 April, *The Sydney Morning Herald* set aside space on its women's page to cover the mood in Victoria St. It noted that the "air of gentility that [previously] pervaded Victoria St had gone" and that women were now learning to be "cautious". Tenant Diane Cleyman complained about strange men hanging around behind the terraces and going into empty flats. "They say the flats are unoccupied … then why do I hear glass smashing in the middle of the night and people walking on floors over my head."[1] During this period, Wendy Bacon also recalled "walking past the office and these guys would be sitting in chairs outside and them talking very loudly about raping me. That was very threatening".[2]

Diane Cleyman's husband Marcel, a seaman, was also an eye-witness to the men's activities. "We had a fairly long period of harassment and silent threats, because Theeman brought in his hired men," Cleyman said. "These blokes, they used to go in and out of buildings where we still had tenants living, carrying crow bars, sticks and things like that. They used to go and ask the old people to give them a specific date when they were going to move out, telling them that they had to move … it was sort of psychological pressure on people."[3]

Cleyman recalled other acts of intimidation. One day, one of the street men told Cleyman that the Commonwealth Police wanted to talk to him. After making a long series of phone calls from a street pay phone, Cleyman returned to his flat, only to find someone had broken into the empty flat above him and broken all the taps and pipes so that his flat was flooded, causing around $2,000 worth of furniture damage. Cleyman also recalled Frank Theeman's agents trucking in a group of derelicts to live in one of the buildings, in a bid to unsettle existing tenants. The derelicts were only removed after the tenants complained to police about this.

On 5 May activist David Cusack told *The Australian:* "There are heavies in the street every day, intimidating residents and members of our committee. Cars have roared down the street early in the morning, with bricks then hurled through windows … the postman has stopped delivering mail on his own violation and somebody has cut the lead on the floodlights outside here, so we don't let the women go out alone now". In response to these claims, a spokesperson for Theeman's

---

1   Fear in Victoria St, *The Sydney Morning Herald*, 30 April 1973, page 13
2   Interview with author
3   Interview with Cleyman in 'Keeping up with the Agents', *The City Squatter* newspaper, 1974

company Victoria Point told the newspaper that "the action group has fabricated every incident to create publicity". However, *The Australian*'s reporter concluded: "The shadows are pretty thick [in Victoria St] these days".[4]

Seaman and musician Mick Fowler was another who experienced these men first hand. He returned from a trip at sea to find he had been evicted from his apartment at 115 Victoria St. When he tried to re-take his apartment, he found the men in his way.

"I borrowed some pliers off a person I knew, tried to cut through the wires, and 5–6 people from the action group came with me, but we didn't get very far," Fowler said.

"Almost immediately [the men] came up, and pushed by me and a few more comrades, but I ignored them and said to the copper 'I am Mick Fowler, a legal tenant and I live here; some bastard has put my gear out, the joint has been broken into, I am very upset; I have come 2,000 miles to come here to find this and you are pushing me aside.'

"The copper said 'Who is this man?' and [one of Theeman's men] said 'This man I want him arrested, he is no longer a tenant and I represent the owner.' And with that I was arrested and handcuffed and taken up there to Darlinghurst Police Station.

"There were always 20–40 [men] in the area … they all had pick handles. They didn't hit anybody with them, they always carried them around. They are walking up the road to buy their sandwiches, in 1973, carrying their pick-handles. Incredible struggle."

Roelof Smilde said the experience scarred him for years after. "Quite often, when I went down to Victoria St and pretty much on my own, I really got a dry mouth … for about four years," Smilde said.[5]

This environment of fear and conflict was exacerbated by the fact that, at the time, Victoria St was unnaturally quiet and eerie. This had

---

4   Street Battle, *The Australian*, 5 May 1973, page number unknown
5   Taken from interview with Roelof Smilde by Martin Thomas, between 2015 and 2016, available in National Library of Australia

come about because the street had been closed to vehicular traffic at its southern intersection with Darlinghurst Rd, as part of the construction of the Kings Cross railway station. In addition to this, most of the tenants in a 250m strip of the street had been forced out, meaning there were far fewer eyes on the street and people coming and going. Even Victoria St's grand rows of plane trees – beautiful as they were – had the effect of enclosing and darkening the street.

Union boss Jack Mundey said he told Theeman that "the actions of [his men] were only inflaming the situation and would prevent any compromise. We were greatly concerned … I remember saying that … if the intimidatory tactics were going to continue, my fear was that someone would lose their life". It should be noted that none of the men patrolling Theeman's property were charged with a crime in relation to their work in Victoria St in the 1970s.

Theeman's apparent decision to use the men may have reflected the fact that he personally feared for his safety. Theeman's architect Ken Woolley said Theeman had confided in him that he had carried a gun while attending a meeting in 1973 with the anti-development activists.

"He and I went to a meeting at the Menzies Hotel with the activists. Before the meeting, Theeman showed me a gun he had acquired to carry around," Woolley said.[6] "He had a little gold-plated automatic … probably a 25 … in a little pocket hand bag. He had clearly been under a lot of pressure, quite upset about it all." Woolley also recalls that Theeman started driving around in a Holden, rather than his regular Rolls Royce, so that he was less conspicuous, and had also claimed shots had been fired at his house.

Woolley also had reason to be fearful. Around the same time as Theeman was carrying his gun, police visited Woolley's Mosman home and told him they had believed his car may be booby-trapped.

"[The police] sat me down in the living room and advised me to keep in the background as much as I could … and advised me to look under

---

6 Interview with author

the bonnet of my car before I drove it," Woolley said. "I wasn't trained in looking for bombs; I took it to mean that there could be something kind of booby trapped." Woolley carried out the police request for several weeks but never found the trap. "With the knowledge that I had of cars, which was not profound by any means, cars were a lot simpler in those days and if someone had wired something onto the battery, you'd be able to see it very easily."

Irrespective of who was scared of whom, and following the Arthur King abduction earlier in the month, it was clear that, by mid-1973, the conflict between the pro- and anti-development forces was growing stronger, with the presence of so-called security men in the street only inflaming the situation.

This environment was not helping Theeman secure planning approval, with Woolley's scheme having been rejected out of hand by a growing chorus of former and current residents, anarchists, unionists and conservationists.

The artists who previously lived in the street had also weighed in with their views. John Olsen wrote an opinion piece in *The Sydney Morning Herald*, stating: "Here are superb houses, full of memories of people from Slessor to Drysdale, homes for people whose careers were no velvet TV success story but who were there allowed to act out their lives with some stance of human dignity. Victoria St bears many resemblances to Montmartre – beautiful plane trees, views of the city, nostalgic steps [and] proximity to the city".[7] The importance of this piece is highlighted by the fact someone handwrote the words "he is supporting us" when saving a copy of the story in the National Trust's file for the street.

Olsen was joined by *The Australian*'s art critic Laurie Thomas, who also wrote an opinion piece calling for Victoria St, along with Woolloomooloo, to be saved. "Victoria and Macleay Sts are historic places and not least because of the artists and writers who lived there

---

7   Selling Out to the Developer, *The Sydney Morning Herald*, 11 May 1973, by John Olsen, page 7

… and whose presence or whose shades would surely join any citizens' action committee formed now to ensure that progress doesn't mean pillage and renewal rape."[8]

In May 1973, after some to-ing and fro-ing, the National Trust decided to place the Victoria St precinct on its conservation list as it was "essential to the heritage of Australia". Clive Lucas had been part of the Trust committee which had walked around and assessed the street.

In a media release, the Trust said the street "possesses a combination of environmental qualities which make it a boulevard unique to Sydney". These qualities, the Trust said, included its cliffside location, the "beauty and scale" of the streetscape, its trees and "quiet and peaceful" atmosphere, its blend of architectural housing types including terraces and its historical associations, particularly with leading arts and cultural figures.

The anti-development activists also started receiving messages of support for high political figures. In late 1972, the Whitlam Labor government swept to power in Canberra with a mandate to improve planning for cities. While it didn't have any regulatory authority to influence the Victoria St outcome (this was the domain of the New South Wales (NSW) – not Australian – Government), the Whitlam government's newly-appointed Urban and Regional Development Minister Tom Uren backed the Victoria St movement. "I love the serenity of Victoria St, with its trees and the human scale of its houses of the last century," Uren said in a statement. "I commend the efforts of those who are fighting to save the character of the street." NSW Opposition Leader and future Premier, Neville Wran, telegrammed a similar comment to the National Trust. Even the State Council of the Liberal party – which was in charge of the political party but not the government of the day – called for Victoria St to be preserved.

Wendy Bacon, Roelof Smilde and the growing number of activists also ramped up their activity, by holding a public meeting on 9 May

---

8   Must Progress Mean Pillage, *The Australian*, 14 April 1973, by Laurie Thomas, page number unknown

chaired by Dr Neil Runcie from the Coalition of Resident Action Groups. The meeting was addressed by Jack Mundey from the Builders Labourers' Federation (BLF) and well-known Australian author Patrick White, and called on the NSW and Australian Governments to come together to preserve Victoria St.

Additionally, on 6 May, activists held a Festival of Victoriana at the street, including dressing up in traditional 19th-century costumes, poetry readings and a Blues singer wandering through the crowd. Guided tours of important historical features were also held.

By this stage, the activists had taken over an abandoned old building known as The Stables – behind 109 Victoria St (artist John Olsen's former home) – as their headquarters. Artists who formerly lived in the area – and other artists from across Sydney – donated valuable paintings and sculptures for a show at The Stables to raise fighting funds.

Theeman couldn't comprehend that the activists would oppose his plans on principle only, thinking that they must have a secret motive. He even publicly floated in a newspaper story, without a shred of evidence, that they were working for a rival developer.

"[Theeman] never understood what it was all about," Smilde said. "He thought at first we might have a particular interest, and that we wanted a cheap place for ourselves and he tried to bribe us, and offer us cheap accommodation."

"Then he thought he must be part of a political party, and that wasn't true, and then he thought we must be working for another developer and screw him, and that wasn't true, and then he threw his hands up and said 'what are you, martyrs or something', and thought we were people who just dropped out of the sky, that we had never been there before.

"In fact, I've lived in Woolloomooloo, Darlinghurst and Edgecliff, two of the places I have lived in have been destroyed, one for the concrete bunker called the Edgecliff Centre and another for the Eastern Suburbs Railway and we don't like the way things are going. So when we got involved in Victoria St, all of that was background [and] we didn't need to even think about it very much. The immediate stimulus was that we had friends in Victoria St who were being kicked out."⁹

Theeman also remained unmoved by the growing choir in favour of retaining the terraces. "Many of the houses in the street are no more than filthy hovels which should have been condemned a long time ago," he said. "Most of the street has been rundown for 20 years and it has been frequented by drunks and prostitutes."¹⁰

However, with the BLF holding its green ban on demolition, Theeman had no real option but to back down from Woolley's plans. On 28 May 1973, Woolley informed the city council that he wanted to withdraw his application "due to objections which do not have an official say".

While the immediate threat of development had passed, it had not gone away. Also ever present was the climate of fear and danger. "The situation has reached the stage where people's lives are being seriously endangered," said novelist Patrick White in early June 1973.¹¹ White would prove to be right.

---

9   Quotes from the documentary film Woolloomooloo: A Redevelopment 1969-1977
10 Labourers Defy Karate Experts in Bid to Save Old Home, *The Australian*, 4 May 1973, page number unknown
11 Residents Intimidated Says Writer, *Daily Mirror*, 3 June 1973, page 15

CHAPTER 20

"He was in big trouble"

If Frank Theeman was in trouble with his hillside Victoria St site, the situation was no better down in the valley for Sid Londish. Londish's dream for a grand new Central Business District (CBD) sprawling across the Woolloomooloo basin was turning into a nightmare.

Londish's case was not helped by the fact that, in August 1972, the Australian Parliament's Standing Committee on Public Works announced it did not support a long-standing proposal to convert the Australian Government's Woolloomooloo land holdings into office accommodation. This was a surprise, given that the then ruling pro-business Liberal and National parties had the numbers on the committee and the proposal was expected to pass. However, one of the government MPs sided with the opposition Labor members to refuse the scheme. The majority committee members felt that the transport-related impacts of new office accommodation would overwhelm the local area and it was more desirable for the government to build new accommodation out of the central city area. This finding turned out to be a severe blow for the concept of turning the valley into a new CBD, and as such made Londish's scheme almost impossible to support.

Around the same time, the Royal Australian Institute of Architects (RAIA) announced it, too, did not support office development in the valley, again because of the transport impacts.

The change of government in Canberra in December 1972 – from a Liberal-National to Labor government – was also crushing to Londish's plans. Labor had come to power with a specific policy to oppose the

Woolloomooloo and Rocks office tower schemes, and instead support the retention of low-cost housing and the creation of new jobs centres closer to Sydney's sprawling and growing western suburbs. "The overbuilding of the centre of Sydney has been one of great tragedies of the last 10 years," said the party's urban affairs spokesperson Tom Uren, while in Opposition.[1]

Also, in late 1972, Woolloomooloo residents met on a street corner and, with the support of a local parish priest, finally formed a resident action group. This in turn gave the impetus for the Builders Labourers' Federation to call a green ban on the redevelopment taking place.

The State Planning Authority's chair Nigel Ashton and his chief planner Peter Kacirek were still trying to resuscitate the scheme, but they appeared to be fighting a losing battle. Kacirek attacked the RAIA analysis, saying it had ignored "economics and practicalities" and that the valley was not suitable for residential uses. In August 1972, Ashton even took the surprising step of writing to *The Sydney Morning Herald*, stating the scheme was still in place.

Londish and Theeman were both now in the doldrums, having been lured into the area with extravagant planning incentives but now treated as pariahs. The two regularly spoke about their collective woes. Londish said it soon became clear that delays were causing significant personal financial strife to Theeman.

"[Theeman] was causing more trouble … because he was in big trouble financially," Londish recalled. "He didn't have a bank like I had supporting me. He used his own money. Having done that, he was in big trouble.[2]

"He used to ring me up – it wouldn't be a day gone by that he wouldn't ring me – [asking] 'What do I do?' And I told him 'For God's sake, sit still! It'll go away. The more you stir, the more they get publicity and the more they'll love doing it to you.'"

---

1 Tom Uren, Labor party spokesperson on urban affairs, Speech on The Rocks redevelopment, taken from Uren files in National Library of Australia, date unknown but presumed 1972
2 Interview with author

In December 1972, Theeman had been forced to refinance his property holdings at Victoria St, after accruing some $600,000 in interest since 1970 but being unable to pay it back. What's more, Theeman was personally on the hook, having guaranteed the entire loan.[3] For him, as each day passed, the stakes became even higher.

---

[3] Victoria St is Financially Quiet These Days, *Nation Review*, 23-29 January 1976, by Malcolm Turnbull, page 369

CHAPTER 21

"They threatened me and prevented me from escaping"

The office environment of architectural firms is ordinarily anything but exciting. The methodical preparation of plans, sketches, reports and drawings is best suited to an atmosphere of quiet contemplation, with the occasional lively discussion during closed door meetings.

Yet on 29 May 1973, the North Sydney office occupied by Ken Woolley's architectural firm was in uproar, with at least 15 uninvited invaders madly searching through drawers and cupboards in an attempt to find something. Woolley himself was desperately trying to escape the fracas through a back door, but his path had been blocked, with the office's 50 staff unable to work for two hours. What was happening?

Woolley's firm had been asked to prepare new plans for Frank Theeman's Victoria St site, in an attempt to appease the National Trust, Builders Labourers' Federation (BLF) and activists. Earlier in the day, Woolley said he had received a phone call from Wendy Bacon, wanting to see the plans, but he refused to commit to showing them. A group of around 30 activists had then gathered around and taken over his office, in an attempt to find the plans.

"I told them I couldn't [show them the plans] because I was bound by duty to a client … when [the client] decides to show it, he will," Woolley said. "They said 'You must do it as an architect' … in fact my duty was quite the opposite. Instead they just charged up the stairs and pushed people aside."[1]

"My staff had been concealing all the material and they couldn't find anything. It was an environment with which they were not familiar, they wouldn't know a drawing from a postage stamp. Then they came back down again, some of them slightly sheepish, and some quite aggressive. A Channel Ten cameraman was there, belting people with his camera."

"They threatened me [and] prevented me from escaping from them, by forcibly holding the door against me. I was trying to get out of the backyard. In the meantime, the staff had called the police." The New South Wales (NSW) chapter of the Royal Australian Institute of Architects issued a thundering statement condemning the invasion. "I deplore the situation where our members are intimidated and impeded in the normal conduct of their business," said Institute President G. Lumsdaine. "Architects are being increasingly blamed for shortcomings in planning and preliminary processes because they are involved in the first basic activity on site."[2]

The incident underlined, yet again, just how heated the Victoria St battle had become.

There was a reason Woolley and Theeman were so keen to keep the plans secret from the activists. This was because, before making them public, they wanted to go on a charm offensive to get support for the plans from the National Trust.

Theeman had scaled back his plans yet again and also committed to preserving and restoring 23 of the 32 terraces. He proposed to construct low-scale apartment buildings on the land where nine terraces would be demolished, with a larger apartment building behind both the retained terraces and these low-scale buildings.

---

1 Interview with author
2 Architect's President Criticises Invasion of Office, statement by NSW chapter of the Royal Australian Institute of Architects, 30 May 1973

Top: Ken Woolley's revised scheme sought to retain some terraces – such as those at the right of this drawing – and demolish others for new in-fill development, as shown in the centre of the image

Above: Ken Woolley's revised scheme as seen from the Domain, with the finger wharf in the foreground

It was a somewhat radical and innovative approach. At the time, such a move by a private developer to blend old and new in a project was unheard of. The prevailing view at the time was that if a historic home was on a proposed development site, the only way it could be preserved was if a public authority purchased it.

Soon after, Theeman made another important concession, by committing that 10 per cent of any new homes at the site (comprising 60 homes) would be set aside for low-cost housing. "Such a concession has never been previously made by a private developer," Theeman said.[3]

Behind closed doors, Theeman met with the National Trust and also with the Australian Government's Urban and Regional Development Minister Tom Uren. While Uren had spoken out publicly against Woolley's first scheme, which demolished all the terraces, he seemed more at ease with the second scheme which retained many of these buildings. "It had been to the National Trust, and Tom's staff rang me and said can we come and see the scheme," Woolley recalls. "So I explained the scheme to Tom Uren. Tom was delighted with it, and he said 'that's terrific, what is everyone arguing about?' He went away very pleased and Theeman went away very pleased."

The National Trust commissioned a report on the scheme from architecture professor Max Freeland, who was also the Trust's Historic Buildings Committee chair. Freeland raved about Woolley's scheme. "It is a very important step forward in Australian architecture," Freeland told the media. "The plan blends the old with the new, retains the beauty and scale of the streetscape and preserves the quiet character of the street in contrast to the general bustle of Kings Cross".[4] Freeland's report went further and stated Woolley's scheme could be "one of the most significant buildings yet to be built in New South Wales and one that has an impact not only on the Australian architecture but on the world architecture scheme".

---

3   Letter from Frank Theeman to Tom Uren, 16 August 1973
4   Victoria St Plan Praised, *The Sydney Morning Herald*, 7 June 1973, page 8

On this basis, and much to the distress of the anti-development activists, the National Trust endorsed the scheme.

Next was the BLF. Theeman thought he had a verbal agreement with the BLF's Mundey that if the National Trust backed the scheme, then the green ban was off.[5] What's more, only a handful of tenants were now still living in the old terraces, making it more difficult for the BLF to argue that a ban was needed to protect these tenants. Even the BLF's president Bob Pringle admitted the National Trust decision put the union in an "invidious position, where up to that stage we had always supported the National Trust".[6]

It was in this environment of uncertainty and doubt that the activists hatched an ingenious scheme in an attempt to convince the BLF that the ban should stay.

---

5   Letter from Frank Theeman to Jack Mundey, 4 July 1973
6   Quote by Bob Pringle in film Woolloomooloo: A Redevelopment 1969-1977

CHAPTER 22

"The best living quarters that I will probably ever have"

By mid-June 1973, Frank Theeman must have been quietly confident that his plans were finally going to get the green light. The National Trust and all three tiers of government backed his plans. He just needed the Builders Labourers' Federation (BLF) to honour an alleged verbal agreement and lift its green ban so work could get underway.

Then, while sitting in his York St office in the Sydney Central Business District (CBD), Theeman received a phone call from one of the activists which yet again put this dream in doubt.

"They rang me up and said 'Frank Theeman, we have now occupied number 57 and 59'," Theeman recalled. "I said 'What do you mean?' and they said 'The building is empty and we have occupied it to prevent it from deteriorating any further, we have taken possession of it'.

"I said 'You are trespassing, get out of there, don't be foolish'. Anyway, they didn't." In fact, before long, the squatters occupied several other buildings on the street, forming a squat.

The Victoria St squat came at a time when the squatting movement in London was at its peak. The London squats began in 1968 and, like the Victoria St squat, involved anarchists working alongside homeless people to take over empty properties in the name of delivering housing for low-income people.[1]

---

1   See the UK Squatters' Movement 1968-1980 by Kesia Reeve, 2009

However, none of the former Victoria St squatters interviewed for this book cited the London squats as inspiration, just as they were also unable to say who led the decision to squat. "Put it down to 'affect theory'. It was there in the air within, we just all said it at the same time," joked Victoria St activist and artist, Ian Milliss, in an interview for this book.

Moving into the vacant buildings, however, had four principal benefits. Firstly, it ensured a residential community was living in the buildings, which would allow the BLF to justify that the green ban should be retained. Secondly, it provided a new story to keep the media interested in the struggle. Thirdly, the squatters would be able to protect the buildings. And finally, the squat had the not inconsiderable benefit of providing free inner-city housing with stunning views.

The squatters were able to easily move into the buildings, given that Theeman had – under pressure from the BLF – removed his provocative "security" men from the street.

Milliss, who was renting at Kensington at the time, recalled how moving into the buildings was stage-managed to maximise media coverage. "Roelof Smilde and I went down the back stairs and we went right around, we came up McElhone Steps and we sneaked into that building. We basically got in there and secured it, we locked up the doors and made sure everything was secure. Then the others had called a press conference up the other end of the street and they marched down the street with banners and things like that. We opened the door and in they came; we hung banners off the front of the building and so we managed to make this big public media event out of it."[2]

Wendy Bacon said the squat was conceived to help the BLF. "My memory is part of the motivation of the squatting, apart from the fact the buildings were being destroyed from the inside, marble removed and all that sort of thing," she said. "We also had to have people in the

---

2   Edited version of Milliss' quote from City of Sydney Oral History interview with Ian Milliss, 2012, pages 18 and 19

Wendy Bacon stands on the balcony of the first Victoria St building to be occupied by squatters, in June 1973 (Photo: Allan Rees)

houses ... to have a live community there that could be protected by a green ban."[3]

According to Bacon, the old terraces provided magnificent accommodation without any price tag. "Various activists, including some builders' labourers, came and made sure the buildings were functional," she recalled. "The place that I lived in, 115 Victoria St, was the best living quarters that I will probably ever have. There was free electricity, free running water, we got the phone on eventually and I was overlooking the whole city. It was absolutely brilliant and very comfortable. It was cold in the winter, but other than that it was extremely comfortable."

Architecture student Val Hodgson, who had worked with Bacon to edit student newspaper *Tharunka* at the University of New South Wales (NSW), was also happy to swap her rundown inner-city rental accommodation for Victoria St.

---

[3] Interview with author

Top: A squatter inside 57 Victoria St (Photographer unknown)

Left: Val Hodgson, front and centre, at the 1973 Vietnam Moratorium march (Photo: Allan Rees)

"I came back to Sydney and I was renting a hole in the wall in Paddington and I'd only been back a couple of weeks. And I went around to visit [a friend] and I complained about having to pay rent and she said, 'What are you doing paying rent? Why don't you go and squat in Victoria St?' And she told me all about it. I went down to the real estate agent the next day and said, 'Okay. I'm leaving.' And I went straight to Victoria St where I selected a flat and I moved in.

"I had two flats, one for my dog, and one for me and my boyfriend. There was never a time where we weren't overlooking the city. Yeah, it was beautiful. Watching the sunset every day."

Around this time, and quite possibly in response to the squatter invasion, Theeman had added notorious former NSW Police detective Fred Krahe to his team.

Krahe had a highly colourful backstory. During his three-decade police career, Krahe solved some major crimes, including murder cases and the arrest of famed criminal Darcy Dugan. He was known to be close to several newspaper police reporters, giving him a level of protection against scrutiny. However, according to David Hickie, author of 1985 book *The Prince and The Premier*, Krahe had a dark side. One of Krahe's former detective colleagues told Hickie that Krahe "was an evil bloke … a big, brooding bastard with an aura of power and evil about him".

In a 1971 police interview, Krahe's former lover – sex worker and brothel madam Shirley Brifman – had made a series of damning allegations against Krahe and 33 other police officers. These included claims that Krahe accepted bribes from herself and other criminals, organised eight bank robberies, destroyed police files, received stolen goods, sold forged banknotes and collected protection money from an Eastern Suburbs abortion clinic. Brifman's allegations appeared to have been sparked by the fact she had been charged for procuring an under-age girl for prostitution, despite paying bribes to Krahe to avoid police attention.

In 1972, Brifman was found dead in Brisbane, despite supposedly being under police protection at the time. Press reports said Brifman's death was either due to a heart attack or an overdose of tablets. No coronial inquest was ever held, causing great conjecture about the real circumstances of Brifman's death, including whether Krahe was involved.

Around the same time, Krahe had retired from the police force at the age of just 52, officially due to thrombosis in his leg. Hickie said the real reason for Krahe's early retirement was due to the fact that "towards the end of his career, [Krahe's] outrageous conduct, near-open as it was, became too much for police headquarters to tolerate".[4]

Whether Theeman knew about the Brifman allegations at the time he employed Fred Krahe, we do not know. But what we do know is that Theeman took advice from Krahe on how to solve the squatter problem. We know this because, at the time, the Fairfax newspaper group was paying Krahe to provide written tip-offs about various sub-surface goings-on around Sydney and NSW, and in these tip-offs Krahe was willing to report on what his client Theeman was up to. These letters are now available in the State Library.[5]

According to Krahe's letter of 24 June 1973, he had arranged and attended a meeting on 21 June between Theeman, Theeman's legal and public relations advisors, and NSW Police Commissioner Fred Hanson, at which it was agreed that the squatters were breaching the Summary Offences Act and should be evicted. The eviction job was given to Darlinghurst Police. "Plans made for doors to be bashed down," Krahe wrote.

However, Krahe claimed that – before the plan could be enacted – Theeman's barrister Kevin Murray had "sailed into" a separate meeting and objected, suggesting any eviction should be first endorsed by the courts. Theeman now had competing advice – with Krahe proposing immediate eviction via the police and Murray favouring the softly, softly court approach.

Theeman had already made a string of errors when it came to his development project.

---

4   *The Prince and The Premier,* Angus and Robertson, 1985, by David Hickie, pages 280-289
5   See MLMSS 9894/Boxes 1532 and 1521, from the Fairfax Media Business Archive, in the State Library of NSW

He'd wasted time and money on a failed development scheme described as "visual pollution". He'd kicked out his tenants before getting a planning approval, which had only aroused the interest of unionists and activists and led to a green ban. Someone had subsequently kidnapped one of the activists, and Theeman then installed so-called security staff to loiter around the street, which had only further inflamed the situation.

Now, Theeman made another mistake – accepting Murray's advice and letting the squatters stay for the time being.

"I had a conference with the police, and I have many, many good friends in the police, and they said 'Go down and remove them'," Theeman later recalled in an interview for a film.[6] "Then my lawyer came in and said 'For heaven's sake, don't do this, you'll upset the union even more, you must prove to them what they are doing is illegal, otherwise you will have nothing but trouble with the union', and I was talked into not asking the police to remove the trespassers but going to court."

Theeman's error was quickly confirmed when, on 15 June 1973, the BLF announced the green ban would stay. The presence of the squatters had helped create the impression that the terraces were still occupied and, therefore, demolition should be blocked. The BLF went on to argue that Victoria St and Woolloomooloo needed to be treated as an "integrated whole" with the need for a "coherent scheme drawn up in the interests of residents and which would concentrate on the interests of low- and middle-income residents".

A few weeks later, in July 1973, Theeman received his development approval from the council and the State Planning Authority but it was – in reality – a worthless piece of paper. With the BLF green ban in place, no demolition or construction work would commence on his site.

And the squatters would only grow in power.

---

6   From film Woolloomooloo: A Redevelopment 1969-1977

CHAPTER 23

"Dead silence" at the auction

In the five years leading to November 1973, Sydney's city centre had echoed to the daily sounds of jack-hammering and groaning trucks as it was completely rebuilt. Huge inflows of foreign capital, an economic shift towards the services economy and a pro-developer planning system, had driven a boom in office buildings.

In a 1972 article headlined 'Save Sydney', the *National Trust Bulletin* bemoaned that "developers are ripping the civic heart out of Sydney … fine old city buildings suddenly become 'obsolete' and are torn down – not because they are no longer serving a useful purpose, but because they do not exploit to the full the earning capacity of the site".[1] Artist John Olsen said he suddenly felt "small and insignificant in these vast, sunless glass valleys" and on a personal note commented that "not one bar or coffee shop that I used to frequent remains".[2]

But when it comes to high-rise development, a boom is nearly always followed by a bust. And the point at which Sydney's property market hit the skids can be traced to an auction held during November 1973.

At this auction, a near-new 16-storey tower located at Woolloomooloo's Sir John Young Crescent was up for sale. The building, which was the first to be constructed as a result of the 1969

---

1   Save Sydney, *National Trust Bulletin*, No. 53, July 1972, page 1
2   Selling Out to the Developer, *The Sydney Morning Herald*, 11 May 1973, by John Olsen, page 7

Woolloomooloo planning scheme, overshadowed a row of nearby historic terraces.

Following a ten-minute sales pitch, during which the auctioneer extolled the building's "tenancy desirability and investment opportunity", attendees were asked to submit a modest $4 million bid to start the proceedings. "Dead silence," the *Australian Financial Review* reported. The starting price was then reduced to $3.5 million. "Again silence," the paper stated.

Soon after, the property was withdrawn from auction, without a single bid being lodged.[3]

The fate of the auction matched the downward trajectory of the New South Wales (NSW) Government's 1969 scheme to turn Woolloomooloo valley into an extension of the Sydney Central Business District.

With the office market going off the boil and the Australian Government wanting to decentralise employment away from central Sydney, there was no appetite among any level of government to resolve the planning scheme's transport headaches. Instead, the City of Sydney Council, and the Australian and NSW Governments, were starting to discuss a new plan for the area.

Even Londish was forced to acknowledge in July 1973 that the 1969 scheme was "not the right solution for the development of the area". In a media release, Londish instead had been forced to beg for the right to redevelop his land for residential apartments. The scheme's lack of progress, according to the *Australian Financial Review*, also meant the Sir John Young Crescent office building now stood out "as an island in a sea of dilapidation".

At the same time, the NSW Government had decided it was time to dismantle the State Planning Authority (SPA). With its political sponsor Pat Morton gone, the organisation – which had concocted

---

3   Near New Office Block Fails to Draw Bid at Auction, *Australian Financial Review*, 28 November 1973, by Derek Hanaghan, page number unknown

the ill-fated scheme to wipe old Woolloomooloo off the map – was now itself being replaced. In March 1973, the new Local Government Minister, Charles Cutler, had ordered a Parliamentary review into the SPA, ostensibly to look at administrative issues relating to its assessment of development proposals. When it made its findings some four months later, the committee decided the "administrative" solution was to get rid of the SPA altogether.

The committee found that the SPA was causing delays, excessively meddling in minor matters which could be dealt with by local councils, was poor at communication, had a narrow 'vertical' management style which made it efficient and was ineffective at working with other State agencies. Although the committee's report didn't actually cite the Woolloomooloo disaster, it did reference some of the issues which had crippled the Woolloomooloo scheme – namely a lack of co-ordination with other agencies and poor communication.

The 16-storey office tower at Sir John Young Crescent – now an apartment building – which soars over terrace homes was a taste of the future of Woolloomooloo if the 1969 scheme had succeeded (Photo: Mark Skelsey)

In ditching the old SPA, the committee began to sow the seeds of what a new planning system might look like. It found that the top-down, directive management style of the SPA was no longer acceptable as planning and environmental issues became more complex and challenging. It said there was a need to "give the public more participation in planning, particularly at the early stages", and for the State planning bureaucracy to co-ordinate a range of expert advice and viewpoints, rather than direct outcomes. In addition, the committee found that local councils needed to be given greater leeway to plan for their local areas.

The demise of the 1969 scheme, and the failed auction, also reflected a deeper malaise spreading across the Sydney property market. After decades of post-war growth and prosperity, Australia's economy was beginning to falter.

In September 1973, in an effort to counter rising inflation, the Australian Government had decided to reduce the amount of money in circulation by buying back more Australian dollars, on either the international exchange rate or bond market. However, in doing that, the government had triggered the start of rising interest rates and a credit squeeze. Within one month of the decision, builders reported being swamped with order cancellations, from buyers who had been unable to secure finance[4] and soon after, real estate advertisements began to appear offering properties as "credit squeeze specials".

However, while the Woolloomooloo planning scheme's vision of a sea of office towers in the valley was now on death's door, its separate support for high-density residential development in Victoria St still had a pulse. This was because Frank Theeman had crucially and quietly secured Tom Uren's backing for his proposal, and continued to enjoy the support of NSW and local politicians. He just now needed to remove the squatters – and the trade union blocking his project.

---

4   Cancelled Orders Swamp Builders, *The Sydney Morning Herald*, 30 October 1973, page 3

CHAPTER 24

"We believed in the potential for a social revolution"

Faithful readers of the *Sunday Mirror* looked forward to their weekly dose of sex, crime and outrage. On the morning of 5 August 1973, they were not disappointed.

"Vice girls on rampage" screamed the front page splash headline, which led to a story reporting that detectives were investigating allegations that "drunken sex orgies" – involving girls as young as 15 – were taking place in homes occupied by Victoria St squatters. "Police have learned that girls have been formed into 'flying squads' to go from one derelict house to another, giving free sex to squatters and protesters," the story reported. The paper also reported that a "certain social disease" was rife among the squatting community, leading people to believe this was a sexually transmitted affliction such as venereal disease.

The story, of course, was complete hogwash – no doubt planted with the paper by Frank Theeman's over-enthusiastic public relations consultants.

Squatter Val Hodgson recalled how the story came about. At the time, the squatters had many different rosters – including for gardening, security, food collection and child care. A fellow squatter had made a tongue-in-cheek suggestion to Hodgson that there was also a need for a sex roster. In an attempt at sarcastic humour, Hodgson decided to

Front page of the *Sunday Mirror*, 5 August 1973

place a few lines about this in *Street Sheet*, the squatters' regular internal publication.

"There's been a few complaints noised about, that not enough ladies are manning the mattresses for the troops," the 17 July 1973 edition of *Street Sheet* stated. "Where are the volunteers for the Street Bun roster?"[1] As for the "certain social disease", this was only the

---

1   Street Sheet, publisher not stated, 17 July 1973, page 1

commonplace skin disease scabies – referred to in the same edition of *Street Sheet*.

"And so that's where [the reporter] got [the story] from," said Hodgson. "But it was horrible what they did ... because we would have weeping parents come around with photos of their runaway 13- or 14-year-old, asking were we sheltering them. And of course we had no runaway 13- and 14-year-olds; all the people that came to us, the homeless people, they were all adults. We had no teenagers. So it was horrible. And they were convinced by ... the *Mirror* that we had them, sheltering them."

Bad and misinformed press was not the only problem facing the squatter commune. Just two days after moving into the street, the squatters saw men they recognised from Theeman's estate agency destroying a fuse box.[2] The squatters also had to contend with "water being cut off, visits from the police and continual rumours about raids".[3]

However, despite all the obstacles put before them, the squatters thrived.

One by one, the squatters occupied additional buildings along the street (in fact, nine buildings were occupied in the first two weeks). The squatters began to restore gas, water and electricity supplies to these buildings and grew their own vegetable gardens.[4]

A food co-operative was formed, whereby once a week everyone put in orders for fruit, vegetables and other groceries which were purchased from markets.

A childcare centre, including swings, a cubby house and a sandpit, was created at the rear of 115 Victoria St. Residents – including those who were not parents – volunteered to look after the children, with

---

2   *Scrounge*, June 1973, page 12
3   A Cross Xmas, brochure produced by squatters, December 1973
4   They Huffed and They Puffed and They Blew Doors Down, *The Living Daylights*, 8-14 January 1974, page 4

mums and dads tipping in $2 each week for play equipment and outings.

Meanwhile, the terrace at 113 Victoria St was turned into a communal area, where film nights were held with a 50c admission (chips and soft drink available), while fences began to be dismantled to create a large parkland between the homes.

To hold everything together, weekly meetings were held in The Stables – the building behind 109 Victoria St. The squatters were even able to use the legal system to their advantage. In July, one of the squatters – John Cox – had been convicted for trespassing, in a decision widely seen as affecting all squatters.[5] However, by appealing this decision to higher court levels, the squatters were able to defer being evicted.

A 'Save Victoria St' sign draped over 115 Victoria St (Courtesy of City of Sydney Archives)

"As the year went on and we got more involved, eventually some of the fences came down and we were planting gardens," Wendy Bacon recalls.[6] "So we went from thinking we're going to be kicked out any moment to thinking we could be here for a long time and we could really build something. If I look back on a period and think there was a really positive, amazing energy [then] it's in the last months of '73

---

5   A Cross Xmas, brochure produced by squatters, December 1973
6   Interview with author

when we're really established and just not knowing what was going to happen and we were optimistic."

The situation was not without its challenges. The commune attracted odd-ball and mentally-ill characters. One of these characters was a man called Miles, who would regularly get drunk and threaten other residents, before sleeping it off and apologising the next day. One day, Miles was sent to the markets to collect the communal food. He never returned and swiped all the cash.[7]

However, as each day passed, a feeling grew that the Victoria St commune was more than just a local anti-development tactic, and in fact could be the launch pad to a future alternative society, both on the site and beyond.

Residents argued that the communal food, housing and child management approach in the Victoria St squat represented a genuine and more environmentally-friendly alternative to a nuclear family-dominated society.

"Victoria St was for me the realisation of an ideal. The dream had been one of a village society, enough room for physical distance, but with a basic community spirit and co-operation, extending most importantly to the children," said one resident.[8] "The nuclear family, on the contrary, is highly wasteful of resources … and unnecessarily pollutive."

"We all had our turns in looking after other people's kids, kids could pop from one house to the other, and they were cared for, we loved all of our kids, no-one person was responsible, we all shared the responsibility of our children and my little girl went ahead in leaps and bounds, socially and in everything else," said another squatter.

In this vein, the squatters published a co-operative housing plan in early December, which would provide the platform for this alternative

---

7   Just Somebody Called Miles, *City Squatter* newspaper, believed to have been published in early 1974

8   The Kids and Me, published by Victoria St Resident Action Group, *The City Squatter*, January 1974, anonymous

society. Under this plan, the Australian Government would be asked to purchase the Victoria St site in which the squatters were residing, and then hand it back to the residents to manage, including rent collection. Rent would be proportional to a person's income and would pay for upkeep of the site.

More broadly, in the heady days of the second half of 1973, there was a feeling that Victoria St was an important part of a brewing but vaguely defined social revolution – one that involved students and low-income workers coming together to reshape society. The social revolution concept was being openly discussed among members of the Builders Labourers' Federation (BLF) and the squatters.

By November 1973, the BLF was at the height of its powers. Through its divisive green ban initiative, it was effectively in charge of the State's building industry by being able to veto the construction of new projects.

Some 44 green bans were in place across New South Wales (NSW), stopping redevelopment in areas including Kelly Bush's in Hunter's Hill, The Rocks, Newcastle's East End, Darlinghurst, Woolloomooloo (including Victoria St) and Waterloo. The State's developers and builders repeatedly and bitterly complained about the bans, including to the NSW Government, but for the moment were powerless to change the situation. In October 1973, at one of its regular meetings with the NSW Government, a representative of the Institute of Real Estate Developers (IRED) told the government that "no amount of money could buy unionists and they were intent on causing disruption". This was a back-handed confirmation that the developers were trying to bribe the BLF, and failing.[9]

However, the union had a radical social agenda which extended well beyond green bans.

In the town planning sphere, the BLF supported residents and communities being able to plan for their own areas, while at the same

---

9   Taken from notes of meeting between IRED representatives and represents of Department of Local Government and State Planning Authority 18 October 1973

time backing the creation of a statutory committee to prioritise the construction of hospitals, schools, kindergartens, and public and cultural buildings, amid concerns there had been a boom in "useless" office buildings.

In traditional industrial relations, the BLF also believed that builders should become permanent employees and, more radically, should also control how building sites were run, including by electing the developer's foreman and then deciding who else worked on the site – a concept known as 'worker's control' or 'union hall hire'. The BLF agenda also extended to "support for blacks", including in Australia and beyond, and greater women's rights.[10] Explaining the union's position, union secretary Jack Mundey said: "Our union believes that workers should have a greater say in the end result of their work. Not only do we demand full employment, but we insist we should have a say in which buildings are constructed. We spend our working lives in the building industry and assert that buildings erected by our members should be socially beneficial to the community at large. As it is now, the sole prerogative in deciding rests with the rapacious builder developer".

In August 1973, as part of a planned power rotation agreement, Mundey stepped down as secretary and was replaced by Joe Owens. Giving an interview later in life, Owens stated that he thought the revolution was close. "Party organisation was very strong … we did vaguely think it wouldn't be too long around the corner before the main event occurred." Asked by the interviewer if the term "the main event" meant "the revolution", Owens replied "Yes". He went on to state, "I don't think we ever believed it, I think we thought it".

Bacon recalls a similar discussion with BLF president Bob Pringle.

"I think the builders' labourers, they actually were exercising so much power over the city they probably did feel they could hang on … all these communities would be able to plan. It was for a few months anyway, and only that, a very optimistic time," Bacon said.

---

10 Workers Formulate Policy, Choose Leaders for Next Three Years, *The Builder's Labourer*, August 1973, page 11

SAVE VICTORIA ST!

"SQUATTING & COMMUNITY ACTION IN VICTORIA STREET"
• MEETING IN PHILOSOPHY ROOM • TUESDAY 1st MAY • 1 pm •
SPEAKERS INCLUDE Ald. DRAPER (A.L.P., City Council), R. SMILDE (Vic. St. Residents' Action Group), GEORGE MOLNAR (Philos.)
DIRECT ACTION IS THE FORM OF THE REVOLUTION!

References to revolution in a pamphlet promoting a meeting, most likely in 1974

"We definitely believed in the potential for a social revolution and I probably still believed that right through the '70s. I think I probably thought we were part of something that could turn into that but I do remember having a conversation with Bobby Pringle very clearly one night. It was when things were getting very doable for the BLF and he said to me 'I really believe we're on the cusp of a revolution'."

However, for the BLF and squatters to achieve this revolution, they would need to dismantle the entire existing concept of free enterprise property development, in favour of a new worker-controlled industry. This was an overly-ambitious and intolerable burden for the union movement and a group of activists to bear.

Not surprisingly, the businesses and government officials which had benefited from, or supported, the free enterprise property development model worked behind the scenes to wipe out the squatters and BLF, and retain the status quo. In doing this, business and government recognised that Victoria St was on the frontline of this battle and therefore must be saved, at all costs, for private development.

By this stage, Theeman had come to the realisation that, while his court action against the squatters was ongoing, it was also time to start planning, with the police, for a mass and forced eviction. In August 1973, Theeman privately met with Deputy Premier Charles Cutler, where he raised the need for action against the squatters and BLF. According to a record of the meeting, Cutler agreed to raise the need for squatter removal with the Commissioner of Police, and the potential for union deregistration with the Minister for Industry. Both men also agreed that turning Tom Uren's informal verbal support into written support was vital.[11]

According to Theeman's security advisor Fred Krahe, Theeman had also donated $100,000 to the re-election coffers of the Liberal party, in part to ensure they supported his project at the State level. Krahe provided a tip-off to Fairfax newspapers that Theeman had also met with Premier Robert Askin in November 1973, seeking action against the squatters.[12]

To keep the pressure on all levels of government, Theeman booked a large ad in *The Sydney Morning Herald*, complaining about the squatters.

A key problem for the squatters, and the BLF, was that there were strong indications that despite the socialist left leanings of the newly-elected Whitlam government in Canberra, it surprisingly wasn't on their side in the Victoria St struggle. In May 1973, as discussed in Chapter 21, Tom Uren had already privately praised Theeman's revised plans. Then, a few weeks later, on 11 June, the squatters met with Uren and pressed him to purchase the land to support the retention of the existing terraces and their use under a co-operative housing model. According to official minutes of the meeting, Uren had avoided committing himself to this idea, and then gone further and said the creation of the Kings Cross railway station meant the area was suitable for redevelopment.

---

[11] Record of meeting between Minister for Local Government and Deputy Premier and Frank Theeman, 15 August 1973

[12] Tip-off letter from Fred Krahe to Fairfax Media, 8 November 1973

> { ADVERTISEMENT }
>
> # ANARCHY REIGNS!!
>
> In Victoria Street, Kings Cross, protected by threats of violence from the Builders Labourers' Federation (BLF), a so-called "Residents' Action Group" (the majority of whom have never been genuine residents in the street) and about 50 squatters
>
> ## HAVE OCCUPIED OUR EMPTY BUILDINGS. They FORCED ENTRY, changed locks, bolted doors, DENY US ACCESS UNDER PHYSICAL THREAT,
>
> advertised for more squatters, collected rents and fight us in court.
>
> All this to enforce a "green ban" on our housing project which was praised by The National Trust and approved by all qualified and elected authorities. Except for a handful of tenants, whom we allow to remain there, practically all original tenants were compensated and left amicably many months ago.
>
> ### The SQUATTERS now are the "RESIDENTS!"
>
> ## I ACCUSE
>
> - Messrs MUNDEY, PRINGLE, OWENS of dragging BLF members and other unionists into ruthless acts of lawlessness.
> - THE FEDERAL GOVERNMENT for knowingly tolerating and ignoring this state of anarchy!
>
> ## CITIZENS BEWARE!!
> ### You may be next to lose your civil rights!!
>
> Issued by
> Frank Theeman, Director,
> VICTORIA POINT PTY. LTD.

Advertisement placed in The Sydney Morning Herald by Frank Theeman, 8 November 1973

After this meeting, the squatters accused Uren of promising to issue a public statement supporting aspects of their cause and then not doing it. There is some evidence to back this claim. The meeting's minutes record Uren as saying he would, in a statement, praise the squatters as "rational people", question the National Trust's processes and call for public discussion on Woolley's design. Wendy Bacon later said she had never seen the statement, and there is no record of it in official files.[13] [14]

---

13 Taken from minute 'Informal meeting with Victoria St residents' group and squatters 11 June 1973', from Australian Government Woolloomooloo Redevelopment file
14 Bacon also stated in an ABC television program later in 1973 that Uren had not kept his commitment to make a public statement

Bacon went on to clash with Uren on an ABC TV show called *Monday Conference*, filmed in November 1973. Bacon told Uren: "Now I think, to you, citizen participation is a necessary phrase, but I don't think it matters". Uren shot back, implying Bacon and her ilk didn't have the right to have a say about Victoria St because they didn't originally live in the area. "Resident action groups have got no more right than anybody else … if they come from outside an area and they try to force their will on anyone else," Uren said.

One of the squatters, Ian Milliss, said the group's lack of success with the Australian Government was due to the fact they were politically inexperienced, along with the fact Uren was far more sympathetic to the tenants who were living in Australian Government-owned homes threatened by redevelopment in Woolloomooloo.

"We were all out of our depth in various ways," Milliss said. "We knew how to get out and fight on the street, but we didn't know how to actually play … that whole bureaucratic game."

In short, the BLF and the squatters now had plenty of enemies and few friends, in a high stakes game. It would prove to be an uncomfortable position as 1974 approached.

CHAPTER 25

Linked by art and blood

At first glance, it seems incredible to compare the geography and history of a downtrodden Sydney street with a European urban icon some 17,000km away. But it doesn't take long to discover that the similarities between Victoria St and the Parisian suburb of Montmartre are quite astounding.

The comparison between Victoria St and Montmartre first arose in May 1973, when the National Trust issued a media release to accompany its heritage listing of the street. The Trust said Victoria St "could be described as the Montmartre of Sydney".

Located 5km north of the Eiffel Tower, Montmartre sits on a 130m high hill which can be easily seen from Paris' city centre. This makes it an urban soulmate to Victoria St, which runs along a 30–40m high ridge above a valley and therefore can also be easily seen from the Central Business District. What's more, both locations are intersected by steep public staircases.

Victoria St and Montmartre were also developed around the same time (mid-19th century) and, by 1973, had both been recognised as historic places to be protected. For most of their lives, the two locations have also sat alongside what could be considered 'red light' districts. They both even share plane trees, with these trees shading Montmartre's main square and Victoria St's footpaths.

When it came to former social connections, both locations had once been home to thriving artist colonies, with artists such as Pierre-Auguste Renoir, Suzanne Valadon and Henri de Toulouse-Lautrec

View from Montmartre back to central Paris (Photo: Mark Skelsey)

calling Montmartre home in the late 19th century while, as explained in Chapter 5, a famous Australian art colony occupied Victoria St in the early 1960s.

The introduction of anarchist squatters into Victoria St further extended these social links, by creating a shared history of revolution and rebellion.

From the mid-19th century, Montmartre had become a popular home to the working class and anti-establishment artists, writers and entertainers, who took advantage of the area's cheap rent after being forced out of central Paris by the grand urban renewal scheme of Seine Prefect Georges-Eugène Haussmann. This scheme constructed wide boulevards and expensive apartment buildings, removing the congested streets and hundreds of rundown buildings in which the lower-income Montmartre residents had previously thrived.

Montmartre's place in world history was then secured due to its role in the creation of the Paris Commune – the two-month, tumultuous working class-led government which ruled Paris in 1871 and is known for inspiring Communist uprisings in Russia and China.

The Commune came about in the aftermath of the Franco-Prussian War. In July 1870, French Emperor Napoleon III declared war on Prussia, yet within a month was taken as a prisoner of war by Prussian

Montmartre's town centre (Photo: Mark Skelsey)

forces after his last forces were defeated at the village of Sedan, northwest of Paris. Joined by other Germanic States, the Prussian forces then marched to and besieged Paris for four months – starving the city of food and killing hundreds by firing shells into homes – while seeking a French surrender.

The terms of the surrender, when it did come, deeply divided Parisians, particularly the working class who resented the folly of the original war declaration by an unpopular Emperor and who, as members of the French military reserve, had been recruited to defend the city during the Paris siege. France had agreed to lose territories, allow a Prussian victory march through the centre of Paris, pay hundreds of millions of dollars in compensation to Prussia and remove the fortifications erected to defend the city.

It was this final point which sparked civil war. Once the Prussians had left, a new conservative French national government had been elected in February 1871 and had sent its army to remove a Montmartre-based cannon, which had been erected by the military reserve. A working-class uprising opposed the claim, leading to the execution of two of the government's Generals and sparking a broader rebellion across the city. To the surprise of many, the national government forces left town, creating a power vacuum which allowed a working-class workers' republic – known as a Commune – to be proclaimed on 18 March 1871. The Commune then promptly took control of the Parisian municipal government.

The Commune had an aggressive and left-wing policy program. Municipal canteens were set up to feed the poor, a minimum revenue was established for all workers, private firms were required to have workers' delegates who met every fortnight, civil partnerships were created, equal pay for men and women supported, freedom of the press was proclaimed and education was secularised. Of particular note to the Victoria St squatters, the Commune also decreed that vacant apartments be given to poor families.[1]

Just like the Victoria St squatters, the Commune had unexpectedly come to, and stayed in, power – after the enemy had quite literally run away. In addition, like the Victoria St squatters, it was also developing radical new policies and programs to transform society. However, as with the Victoria St squatters, the Commune was despised by the rich and powerful, who watched as their property was appropriated and fortune threatened.

On 21 May 1871, the national government's army managed to break back into Paris. An estimated 20,000–25,000 supporters of the Commune were slaughtered without trial, in what became known as the 'Bloody Week'.[2] Another 10,000 supporters were sent to prison and 5,000 more sent to labour camps in New Caledonia, an island in the South Pacific (one New Caledonia internee was artist and future Victoria St resident Lucien Henry, who was featured in Chapter 3).

All this was an unsettling harbinger to the future of the Victoria St squatters. Just as the Commune had only remained in power for less than two months, the squatters also knew their time in power would be limited. And just as had been experienced by the Commune, the squatters' demise would also come about by violence.

---

1   La Commune: A Lesson in Audacity, *The Guardian*, 1 August 2011, by Agnes Poirier
2   *The Fall of Paris - The Siege and the Commune 1870-71*, Macmillan, 1965, by Alistair Horne, page 418

CHAPTER 26
"It felt very much like war"

Looking down from the window of a tiny attic apartment three floors above Victoria St, journalist John Clare could not quite believe his eyes. While peering through the dim dawn light of 3 January 1974, Clare watched as hundreds of police slowly marched into the street. "A wagon slid round the corner from Hughes St, followed by a long blue line of cops," Clare later wrote. "It was a mesmerising and unbelievable thing to see cop after cop marching around the corner and forming a line beneath the trees."

While he didn't live with the squatters, Clare's eagle's nest-style vantage point, on the opposite side of the street from the occupied buildings, meant he had been appointed by the squatting community as a lookout for police activity. This meant Clare had been given a siren with a "deafening wail", which he repeatedly pressed into action as 200 police assembled in the street. At the time, an observer noted: "Wailing up and down the street, the sound evoked every World War II novel, every air raid description, you'd ever read".[1] "It felt very much like war," Clare later wrote.[2]

Clare had witnessed the start of the battle of Victoria St.

The squatters knew this day was coming. During December, there had been a flurry of court hearings, as test case squatter John Cox tried

---

1   We'll Strangle You with Barbed Wire, *The Digger*, published by High Times, January 1974 edition, page 5
2   *Low Rent: A Memoir*, The Text Publishing Company, 1997, by John Clare, page 160

to avoid being convicted for trespass and, in rapid succession, the courts sought to quash all his appeal avenues. "Such haste in light of the usual sluginess of the court system is breath-taking," a squatter pamphlet stated.[3] On 21 December, the New South Wales (NSW) Chief Justice Sir John Kerr had dismissed the final appeal made by Cox. Activist Roelof Smilde remembered the case as an utter shambles. Smilde recalls Cox turning up to court wearing thongs. "He was very distinctly badly dressed, you might say, for the occasion," Smilde recalled. "They asked Cox a few questions which he wasn't able to answer as to why he should be legally allowed to stay in Victoria St. Kerr was obviously keen to get it all over with. At one stage Cox sort of faltered in this statement that was going nowhere."

At this point, the last legal hurdle getting in the way of the squatters' eviction was removed. Shortly after, Kerr would soon be given a knighthood by Premier Askin and fatefully appointed as Governor-General by Prime Minister Whitlam.[4]

"After six months of squatting, the Victoria St action group expects police action will be taken against the squatters between now and the New Year," the squatter pamphlet warned.

Just like Paris at the end of the Franco-German War of 1870–71, the squatters began to prepare for a siege. "We were already starting to batten down the hatches by that stage," said squatter Ian Milliss.[5] "We knew it was going to be all over. It was just a question of when they'd move and how they'd move and stuff like that. And we were already investigating all these things about how we could barricade stuff. How much of a fight could we put up at the end? And also how we could keep track of what they were doing? We actually had people watching the police stations, so we knew what the police movements were."

By this stage, the occupation had reached its peak, with 80 squatters in place across 13 buildings. The squatters used their growing population

---

3   A Cross Xmas, anonymous pamphlet
4   As Governor-General, Kerr dismissed the Whitlam Government in November 1975
5   Interview with author

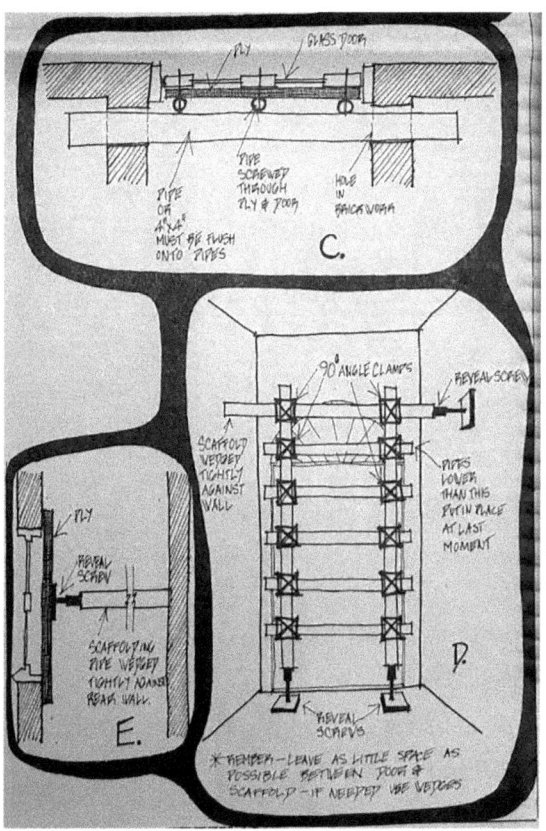

Diagram of the barricades in the City Squatter newspaper published in early 1974

to assemble wood or metal scaffolding leftover on city building sites, or helpfully 'donated' to them by builders' labourers. They also collected corrugated iron from the roof of a burned out building in the street.

With basic tools, such as hammers, tape measures and saws, and with little construction experience, they began to assemble intricate barricades behind windows and doors, and installed barbed wire on balconies.

Milliss said the squatters knew that it was unlikely they would be able to ultimately repel an eviction, but they did know that the barricades would have the effect of causing a major public spectacle which would only help their arguments and principles.

"You stage something which makes power expose itself as to how it is," he said. "And so you create this set of conditions which means power has to actually reveal what it is and how it works. And so the barricades did that. The barricades meant you had to have people on the other side with axes and sledgehammers smashing their way in to get to you."

Another squatter, Val Hodgson, concurred with this viewpoint, saying the barricades would help buy valuable time – including television airtime.[6]

"We needed to get our political statement out," Hodgson said. "We needed to get the max amount of time, and fill the street with spectators, and the press. We needed time for everyone to get there. Otherwise we were just a bunch of no hopers being thrown out of empty houses."

On 2 January 1974, Wendy Bacon received a tip-off – via a Builders Labourers' Federation (BLF) member whose brother was a policeman – that a massive police operation to evict the squatters would happen the following day. This crucial information allowed the squatters to work around-the-clock to strengthen their barricades, and call for friends and colleagues to bolster their numbers.

The BLF's secretary Joe Owens phoned Frank Theeman at his Surfers Paradise holiday home on the Gold Coast, demanding to know what was happening. Apart from confirming he wasn't going to immediately demolish buildings, Owens' notes state that Theeman was "extremely curt" and "would not answer any further questions and hung up".[7]

Which then led to the early morning events of 3 January 1974.

While it was confronting enough to have hundreds of police in the street, what was even more frightening was that they had come to Victoria St with dozens of burly security men, reportedly paid $100 for their services by Theeman. The job of these men was to break through the barricades with axes and other implements, to allow the police to remove the squatters.

According to Owens "the guys employed by Theeman to smash down the doors, those guys all worked at the strip joints and blue

---

6   Interview with author
7   Note in Joe Owens collection, Noel Butlin Archives at Australian National University

movie theatres, and areas around the Cross".[8] Theeman called the men 'controllers' – the squatters called them 'thugs' or 'goons'.

Well-known journalist and commentator Anne Summers was among the throng which had joined the squatters in the days before the eviction, and witnessed the mobilisation of police and Theeman's security men. "We peered over the balcony and were confronted with the terrifying sight of a bunch of burly men in shorts and singlets, carrying crowbars. Behind them, standing guard, were dozens of uniformed policemen," Summers recalls.[9] Another witness described Theeman's men as "huge flabby fellows, like prize bulls gone to seed, crammed in tight jeans and shorts".[10]

To this extent, and in line with Milliss' point, the squatters had successfully forced power to expose itself. This power display involved the highly unorthodox sight of police publicly coming together with underworld figures.

Theeman was, however, unrepentant about his decision to employ the men. "I am sorry I didn't think to call the Salvation Army to get these people out ... [it] would have been the right thing," he said.[11] "I had to find people to bash down these doors."

At precisely 7:07am, after police and Theeman's men were seen shaking hands, and Theeman's men read out a prepared statement, the battle began.

On this still and humid mid-summer's morning, Victoria St echoed with the sound of axes and sledgehammers pounding into doors, windows and roofs, and the smashing of windows. The squatters fought back with anything they could find – including by thrusting poles through holes in the doors or throwing vegetables, rubbish and vats of paint at Theeman's men.

---

8   Quote taken from film Woolloomooloo: A Redevelopment 1969-1977
9   *Ducks On The Pond*, Penguin Books, 1999, by Anne Summers, page 306
10 We'll Tangle You in Barbed Wire, *The Digger*, published by High Times, January 1974 edition, page 5
11 Quote taken from film Woolloomooloo: A Redevelopment 1969-1977

Milliss says the experience was terrifying. "It was fucking chaos," he said. "There were people smashing things up around you and doors being smashed in, in front of you. In the end, we just thought, okay, safest thing here to do is just all retire to the back room and just sit and wait till they're in. Just don't be in range of any flying objects or anything like that. It was just a safety shift. And then the cops came in and read us the riot act and then carted us out. And of course the thugs might have done all the nasty shit of smashing stuff up. But it was the cops who had to do quite literally the heavy lifting, pick you up and carry you out."

In the end, many of the squatters were actually thankful the police were on the scene, as they felt their lives were in danger if they were left alone with the thugs.

"I felt happy the police were there," Val Hodgson said. "And when their time came to arrest me, I refused to walk. I made them carry me. But I was very cheery and thanked them for the lovely way they'd carried me into the paddy wagon. But they were doing their job, and I didn't feel any hard feelings to them. In fact, I was grateful they were there."

Or as another unnamed squatter was recorded as saying: "One of the thugs was making karate things to me, I didn't know what was going to happen, I thought he was going to flatten me at any minute, then a copper came in and said you go here and you go over there, and I was saved".

Anne Summers was photographed being carried outside the buildings by three police. The photo shows Summers laughing – which she attributed to being relieved at being out in the street and therefore not at risk of being bashed by Theeman's men.

The barricades were only partially effective, with some holding out for just 20 minutes but others for more than an hour. The delay gave enough time for media crews to twig that a big story was brewing in Victoria St, then travel to the street and capture dramatic images of the action and yelling squatters being carried away from the scene.

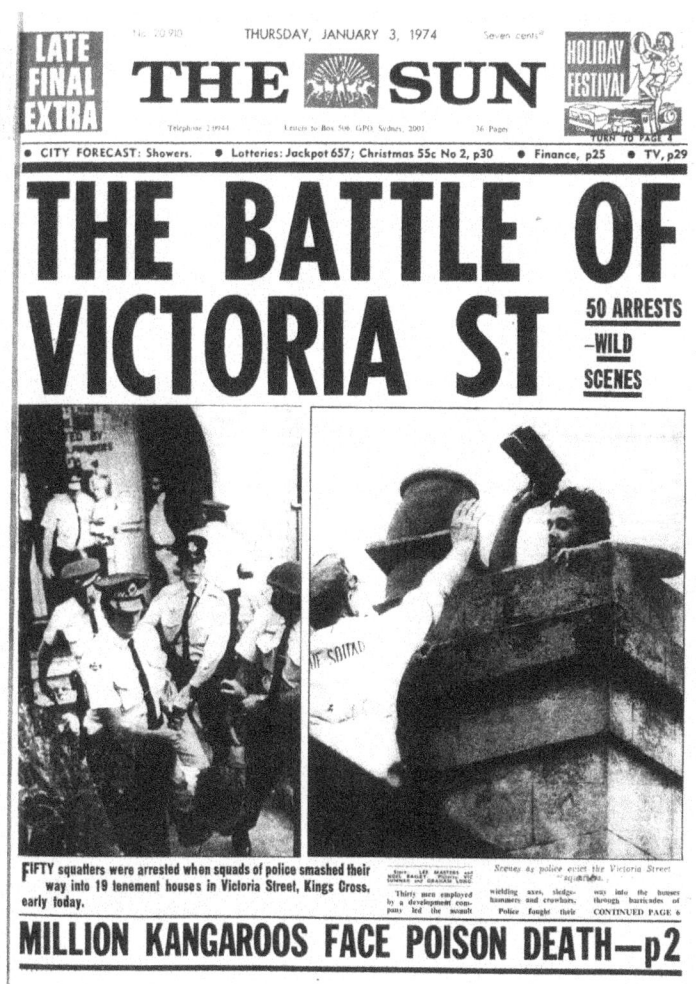

Front page of The Sun, 3 January 1974

Importantly, the delay also gave some squatters enough time to consider an alternative way of avoiding capture.

"It quickly became apparent how flimsy the barricades were in the face of attack. Someone shouted … 'to the roof'," one squatter said.[12]

---

12 Quote from story in *The Digger*, published by High Times, January 1974 edition, page 5

"It felt very much like war"

Top: Police try to arrest one of the squatters on the rooftop of 115 Victoria St (Source: The City Squatter)

Above: Police and onlookers mill in Victoria St as the eviction gets underway

At 113 and 115 Victoria St, two squatters – Keith Mullins and Con Papadatos – clambered to the rooftop. By disappearing into chimney shafts when police approached, and through daredevil clambering over rooftops, the two men were able to evade capture.

The cat-and-mouse game between the two men and the Police Rescue Squad added a note of levity and farce to what had started as a terrifying day. The spectacle attracted around 100 people to the street, and in turn a party-time atmosphere began to develop, particularly as squatters who'd been arrested earlier in the morning were bailed and returned.

"As the evening wore on the crowd continued to watch Keith and Con," Wendy Bacon wrote.[13] "They [the two men] asked for music: no power was available, so we began to sing. Our repertoire was slight but soon we began to invent our own words.

"Later a man took the guitar, and in a voice half spoken, he wailed a saga of flats too expensive to rent, of green bans and squatters, of high rise and disappearing cities. Soon he was joined by the percussion of saucepans. Gradually, first a few feet and then much further, we emerged dancing onto the road. Dismay had turned to enjoyment. The energy of the squat had not so easily been destroyed."

It wasn't until around 1am on 4 January that the two men decided to surrender and come down from their perches.

There was then a final flurry of activity at dawn on Friday 4 January, when Elvis Kipman, a former squatter, climbed onto a chimney at 113 Victoria St. The controllers attempted to shift him by lighting a fire below, but Kipman shoved his pillows and blankets down the chimney and smoked the men out of the building. The police climbed onto the roof, handcuffed him and proceeded to demolish the chimney around him.

Twenty-one hours after it began, the battle of Victoria St was over.

---

[13] They Huffed and They Puffed and They Blew Doors Down, *The Living Daylights*, 8-14 January 1974, page 3

Front page of alternative newspaper Living Daylights reporting on the squatter eviction

CHAPTER 27

"Residents and developers alike are victims of inadequate legislation"

From an early age, Andrew Jakubowicz had understood that, if a community worked together, it was likely to become stronger and more resilient. This was, in part, because of the experience of Jakubowicz's parents, who were Polish Jews who had fled their home country in 1939 before being interned by the Japanese in Shanghai.

"[My parents] were both very active in various points during the war in refugee survival groups," Jakubowicz said. "They saw there was a real relationship between the survival of the community and their personal wellbeing."

"In Shanghai, my father was the treasurer of the Polish Jewish refugee group. My mother was the manager of the sort of community kitchen, and my grandmother was the director of the community kitchen. They didn't have much glamour but they had a lot of responsibility. And I think that perspective … seeped into me."

Jakubowicz's parents continued their influence as he grew up in inner Sydney in the 1950s and 1960s. Jakubowicz's mother ran two clothing shops in Kings Cross, and his father a dry cleaning shop in Darlinghurst and then Bondi. Jakubowicz would visit both shops after school or on weekends, where he'd take part in the inevitable political debate with customers. Through the shops, Jakubowicz met Juanita Nielsen, with whom his mother advertised her shops, and senior Australian Labor party left-wing figure Ernie Page, a Mayor of Waverley and eventually a New South Wales (NSW) Government MP and minister.

Given the above, it was no surprise that Jakubowicz was drawn to a career in sociology, with a bent towards left-wing politics and community organisation.

After leaving Sydney Grammar School at the tender age of 16, Jakubowicz studied arts for three years at the University of Sydney. In a sign that Sydney was much smaller in the 1960s, Jakubowicz both went to school with Frank Theeman's sons, and while at university, wrote stories for Nielsen's Kings Cross *NOW* paper.

In 1970, Jakubowicz decided to pursue a Doctor of Philosophy (PhD) degree in urban sociology at the University of NSW. Jakubowicz's PhD supervisor, Sol Encel, let him know that the City of Sydney Council was preparing to create a new strategic plan, which would set a new long-term vision for the council area. Jakubowicz thought the plan was likely to have implications for his home suburb of Surry Hills and decided to organise the Surry Hills community, at the same time making it his PhD research subject. It was, as Jakubowicz put it, a form of "participant observation and sort of action research".

Jakubowicz felt that, given the plans being launched to completely redevelop The Rocks and Woolloomooloo, Surry Hills could be next.

"I guess it was partly the sense of, [Surry Hills] is a really valuable social space and people get on really well," he said.[1] "There's all these different mixed groups. I liked living there. My friends liked living there. We'd seen what was coming, and what was proposed in The Rocks. We saw what was happening elsewhere in the city. There was also, I think, because of the City of Sydney strategic plan, there was an opportunity, a discourse of participation around … a chance to see, if you didn't stuff [Surry Hills] up, what would happen?"

With local school teacher Enid Cook and others, Jakubowicz formed a resident group called the Planning for People campaign, which held public meetings to discuss the upcoming strategic plan. Before long, Jakubowicz and his group joined the surging Coalition of Resident Action Groups (CRAG), which had been formed in 1971.

---

[1] Interview with author

By the time early 1974 came around, the Planning for People campaign had scored some big wins. These included preserving most of Surry Hills as a residential area, successfully obtaining a green ban to stop office expansion, securing additional community facilities for young families, convincing the City of Sydney Council to reduce through traffic and requiring a developer to provide low-income housing.[2] In addition to this, Jakubowicz found himself as chair of CRAG – representing resident action groups across Sydney – at a crucial and tumultuous time in the organisation's and the State's history.

Since April 1973, and particularly during the siege of January 1974, the Victoria St development issue had helped influence a public perception that the planning and development in NSW was being badly managed, if not completely out of control.

It had done this by exposing the lack of mechanisms available for the general public or even other State agencies to participate in planning decisions or to protect heritage or affordable housing. When combined with ongoing green bans on dozens of other sites – including at the major Rocks redevelopment – and a raft of other development controversies across Sydney and regional NSW, public sentiment was in favour of a radical overhaul of the State's planning system.

A few days after the siege, CRAG issued a media release calling for a Royal Commission into Theeman's Victoria St development. This release laid the blame for the squatters' violent eviction squarely at the feet of the NSW Government, stating that it had tolerated Theeman's forced eviction of the original tenants by "coercion and harassment", not followed up on the disappearance of Arthur King and allowed Theeman to use "para-military force" to evict the squatters. "The crisis was also the result of piecemeal town planning and the failure to equip any authority with the power to control demolitions," the statement said.[3]

---

2 Surry Hills News, published by the Planning for People Campaign, August 1974
3 Request for Royal Commission into Victoria St, Kings Cross, media release by Coalition of Resident Action Groups, 6 January 1974

Andrew Jakubowicz in the 1970s

It wasn't only resident action groups who thought the NSW Government had lost its way. The developer lobby group, then known as the Institute of Real Estate Development (IRED), had also been quietly working on a reform agenda. Stung by the shutdown of dozens of building sites through Builders Labourers' Federation (BLF) green bans, IRED's executive had in November 1973 endorsed a project to work on a "policy, platform and course of action" to "resolve the industry's conflict on the green ban problems".[4] This project included meeting with Jakubowicz and his CRAG colleagues, and also the Victoria St squatters.

IRED endorsed its senior vice-president Bruce McDonald, a Sydney townhouse developer, to lead and be the spokesperson for this project. Jakubowicz said McDonald did away with the organisation's previous

---

4   Confidential Institute of Real Estate Developers report, on 'Green bans generally and the evolution of the Institute's redevelopment policies', published around 10 December 1973

"table thumping" approach to resolving green bans, and instead brought a new and more conciliatory tone.

"He was quite silver tongued," Jakubowicz said of McDonald. "He was well educated, quite polished. His negotiating style was much more empathetic. I don't think he was any less tough. He basically thought 'This is stupid, what we're involved in. We can give a lot on this and still be ahead of the game by miles, and why wouldn't you want locals to have a say in all this stuff, to some extent? As long as they can't control it.'"

IRED went public with its project in late 1973. "Those of us involved in development have learned a lot in recent years, but legislation hasn't caught up with learning, or the compounding rate of social change," McDonald said. "In the meantime, residents and developers alike are victims of inadequate legislation, and are trapped in problem situations for which there is no solution in existing government machinery."

The violent eviction of squatters from Victoria St in the first week of 1974 only lent weight to the view that the NSW planning system was failing to provide the right environment for difficult development issues to be amicably resolved.

Issuing a media release in early 1974, IRED's McDonald was happy to concede that "recent events of violence, harassment and police involvement in tenancy evictions and building site confrontations are to be deplored" and that the "present Victoria St confrontation must be defused, and other similar incidents must not be allowed to develop".[5] McDonald then pronounced that 1974 would be the "year for planning changes". It was a statement that put Victoria St squarely at the centre of the reform push.

To be fair, the NSW Government had also realised change was needed. In October 1973, Deputy Premier Charles Cutler announced that a new body would be set up to replace the State Planning Authority (SPA), and that this body would be required to set up a new planning system which gave greater powers to local government.[6]

---

5   News Brief to members, Institute of Real Estate Development, 15 January 1974
6   One Department for Land and Environment, *The Sydney Morning Herald*, 25 October 1973, by John O'Hara, page 1

In a fact that has to date escaped public attention, Cutler even went as far to propose, via a draft Cabinet minute still sitting in the NSW archives, that a member of the "trade union movement" should be appointed to the planning body proposed to replace the SPA. A subsequent internal government report confirmed that this appointment was planned as "one of the steps that the government might take towards a solution of the 'green bans' situation".[7] The proposed appointment was also somewhat ironic, given that the SPA had, since April 1973, been stoutly resisting an attempt by the Building Trades Group (which represented all building unions) to have regular meetings to discuss planning issues.[8] The proposal also illustrated just the level of pressure on the NSW Government, by developers, to resolve the green ban issue.

Needless to say, most Ministers in this highly conservative government blanched at the prospect of appointing a member of the communist BLF – or their socialist union ilk – to a new government body, and Cutler's minute was deferred. In December 1973, the NSW Government did, however, appoint the State's first Minister for Planning – John Fuller, a grazier from central-western NSW.

In early 1974, resident action groups, the developer lobby group and the BLF began to discuss what a revamped planning system could look like.

Jakubowicz noted that the developers' position was to "order the situation, to negotiate and achieve consensus", so they would be able to continue to develop land in an environment free of highly disruptive union green bans. He also noted that CRAG was somewhat surprised that it was finally being brought into the "confines of power".

"Nobody had a clue what all this was going to do," Jakubowicz said. "We had three years of people being beaten up, people disappearing

---

7   Report of the Committee to Consider Matters Relating to the Combining of Planning and Environmental Matters, NSW Public Service Board, February 1974
8   As explained in memos found in Liaison with Community Groups file (file number J17/5) which forms part of Department of Planning functional file series in NSW Government Archives

at the worst end of it. Down at The Rocks people have been arrested, buildings have been destroyed, bulldozers have been pulled in, people are being evicted all over the place, so it was like 'what do you say?'"

On 18 February 1974, CRAG prepared a paper – under Jakubowicz's name – which laid out how a new planning system could operate. The paper was a work in progress, stating it "did not represent co-ordinated CRAG policy" and that it would be distributed to individual resident action groups for feedback. Jakubowicz has kept the original version of this paper, which recorded the initial feedback on its ideas from the BLF and IRED.

Jakubowicz's notes show there was broad agreement between the parties that people should be able to more easily have their say about planning issues, including through the improved notification of planning schemes and development applications, and the greater use of open forums. Somewhat surprisingly, CRAG was also able to secure the developers' reluctant endorsement for the concept of objectors to development applications being able to appeal – and potentially overturn – any council approvals in court.

When it came to heritage protection, there was agreement that demolition contractors should be registered and planning approvals should be required to demolish buildings. It was also agreed that local councils should prepare registers of historic buildings and precincts, and that substantial penalties should apply for people who demolished these buildings without approval.

The paper then turned to the protection of low-cost housing. This was a more difficult problem to solve. CRAG pushed for developers to be required to provide a guaranteed proportion of rental housing for people on lower incomes in any new development, or at least pay levies to allow the relevant council to buy this housing. IRED blanched at this prospect.

Separately, CRAG wanted developers to ensure that alternative accommodation was supplied to tenants evicted from low-cost housing. IRED sought to water down this commitment, so that developers only needed to take "reasonable steps" in this direction.

In a media release published on 19 March, Jakubowicz was positive about the discussions. "There are concrete proposals emerging that [the NSW Government] can take action on, to generate positive community planning, environmental responsibility and an end to situations that provoke green bans," he said.

The media got wind that consensus may be close. On 29 March, *The Sydney Morning Herald* reported that more than 200 of IRED's members would be meeting on 8 April to consider whether to endorse the initial policy proposals. In the story, Jakubowicz was quoted as saying the "proposed legislation could make green bans unnecessary", while McDonald was quoted saying "we are at the breakthrough stage in overcoming these problems".[9] A separate CRAG meeting was to be held on 9 April.

Some time in late March, Jakubowicz distributed IRED's formal response to CRAG's initial ideas to CRAG's resident action group members. In this document, IRED contended that, once residents were given the right to seek to overturn development approvals in a new planning appeals board, green bans should no longer be tolerated. IRED had also somewhat provocatively and prematurely added CRAG's name and endorsement to this proposal.

At its meeting of 2 April, at which the IRED document was discussed, CRAG imploded. Groups from Victoria St, Woolloomooloo and Darlinghurst – which included a number of anarchist activists such as Wendy Bacon and Val Hodgson – were unwilling to support a position seen as aligning with developers and undermining green bans. The meeting resolved that CRAG should disassociate itself from the IRED document and at any rate was "not representative of all resident action groups".[10] Just when the discussions were looking promising, it was a humiliating backdown.

---

9 Meeting to Discuss Green Bans Future, *The Sydney Morning Herald*, 29 March 1974, page 3

10 *Twentieth-century Sydney: Studies in Urban and Social History*, Hale & Iremonger in association with the Sydney History Group, 1980, chapter entitled The Coalition of Resident Action Groups by Zula Nittim, page 244

On 8 April, Jakubowicz was forced to write to McDonald, stating that CRAG wanted its name taken off the document, until it had more time to talk to its members. The letter also requested that IRED members should continue to respect green bans. In the coming weeks and months, neither party showed any appetite to return to the negotiating table.

When asked why no more negotiations took place, Jakubowicz said: "[IRED] were hoping to get [our] endorsement, but they don't really care one way or the other and they're moving forward ... and I think CRAG is basically saying, this is too hard to take any further. We are not an organisation that can deliver anything more than this".

The whole episode had illustrated how difficult it was for a volunteer and highly fragmented organisation like CRAG to achieve consensus on sensitive policy proposals.

However, despite the slightly shambolic nature of the discussions in the first half of 1974, they unearthed something of real value. In these discussions, it is possible to discern the formation of the modern town planning system, which came to be enacted later in the decade. Since the late 1970s, issues such as public participation in planning outcomes, protection of heritage and affordable housing protection and provision have been important elements of the State's planning system. And here they were, being discussed and debated in the aftermath of the Victoria St siege.

Jakubowicz argues that acting on its own, the NSW Government would have been unlikely to have delivered the same outcome.

"The planning space emerges in those conversations ... and really gets taken up fairly much in the legislation that emerges out the other end," Jakubowicz said. "There was no way government would set it, because there were too many things in there that government wouldn't even think about. Not that they wouldn't consider it if someone put it forward, but it would never cross their minds. So I think the fact that it was forced into the sphere actually produced ... the valuable outcome."

At the same time that these discussions were happening, the NSW Government was trying to get its own house in order. In late March and April 1974, it introduced legislation to create a new Planning and Environment Commission to replace the SPA and reform the State's planning system.

Around this time, government figures cited the Woolloomooloo planning scheme debacle as a reason to create this new system.

During parliamentary debate on the Planning and Environment Commission legislation, John Barraclough, the State MP for the inner-Sydney seat of Bligh, said: "The State Planning Authority had a plan for Woolloomooloo … in effect the people in the Authority sat behind closed doors, something like members of the Ku Klux Klan, planning. These were planners who could not be seen. These planners were not planning for the environment or the people. That is the reason why the system must be changed. As a result of this bill, the people will be involved in planning".[11]

Around the same time, the Minister for Planning and Environment John Fuller echoed similar sentiments. In a speech discussing the need for a new planning system, he asked: "Could the situation in Woolloomooloo have been averted or greatly minimised if community interests have been accorded greater participation in the planning process and if greater attention had been paid to socio-economic appraisals?"[12]

---

[11] Debate on NSW Planning and Environment Commission Bill, NSW Legislative Assembly, 2 April 1974, page 2307

[12] Speech by Sir John Fuller to Institute of Real Estate Development, 1 May 1974

PART 4
JUANITA'S DEFIANT STAND

CHAPTER 28

"Green ban soup"

If there was one thing that Joe Owens knew from a young age, it was that he wasn't going down the pits. Owens grew up in the appropriately-named Black Hill, a grimy mining village surrounded by slag heaps near Durham in northern England.

While Owens' father was a miner, and later died of black lung, Owens found he was mildly claustrophobic and not suited to a career underground. Nor, as it turns out, was he suited to another characteristic of his father – alcohol abstinence.

With a propensity for drinking, along with fighting, Owens quickly found his way out of Black Hill – and his way into trouble.

While undertaking his compulsory period of National Service, Owens was sentenced to three months in jail after assaulting a sergeant in a pub, and stealing goods. On his release, he headed out to sea as a deckhand, where he continued to find trouble. During his travels, Owens visited a bar frequented by Black people in South Africa, only to be assaulted by the local police for allegedly "being in the wrong place".

Owens quickly tired of his seagoing life. "All you see is ports and fucking pubs," he said. "You don't see anything. You see pubs in ports and the women that hang around pubs in ports."

Owens then jumped ship in New Zealand, where he finally found his calling. Owens may have been claustrophobic, but on the flipside, he also discovered he had a "head for heights". He began working as a rigger on the construction of the Auckland Harbour Bridge, and later moved to Sydney where he worked as a 'dogman', organising and riding crane-hoisted building material loads on construction sites.

This brought Owens into the orbit of the New South Wales (NSW) branch of the Builders Labourers' Federation (BLF). In the early 1960s, he met future NSW BLF secretary Jack Mundey and president Bob Pringle. Owens came to the conclusion that they, and the Communist party of Australia, were "doing great things". By 1972, Owens had been elected as a full-time union organiser and was part of the BLF's leadership team.[1]

"I'm not an intellectual ... I was a working bloke that was first attracted to Communism because they were an active lot and they got stuck into the bosses and they knew how to organise," Owens said.

In August 1973, Owens stepped up again and became the union's full-time secretary, after Mundey's six-year term in the role expired.

Owens took control of the union at a time when its future was at the crossroads.

Under Mundey's leadership, the union had seemed to be invincible. It had become notorious for its militant pro-worker policies and attitude, and its headline-grabbing green bans which had shut down dozens of development sites. As of mid-1973, this included the ongoing ban on development on Frank Theeman's Victoria St development site, and another 45 or so sites across NSW. The BLF appeared to have Sydney at its mercy.

Around the time Owens took control, and as noted earlier in this book, he and Pringle were even starting to speculate that the BLF may be at the centre of a new social revolution – one that involved workers and students coming today to re-order and reshape society, with capitalists the losers and the under-privileged and under-paid the winners.

However, soon after this time, the union's future came under a cloud.

---

1   This information is taken from an interview between Joe Owens and Ann Turner, August 1996, National Library of Australia Oral History Section

In October 1973, the Master Builders Association (MBA) – the industry body for developers and building contractors – applied to deregister the BLF at the national level. The MBA argued the BLF's NSW branch – as a creature of the BLF's national federation – had undertaken excessive and unpredictable strike action and unreasonably shut down large sections of the building industry with its green ban policy. If successful, the deregistration move would mean BLF members across Australia, including NSW, would not benefit from arbitrated wage and condition deals, and other unions would be able to steal the BLF's members. It also increased the political and policy tensions between the union's NSW branch led by Owens and its national branch, led by Norm Gallagher.

Meanwhile, in September 1973, the Australian economy was hitting stormy weather as a "credit squeeze" was beginning to form. This had serious implications for the building industry, which relied heavily on finance, and in turn the BLF and its green bans program.

Green bans had brought positive publicity and community support for the union, and had been easy to justify to the union's membership when the economy was riding high and therefore work on building sites was plentiful. There was no issue banning work on one site, when workers could easily access work on another site operating down the road.

However, the good economic times were now coming to an end, and therefore there was less work around for builders' labourers. Suddenly, what had been touted as a workers' revolution was starting to look like a workers' nightmare.

A meeting of the BLF's NSW executive in January 1974 noted that the "labour situation was getting tight" and some members were defaulting on their dues.[2] A week later, a BLF meeting discussed the need for a "settlement procedure" on green bans, while one of the executive members announced he was taking leave of absence for a year because of "the pressure".[3]

---

2   Minutes of NSW BLF Executive meeting, held 23 January 1974
3   Minutes of combined organisers, activists and branch meeting, NSW BLF, 30 January 1974

By mid-1974, large builders were starting to collapse. In July 1974, Home Units Australia – then Australia's largest builder of home units – became the first victim of the credit squeeze and had to be rescued by two other companies.[4] After having denied it was in trouble in April 1974, another major developer Mainline collapsed in September, while a further developer Cambridge collapsed the following month.

The problems spilled over into an acrimonious meeting of the NSW BLF branch in June 1974. The issue related to a proposed high-rise complex in Darlinghurst, which was covered by an existing green ban. The site's developers wanted to lift the green ban so they could begin construction. A site meeting of BLF members had backed this proposition, because the job would provide work for them, but this motion had to be ratified at the branch meeting.

At the meeting, Owens strongly argued against immediately lifting the ban, stating that a "split in the union" would only help the BLF's enemies and the decision should be deferred for a month to allow further consultation with residents. But the rank and file could not be swayed and voted 60 to 40 to lift the ban there and then. "These issues will probably arise in other areas as development slows down," a meeting of the BLF executive on the same day stated.[5] Soon after, the union issued a media statement saying it was going to establish a three-man panel to review existing green bans.[6]

Owens realised thoughts of a revolution were just a mirage. "You know, we vaguely thought that the revolution was in sight," he said. "We were fucking wrong. It wasn't in sight … it was never to be in sight."

However, for the union, the last-minute green ban backdown was too late. In June 1974, the Australian Industrial Court decided to deregister all BLF State branches, and its Federal arm, citing the NSW union's

---

4 Major Building Group Rescued, *The Age*, 20 July 1974, page 19
5 Minutes of the NSW BLF executive, and branch meeting, 4 June 1974
6 $3,000 million Green Ban Review Promised, *The Sydney Morning Herald*, 15 June 1974, page 3

Joe Owens addressing a pro-BLF rally held at Circular Quay in 1974 (Photo: Andrew Jakubowicz)

"industrial lawlessness" over the previous four years, including the green ban policy. Deregistration meant the union was still in operation, but had vastly reduced powers when it came to seeking wage increases and condition improvements for its members.

In October 1974, the Federal arm announced it would take over the NSW branch.

The Federal intervention was, as would be expected, a heated and volatile affair. Gallagher and the Federal branch argued the NSW leadership had to go because it was not following proper record-keeping, selling motor cars to members below their true value, providing improper payments to members and their families, not co-operating with auditors and had "gone too far" with green bans. Not surprisingly, Owens and the NSW branch argued that Gallagher and the Federal branch were "lining up with" the Master Builders Association and developers so the union could be re-registered, and were part of a larger power play that would allow Gallagher to become the top dog among all building unions.

Gallagher moved from his usual Melbourne base to Sydney, where he stayed in a Central Business District hotel and declared to the media that he was having "green ban soup" for breakfast.[7]

Just as it had in earlier life, violence then once again entered Owens' world. He clearly feared for his life and hid in the homes of friends. "I don't think they were going to come and kill me but some were sent up [from Melbourne] to try and spook us … if they knocked one of us off it would have been interesting," Owens said.

Several documents in a collection provided by Owens to a Canberra-based trade union archive show why he was fearful.[8] One document purports to be a court affidavit from a Melbourne man, who says he was flown to Sydney by the Federal branch to take over building sites occupied by BLF members loyal to the deposed executive. The man says he was taken to a motel near the University of Sydney, where several other men with the same task were based.

In one of the motel rooms, the man says he found an interesting discovery.

"[One of the men] opened a wardrobe door and inside I saw a rake of artillery that the Irish Republican Army would have been proud of," the man said. "I said to him 'what sort of guns are they?' He said 'they're doctored' and took one of them in his hand and said 'it's just about equal to a machine gun'. I reckon there were about four rifles in the wardrobe."

In the end, Owens was not harmed, in part he says because of his hiding and also because NSW Police didn't take kindly to Victorian criminals being flown to Sydney.

---

7   Labourers' Split - Tale of a Takeover, *The Sydney Morning Herald*, 14 October 1974, page 2
8   This is the Joe Owens Collection (Z235) in the Noel Butlin Archive at the Australian National University

As each month went by, however, Owens lost his grip on the union. Major building contractors sided with Gallagher and would not allow union members aligned with the Owens leadership team to work on their sites. This meant members who were formerly loyal to Owens had a grim choice – either become a ticket holder in the new Gallagher-aligned union branch or be out of a job. It's also often been speculated that Victoria St developer Frank Theeman subsidised Gallagher's adventure in NSW so that the green ban could be lifted on his project, although this has never been proven. What is known, however, is that Theeman's security advisor Fred Krahe reported in a tip-off to Fairfax Media that, in November 1973, Theeman flew to Melbourne "where he has a secret appointment with Gallagher … and it is hoped that Theeman can talk him into talking action against the NSW brigade". This meeting certainly appeared to have had a positive outcome.

The irony was that, as the former NSW branch leadership was "having its wings torn off" (as one observer of the times said during an interview for this book), the results of its urban environment policy agenda were finally bearing fruit.

In November 1974, the NSW Government had, somewhat belatedly, reacted to the root cause of the green ban era – the public outcry over poor development – by issuing a paper outlining options to reform the planning system. The paper, *Towards A New Planning System*, conceded that the existing planning system had become obsolete. This paper found the planning system was almost exclusively focussed on what individual property owners could build on their land, but failed to consider broader issues such as transport movements and environmental protection. The paper also found that there was a lack of effective public involvement in planning issues, and that too many decisions were concentrated at the State – instead of local – level.

"In recent years the Australian public has become increasingly interested in participating in various areas of government and decision-making," the paper said. "This has been evident, for example, in persons wanting a say in their children's education, in factory workers participating in management and in students influencing the content of their courses. In [the NSW planning system] the movement towards public involvement has been manifested in particular in the formation of resident groups concerned with planning and environment issues."[9]

The paper was helping to usher in a new era in town planning, one where the rights of individual property owners were being eroded as communities sought to better protect their local environment and have their say about development in their suburb.

Most Sydney residents welcomed this new State-sanctioned platform to debate and challenge local development. For one Kings Cross local, however, this new-found power would hardly be a blessing, and in fact would turn out to be deadly.

---

[9] Towards a New Planning System, Minister for Planning and Environment, November 1974, page 20

CHAPTER 29

"There is very little of the old Cross now"

As far as newspaper publisher Juanita Nielsen was concerned, her beloved home suburb of Kings Cross was heading in the wrong direction. Nielsen had known and loved the suburb for three decades and, when she permanently moved into the area in 1968, had declared "there was no question I would live anywhere else".

Six years down the track, however, Nielsen was becoming deeply disenchanted with the state of the local area. "I think, what happened to the Cross is what has happened to the rest of Sydney, what has happened to the Quay and the centre of the city, there is just too much money around," Nielsen told a radio journalist in 1974. "When the real estate became so valuable, and when overseas investment poured in, it was bad news for Sydney."

Nielsen's gripe was not that this development was bringing too many people into the area, but it was doing precisely the opposite. She argued that the construction of huge road and rail infrastructure projects running through the area was resulting in hundreds of homes across large sections of the suburb being demolished. At the same time, she argued, developers like Frank Theeman were moving in and evicting tenants for their building projects, which again was resulting in depopulation.

"So gradually the people started leaving, they left in great swathes along the line of the Kings Cross road tunnel, they left in a body from the area of the railway station itself; in the meanwhile individual developers were systematically emptying Kings Cross. This has continued to this point," Nielsen said. "There is very little of the old Cross now. Some of the buildings remain, they get a little bit shabbier every year, but the spirit has almost entirely gone, because the people have gone. It didn't take very much to get it back, you just needed the people."

Nielsen's concern was that, with this depopulation, the area's criminal elements and remaining local residents were coming into contact more often. "With the numerical depopulation of Kings Cross, it's left a very strange situation, where you have the remnants of the thousands of people who used to live here, which means you still have a number of wealthy people, very genteel folk, you still have a number of small localised criminals, you still have people from every walk of life in between, but they can't avoid each other anymore, they don't get lost in the crowd, and you have the situation where they are trying to live with each other, or avoid each other, or in spite of each other. This has created a situation where the different factions are trying to get rid of the other lot."

Nielsen also noted that this depopulation was impacting her own business. "As the owner of the local newspaper I can tell, purely in selling advertising, that although there is still a reasonably large population here, the shops don't have the money to advertise, they don't have the money to buy fresh stock, or to change their stock or change their image, because the rates or the rents they are paying are far too high, so every year it gets a little bit seedier, the shops are slightly less well-stocked, because they are less well-stocked they are less attractive.

"So more and more people go to Double Bay. The incidence of fly-by-night shops such as sex shops at the ground level, with the sort of facades nice people avert their eyes at, well they avert their eyes when they pass the next shop; this is definitely not helping."

Nielsen's business and romantic partner David Farrell had witnessed the same change, which had seen Kings Cross become a less populated, sleazier and arguably more dangerous place.

Nielsen had moved into the suburb soon after the Australian Government agreed to include Sydney in the United States' Rest and Recreation (R&R) leave program. Between October 1967 and December 1971, the program brought around 280,000 American Vietnam War servicemen into Sydney. Most of these servicemen found their way to Kings Cross, where they sought out its earthly delights, including sex, alcohol and drugs.

"When R&R came, the money flowed, the criminal element lifted substantially and the drugs came in too," Farrell recalls. "The girls came in, the younger prostitutes, with R&R. What happened is that some of the old apartment buildings, opposite where we lived ... they were both turned into brothels. Full bore, packed, that happened rather quickly, you could see they were making big bucks."

The R&R program, along with the destruction of around 300 homes for road and rail projects, and the emptying or destruction of more homes for development projects, meant that in just four years Kings Cross had gone from an eclectic and diverse all-hours centre which serviced a dense residential population, to a red light district which serviced the rest of Sydney. In other words, it had gone from cosmopolitan to crass, from bohemian to a brothel.

Popular media also noticed the change. "It is as if the sleaziness has taken over, crowding into family time and gobbling up anything there was of a much-dreamed heyday," journalist Dennis Minogue wrote in early 1975.[1]

Farrell said Nielsen became concerned that the "little people" – the long-term and low-income bedsit tenants or the small family businesses – no longer had a place in the suburb thanks to the work of governments and developers. "[She was] very much for business but small business; she hated big business and multinationals," Farrell said. "She had been bitten by the whopping big businesses and people who had taken over Mark Foy's. The paper was about small business; she

---

[1] The Changing Face of the Cross, *The Age*, 8 February 1975, by Dennis Minogue, page 13

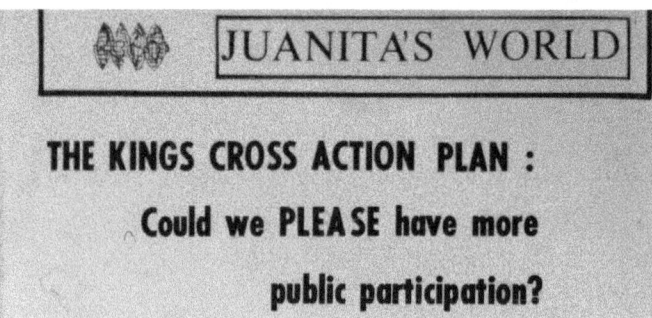

Top: By the mid-1970s, Kings Cross was beginning its shift from bohemian to sleaze, as shown in this 2004 photo (Courtesy City of Sydney Council)

Above: Headline from NOW newspaper, February 1973, which accompanied a story from Juanita Nielsen calling on the creation of an information centre for Kings Cross

believed in the right of people to make their own life and business, uncorrupted and unhindered."

Nielsen was firmly of the view that Kings Cross locals should use their voice to change the suburb's direction. What's more, as a local newspaper publisher, Nielsen also increasingly recognised her power as an individual to influence the debate. In a series of articles published during 1973, Nielsen pleaded with Kings Cross locals to participate in an action plan being created for the suburb by the City of Sydney Council, and for the council to improve efforts to engage with said locals. "Where, and how soon, will the city council establish an information centre to show the progress of the Kings Cross action plan?" Nielsen wrote in February 1973.[2] Asked whether Nielsen wanted people to participate in planning, Farrell said: "Yes, she did talk about them having their say; she felt that many of them were voiceless, and she could give them a voice, and she was giving them a say by what she was doing".

Nielsen's newspaper, *NOW*, had not always carried such content. At the time of its inception, Farrell noted that paper was "100 per cent sold", with even front pages being set aside for clothes shops who wanted Nielsen to model items or restaurants paying for "reviews".

However, with declining advertising demand, and Nielsen's new-found anger at her suburb's change, the paper slowly turned into a strange blend of advertorial puff pieces and thundering editorials by Nielsen. "We talked about [*NOW*'s campaigning], she said to me 'this is going to impact our profit, but I've got to do it ... I hadn't planned to be an activist, but I can't sit by and let this happen, but I've got to do it my way, not going to do it anyone else's way' and that is what she did," Farrell recalls.

Nielsen implemented this advocacy in her own peculiar and somewhat overly excitable writing style – using lots of rhetorical questions, capitalisations and exclamation marks. "I write as I think,"

---

[2] The Kings Cross Action Plan: Can We Please Have More Public Participation, *NOW*, 27 February 1973, by Juanita Nielsen, page 2

Juanita Nielsen, photographed outside her home and office at 202 Victoria St, in October 1974 (Courtesy of Fairfax archives)

Nielsen told *The Sydney Morning Herald* in 1974. "I don't revise or change anything."[3] In short, Nielsen's style of journalism felt more personal than professional.

Nielsen didn't just focus on Kings Cross. She very much understood that what was happening in the Cross was part of a deeper malaise affecting the entire inner-Sydney area.

---

3 The Editor who Models the Fashion, *The Sydney Morning Herald*, 12 October 1974, by Lenore Nicklin, page 12

She wrote about redevelopment plans and issues in The Rocks, Woolloomooloo, Paddington, Darlinghurst, Edgecliff and the Haymarket area. Farrell recalls Nielsen regularly meeting activists from right across Sydney. "Quite apart from what she did in the newspaper, she was meeting lots of people, many things I didn't know about, she was off every day, saying 'I met these people and those people', she was very active," Farrell said.

One of those regular minglers was Michael Llewellyn-Smith, who in 1971 was appointed the chief planning officer for the City of Sydney Council at the age of just 29. Llewellyn-Smith saw that Nielsen was someone who had the pulse of the community, and therefore could give useful information to guide council decisions.

In an interview for this book, he said: "From my point of view, it was useful to get some sort of local feedback on how things were being perceived as to what was going on ... [Nielsen] through her articles and her position had her roots and contacts in the community ... so it was useful to be able to figure out what was happening from the community perspective by talking to her. I was careful not to release any obviously confidential information but there were fairly robust but interesting chats, philosophically, as to where Sydney was going, and why it was going in that direction.

"I mean, [Sydney] was beginning to see the rise of sort of citizen power in the sense that the old master planning approach of deciding on a plan and just imposing [that plan] was beginning to be questioned by the community [which was] saying hang on, we want a say in this.

"And so, I think people had a great deal of time for all the sorts of things [Nielsen] was saying, which was along those lines."

However, while Nielsen had focussed her writing on Kings Cross and inner-Sydney issues, there was one project which increasingly caught her attention.

In her newspaper, Nielsen had failed to cover the April 1973 eviction of tenants to make way for Theeman's Victoria Point redevelopment, along with the squatter's occupation in mid-1973. The omissions were somewhat curious, given that the project was just a few hundred metres from Nielsen's home, but perhaps reflected the fact that Nielsen had little in common with the anarchist activists who dominated debate during this time, plus the fact that Nielsen's views and therefore editorial policy were still evolving.

However, as Nielsen became more convinced that Kings Cross, and inner Sydney, were being subjected to unwanted changes from government and developers, she turned on the Victoria Point project as exemplifying everything that was going wrong. Here was a project that had left rows of vacant homes, after evicting low-income workers and pensioners – in other words a key contributor to the suburb's depopulation and social change which Nielsen detested. From August 1973 onwards, and particularly in 1974, Victoria Point regularly featured in Nielsen's strident editorials.

"What becomes of the original inhabitants of a development or newly-trendy suburb?" Nielsen wrote in her first story that touched on the Victoria Point project. "When cars become redundant, they're crushed into scrap metal. But what happens to redundant people?"

Nielsen's campaign had just begun.[4]

---

[4] More Evictions in Victoria St, *NOW*, 28 August 1973, by Juantia Neilsen, page 2

CHAPTER 30

"The whole house started to smell like someone had thrown up into it"

It was a clear and mild autumn evening in April 1974 when around 500 members of Sydney high society gathered at Frank Theeman's Bellevue Hill home for his annual La Bella Italia charity bash. The black tie event was a must-attend on the Sydney social calendar, with the 1973 event attracting famed and extravagant American entertainer Liberace.

The week before, the *Sun-Herald* social column had broadcast the event to the world. "This is the week when it's all happening," the paper said. "At Bellevue Hill, there's La Bella Italia at the Frank Theeman's – that extravaganza on an Italian theme with marquees, two dance bands, prizes for the most elegant guests and the target of raising funds to send young Australian singers to study in Milan."[1]

The former squatters, still smarting from their forced eviction, took the newspaper story as a formal invitation.

Around 9:30pm, around 50 former squatters and their supporters began protesting outside the event, including shouting at guests. This sent Theeman's security personnel rushing to the front of the home, when in fact the real action was happening inside the event itself.

As activist Ian Milliss tells the story, the protesters had managed to score 10 tickets to the event courtesy of an Eastern Suburbs high-society

---

1   Happenings … Here, There and Everywhere, *Sun-Herald*, 31 March 1974, page 95

> Tonight's social ball has a nasty twist. Along with the usual network of politicians, judges, developers, other capitalists, opera lovers (sic) and their police and security men (bouncers minus crowbars), you have us - 8 ex-squatters and two builders labourers. The person sitting next to you might be a squatter!

Excerpt from a leaflet handed out by protesters at Theeman's April 1974 party

housewife, who had strong leftish political views and was once married to a French anarchist. These tickets were distributed to eight former squatters and two builders' labourers, including Builders Labourers' Federation (BLF) secretary Joe Owens.

"People with fairly ill-gotten gains want to transfer financial capital into cultural capital, and sucking up to ... the Opera ... was one way of doing that, it was [Theeman's] entry into high society," Milliss said. "We managed to mix the ages up enough to make our table look plausible; we all had evening wear, I was the youngest, then we slowly started infiltrating the party."

Milliss then set about sabotaging the party by leaving portions of butyric acid – which is naturally found in rancid butter, parmesan cheese and human vomit – around Theeman's home and garden. "I'd been rigged up with this little system where I could drop butyric acid around the place, so the whole house started to smell like someone had thrown up into it."

Other activists also began to distribute pamphlets which attacked Theeman and told the activists' version of the Victoria St story. "The difference between the lifestyle of the guests at this do and the tenants in Victoria St is more than economic," the pamphlet stated. "On your side is power and prestige, on their side are poor educational and social facilities, police oppression and rough justice in the courts."

The disruption worked a treat. "As we slowly slipped pamphlets into things and under and around things, there was a big demonstration going on out in the street, more of a diversion, which meant they had security people out there," Milliss recalls. "Suddenly it dawned on them that there were protestors inside as well, you got a tap on the shoulder, and then were taken out the back gate. We wanted to quietly do things to make the whole thing rather unpleasant, and a bit embarrassing, we didn't want him to get away with making out he was a respectable person."

In a letter to *The Sydney Morning Herald*, Theeman raged against the activists, claiming they had also slashed and deflated the tyres of cars outside his home. "Can this frightening state of affairs be allowed to continue, when a family in their own home, and their guests are intimidated by aggressors trying to enforce mob rule on the community?" he thundered.[2]

The party fracas was a sign that, despite the slow dismantling of the BLF and the eviction of the squatters, Theeman's project was still controversial and in deep trouble. It was as though as soon as Theeman tried to solve one problem, another was created. This meant that his development project, which had initially seemed like a sure-fire money spinner, was increasingly turning into a money pit.

In July 1974, Theeman had sought to extend the timeframe for his development consent, granted the previous year, but in the following weeks and months had heard nothing back from the council. The application letter illustrated Theeman's concern.

"May I again point out to the council once again that the holding charges for this project amount to $1 million per annum, or $3,000 per day," Theeman wrote. "If we are not able to proceed with the project within the very next few months, this company, and this writer through personal guarantee, faces an extremely serious situation in which we have innocently been placed by the complete change of the Woolloomooloo plan."[3] Later in 1974, Theeman confided that he had lost $2.5 million in interest since purchasing the site and, at best, could hope to "break even".[4]

---

2 Charity Party Disrupted, *The Sydney Morning Herald*, letter by Frank Theeman, 15 April 1974, page 6
3 Letter from Frank Theeman to Alderman Leo Port, 10 July 1974
4 Letter from Frank Theeman to NSW Premier Elect Tom Lewis on 5 December 1974

Theeman's security advisor Fred Krahe was reporting a similar story. "Frank is in desperate trouble ... he is endeavouring to negotiate the transfer of the entire Victoria Point set up to CAGA [Theeman's financier] and in the process will drop $2.5 million dollars," Krahe said in a tip-off letter to Fairfax Media in August 1974. In a separate letter around the same time, Krahe also revealed that Theeman's financial pain was so bad that he had been forced to initiate the secret sale of his beloved Bellevue Hill house.[5]

What's more, Theeman's financial problems were not solely related to the Victoria St site. Just before Christmas 1973, it was revealed that a related group of property and mining companies, in which Theeman was a major investor, had collapsed. A liquidator had been appointed to the Vale Corporation group of companies, amid media claims that investor funds may have been misappropriated and a company director had fled the country.[6] Theeman was said to have invested around $500,000 into the companies.[7]

The problem for Theeman was that, as the debate about what constituted good town planning evolved and matured, a new breed of town planners was again questioning his project and potentially forcing down his development yield.

Three years earlier, in 1971, the council had been lobbying Premier Robert Askin to overrule his own State Planning Authority to allow three soaring 45-storey apartment towers, with the ability for Theeman to construct and sell new floor-space which was 10 times the size of the original land parcel.

Now some council staff were contemplating only allowing Theeman to build piddling four storey towers, and build just two times the size of the original land parcel. The change in sentiment from the council was remarkable, and a reflection of the rapidly changing attitudes to town

---

5   It does not appear that the actual sale happened until early 1975
6   Trustee Wants to get Public's Money Back, *The Sydney Morning Herald*, 29 December 1973, page 20
7   Managing Director Sold Shares Six Weeks Before Munga Creek Went into Liquidation, *The National Times*, 31 December 1973, page 38

planning and the growing belief that new development should be more intensely scrutinised and more responsive to its surroundings.

Part of Theeman's issues stemmed from what was happening in the Woolloomooloo valley below his site. By May 1974, the City of Sydney Council and New South Wales (NSW) and Australian Governments had come together to formally dump the previous flawed 1969 Woolloomooloo valley high-rise office tower plan, and instead exhibit new development options which preserved most of the valley as low- and medium-rise housing. At the same time, the Australian Government was beginning to float the idea that it purchase large swathes of land in the valley, so that it could be turned into public housing.[8]

Residents in Woolloomooloo, who had been saved from being redeveloped themselves, now realised they faced being overshadowed and overlooked by Theeman's soaring project. "Can you imagine the utter ugliness of this enormous wall that will face one when he looks up?" said community group the Residents of Woolloomooloo in a submission dated July 1974. These objections were beginning to influence the council's planners.

Nielsen was more than happy to stir up opposition to Theeman's project. She worked closely with Woolloomooloo activists, including Nellie and Gerry Leonard who had been long-term low-income tenants in a cluster of homes owned by the Australian Government in the east of the suburb. In May 1974, Nielsen published a petition from resident activists in her newspaper, which among other things requested the "total preservation" of the existing Victoria St terraces.

"Nellie and Gerry [Leonard], she was very close to them; they knew everything that was happening in Victoria St, they were spies for her talking to Victoria St residents," said Nielsen's partner David Farrell. "From that perspective, the Woolloomooloo people were helping her with Victoria St."

---

[8] Federal Funds for Homes, *The Sydney Morning Herald*, 15 May 1974, page number unknown

The new mooted council planning controls would have spelled absolute disaster for Theeman. "The writer now hears that under the new Woolloomooloo scheme under consideration, the plot ratio is to be further reduced to 2:1. Such reduction would result in a loss of $5 million to us, and bankruptcy for this company," Theeman wrote to incoming NSW Premier Tom Lewis.[9]

However, just as things looked their bleakest for Theeman, an unusual white knight yet again came to his rescue. In short, this book finally reveals the unusual role played by the Labor government of Prime Minister Gough Whitlam, which ruled Australia between 1972–1975, to back Theeman.

Whitlam and his Urban and Regional Development Minister, Tom Uren, had come to power in December 1972, with a mission to clamp down on the worst habits of private property speculators and developers. Indeed, in official speeches and articles, Uren was happy to describe himself as a socialist.

The government's argument was that uncontrolled land and property speculation needed to be brought to heel as it was increasing the divide between rich and poor, and ruining the environment of inner-city areas. Uren opposed the construction boom in inner Sydney, stating that "we are over-building the Central Business District (CBD) of Sydney, North Sydney, The Rocks, Woolloomooloo and Kings Cross" and that "the complete destruction of existing communities in our cities, particularly those in our older suburbs, can never be excused".[10]

Uren threatened to use the government's power over foreign investment to "siphon funds away from further over-development of the city centres".[11] On the city's fringes, to control spiralling new home block prices, Uren threatened to establish new government bodies which would buy land and then subdivide and sell it on a leasehold

---

9   Letter from Frank Theeman to NSW Premier Elect Tom Lewis on 5 December 1974
10 An article by Tom Uren MP, Labor's Federal Spokesman on Urban Affairs, published in the Daily Telegraph on 20 December 1971
11 Opinion piece by Tom Uren MP, Federal Labor Spokesman for Urban Affairs, submitted to Daily Telegraph for publication on 5 June 1972

basis – effectively putting a cap on prices and cutting developers out of the equation. This final policy was deeply unpopular among developers, who accused Uren of looking to make homeowners "tenants of the government" and that removing developers "would not solve the problem".[12]

Given the above policy position, and after taking into account widespread publicity about Theeman's use of intimidation to remove working-class tenants, and violence to evict anarchist and left-wing squatters, there would seem to be little chance that Uren and the Whitlam Government would support Theeman's Victoria Point project. And yet that is exactly what happened.

As revealed in Chapter 21, in a meeting in mid-1973, Uren had privately praised Theeman's revised plan, even though he had no official approval role in relation to this plan. In the same year, Uren had avoided committing to a proposal by the squatters that the Australian Government buy the site.

In 1974, as the Australian and NSW Governments and City of Sydney Council regularly came together to decide the future of Woolloomooloo, Uren switched his in-principle support into action, and was able to deliver a major coup for Theeman. In August 1974, Sydney Lord Mayor Nicholas Shehadie and NSW Minister for Planning Sir John Fuller came together with Uren at a planning meeting for Woolloomooloo. At this meeting, Uren remarked that it was not "economically viable" for governments to acquire land in Victoria St, thereby releasing Theeman from the ignominy and potential financial disaster of having his land acquired for low-rise public housing.

At a later meeting of the same parties in November 1974, attention turned to what planning controls were appropriate for private development in Victoria St, given the land was not going to be acquired. A council planner proposed that they should limit development on Victoria St – including Theeman's site – to just four storeys, so as to not create a "visual barrier" on the edge of the Woolloomooloo basin.

---

[12] Comment by Allen Vogan, President of the Urban Development Institute of Australia to the Institute's Second National Congress in 1974

Of the participants at the meeting, Uren was the first to baulk at the idea. "In some ways I am sympathetic to the exhibited Woolloomooloo scheme for Victoria St, because it is close to public transport and there has to be a reasonably rational development," Uren said. Upon hearing Uren's remark, Alderman Briger stated "the figures could be left open-ended" and Lord Mayor Nicholas Shehadie then said "we could agree to what you say".

Later in the same meeting, Briger noted that it appeared to have been decided to make two major alterations to the draft planning scheme, one of which was that "four storeys does not seem to be a reasonable one" for Victoria St. To this, Uren replied "I am prepared to accept that".[13] The meeting resolved to decide the Victoria St controls at a later time.

From reading the record of the meeting, there is little doubt that Uren's intervention – with the support of the NSW Government and council – had led to Theeman being able to achieve a significant development uplift on his site. What's more, Uren's stated support for the exhibited 1969 Woolloomooloo scheme is an extraordinary statement, given this scheme supported CBD-scaled towers in quiet, low-rise Victoria St, with no building height limit and no retention of existing terraces.

While we don't know whether this was related to Uren's intervention, soon after Theeman decided to make a bold bid to boost the development potential on his site. In January 1975, he brought in Neville Gruzman as his new architect. Gruzman had received some kudos for preparing an informal 'people's plan' to help preserve the historic area of The Rocks and had also been nominated by the BLF in mid-1974 to sit on a green ban review committee. Theeman clearly thought Gruzman may have the right contacts to finally solve his approval and construction woes.

Gruzman's new application sought an 18-storey development at the site, which contained 50 per cent more floor space and around eight

---

[13] Taken from the record of a meeting relating to the Woolloomooloo Action Plan, 1 November 1974, held at Sydney Town Hall

additional storeys compared to the project approved in mid-1973. However, the new application seemed to once again bring sinister forces to the fore.

Around 7:30pm on 6 February 1975, Woolloomooloo activist Nellie Leonard – Nielsen's close confidante – was approached outside her Forbes St home by two strangers driving a light green 1966 Ford. One of the men menacingly told Leonard that her husband, herself and her friends needed to "slow up and drop off" or "you know what will happen" – without naming the matter they wanted to be "dropped". The two men then sped off into the night.[14] In his book *Killing Juanita*, author Peter Rees speculates that the threat may have come from developers in the Woolloomooloo valley, rather than from Theeman.

However, in light of the opposition from Woolloomooloo residents to Theeman's plans, Nielsen's friendship with the Leonards, and the previous history of Victoria St-related violence in 1973 and 1974, it seems plausible that the threat was linked to Theeman's Victoria Point project. This theory is further reinforced by the fact that, at Nielsen's inquest in 1983, Leonard said that Nielsen had told her that the two men in question matched the description of men who had also previously threatened her and had told her that she needed to "drop off or she would disappear from the face of the earth".

Whatever the reason, it was a small taste of the final violent act which would visit Victoria St and Kings Cross in mid-1975.

---

14 Statutory declaration by Mary Ellen Leonard, dated 8 February 1975

CHAPTER 31
"A class war going on"

As far-fetched as it sounded, Juanita Nielsen had managed to find a connection between a lonely temple in the harsh empty desert of central Iraq and a development proposal in the chaotic, crowded streets of Kings Cross.

The Great Ziggurat of Ur rises up from the Iraq desert, around 340km south of Baghdad. Constructed some 4,100 years ago as a 30m high tiered temple to a local goddess, and re-built several times over its long life, the Great Ziggurat is sometimes described as Iraq's answer to the Great Pyramids of Egypt.

As far as the well-educated Nielsen was concerned, the Great Ziggurat shared an uncanny likeness with Frank Theeman's latest development proposal, prepared by architect Neville Gruzman.

"It is not only an eyesore in its own right, but would block sun and vital cooling breezes into the Woolloomooloo basin," Nielsen wrote of Theeman's plans in her 6 May 1975 edition of *NOW*. "It resembles the Great Ziggurat of Ur – viewed through a bad case of double vision." Theeman denied the proposal was ugly. "It rises and falls from six storeys to nineteen storeys, thus providing more balconies and roof terraces, better air circulation and a better aesthetic aspect," he told the National Trust.[1]

---

1   Letter from Frank Theeman to National Trust, 28 April 1975

Top: The Great Ziggurat of Ur, following its restoration by Iraqi leader Saddam Hussein in 1980 (Source: Wikipedia Commons)

Above: The 1975 development application proposal for the Victoria Point site

Nielsen's comments filled an entire page of *NOW*, which she had devoted to analysing the Victoria St situation. Around a third of the page focussed on the alleged evils of Theeman's proposal, including that it had evicted 400 low-income tenants but only offered 40 new low-income units and would also cause traffic issues. Another third of the page looked at other potential high-rise projects in the street, including the 28-storey tower which Nielsen said would be next door to her home, and the final third represented a desperate plea to building unions to continue to protect the street.

Nielsen had ramped up her Victoria St coverage after the collapse of the former leadership of the Builders Labourers' Federation (BLF).

Under Joe Owens, the New South Wales (NSW) BLF leadership had fought a brave battle against a takeover by the union's Federal branch. However, by March 1975, the NSW branch was in a parlous financial state, with $48,000 in debts but only $20,000 in hand to pay them, due to the defection of members to Norm Gallagher and his Federal branch.[2] After Owens told his colleagues the situation had become "untenable", the executive voted to capitulate, including handing over membership dues and property to the Federal body.

The importance of Victoria St in the union power struggle appeared to be underlined when, on 16 April, Gallagher announced that Theeman's Victoria St site would be the first BLF green ban to be lifted in NSW. Gallagher said the site would bring "badly needed work for building workers".[3]

Nielsen knew that, with the collapse of the green ban, everything had changed. She now needed to act with haste to find new allies to back her fight, including politicians or other unions involved in the construction industry. And while she had some friends in the Woolloomooloo basin, Nielsen was largely fighting this battle on her own.

"[Nielsen] did have lots of friends, she wasn't alone as you think, but because she wasn't part of a Push or group, she operated as a clear lone

---

2   From minutes of Executive Meeting of NSW BLF branch, 20 March 1975
3   Union Lifts Victoria St Ban, *The Sydney Morning Herald*, 17 April 1975, page 1

front," noted her business and romantic partner David Farrell. Farrell said Nielsen's alleged "Victoria St Ratepayers' Association" was in fact made up of Nielsen, a local chemist and "the women in the clothing shop".

It seemed that Nielsen knew that every day, if not every hour, was valuable to take on Theeman and anyone else trying to destroy her beloved Victoria St. Nielsen's activity became more frenetic; her writing more shrill, eccentric and excitable.

Nielsen claimed that, with the green ban collapse, the "developers began to gather like vultures".

"While every green ban area represents a different problem, Victoria St seems to have a little of everything that is ailing the inner city and the Australian way of life in 1975," Nielsen wrote in her 6 May edition (in capitals). "We want [Victoria St] to stay as it has been for more than a century, an interesting community of workers, students, eccentrics, the wealthy, the middle class and the pensioners, and because of this, a magnet for tourists!"

Nielsen turned her attention to the Building Trades Group (BTG), the umbrella group for building unions. While the BLF green ban had collapsed, Nielsen felt other unions in the building industry, such as those representing carpenters, plumbers, bricklayers or painters, may instead take up the fight and keep the ban on.

After a meeting between Theeman and Gruzman on 30 April, the BTG decided to invite submissions on Theeman's proposal from residents. Such submissions needed to be in the hands of the BTG before its next meeting on 14 May. Nielsen sought to curry favour with the BTG by publishing an interview with its secretary Sid Vaughan, which noted that the BTG had maintained green bans on high-rise buildings in Cook Rd, Centennial Park and in Bankstown.[4]

On 12 May, Nielsen sent a three-page letter to the BTG, allegedly on behalf of the "Victoria St Ratepayers' Association" – complaining that the Theeman proposal would turf out lower income workers, increase rates and cause traffic gridlock. A particular bugbear for Nielsen was that Theeman's proposed new affordable housing units would be located

---

4   The Building Trades Look at Breen Bans, *NOW*, 6 May 1975, by Juanita Nielsen, page 3

> And we urge the Housing Commission to carefully assess the effect, physical, economical and environmental, of the proposed Victoria Street development on their own very creditable Woolloomooloo housing plan.
>
> And to ask themselves just how desirable is Mr. Theeman's proposal to offer the Commission 40 units at the "bargain basement" level of the Complex, between two huge heavily trafficked gasoline exuding car parks – the Victoria Point 400 car Garage and the Commonwealth Car Park across the road!
>
> On the surface of it, wiping out upwards of 400 "living units" – the residential rooms and flats of Victoria Street, for a level swap of 40 "living units" down in Cancer Country, doesn't seem to be a good bargain – environmentally speaking.
>
> signed,
>
> *Juanita J. Nielsen*
>
> Juanita J. Nielsen,
> Secretary,
> Victoria St. Ratepayers' Ass'n.

The final portion of Nielsen's 12 May 1975 letter objecting to Theeman's latest plan

at the building's less desirable basement levels, near carpark entrances, which she described as "cancer country". The letter was to no avail.

At its meeting on 14 May, the BTG announced it would not maintain a green ban on Theeman's proposal, given the City of Sydney Council was conducting an "environmental impact study" on it. While this was obviously a bitter blow for Nielsen's campaign, she showed no sign of accepting defeat in the next edition of *NOW* – twisting the BTG decision to state that it represented a "reprieve" from the "imminent demolition" of Theeman's Victoria St terraces while the study was undertaken.

As Nielsen's anti-development activity ramped up, so did the threats. Just as the spectre of violence had reared its head against Arthur King in 1973, against the squatters in 1973 and 1974, and against Nellie Leonard in early 1975, Nielsen reported to friends in May 1975 that she had begun to receive threatening phone calls.

However, as tears began to well in his eyes and as his voice began to quiver, Farrell told this author in an interview that Nielsen was unlikely to be intimidated by such actions.

"She had a confidence that she could not be stood over, she could not be conned or exploited or intimidated, she simply couldn't, she could not be intimidated by class; everyone was equal, as far as she was concerned, very much egalitarian," he said.

In line with this defiant stance, Nielsen shrugged off the BTG rejection and the threats, and shifted her campaigning to the political arena. At the same time that the brakes were being put on green bans, the planning system was responding to the community triggers which had caused green bans in the first place, by allowing greater public participation in decisions, and more detailed and careful examinations of new projects. This new policy approach meant that, for the first time, members of the public – including Nielsen – had the opportunity to formally comment on Theeman's plans and what's more, his plans came under close scrutiny from the council's town planners.

With Mick Fowler, the sole remaining tenant in Theeman's development site, and the Woolloomooloo Resident Action Group, Nielsen submitted a four-page objection to the proposal to the City of Sydney Council and the NSW Government's Planning and Environment Commission. The letter was received by the authorities on 14 May.

In the objection, Nielsen and her colleagues list the occupations of the low-income people they said lived in Theeman's terraces before the April 1973 eviction, including 80 unemployed people and 10 sex workers. "What was happening on the western side of Victoria St was not an isolated event," Nielsen said. The objection stated: "All round the inner city, The Rocks, Pyrmont, Woolloomooloo, Darlinghurst, Surry Hills, the same type of thing was happening. Low-income earners were being evicted … there was a class war going on; the State Government, the City Council, the businessmen and the developers were working hand-in-hand to turn the city and its surroundings over to the wealthy."

Nielsen supported the preservation of the terraces, but said this should be extended to buildings at the rear of the site. However, she raised concerns that "the expense now necessary to restore the Victoria St frontage will mitigate their occupation by former tenants" and also cause increases in property values and therefore council rates for all Victoria St properties, further driving out low-income tenants. Nielsen also claimed the scale of the project would cause over-shadowing and air pollution in the Woolloomooloo basin below.

The objection letter made a series of demands. It called for the development application to be rejected, and then a series of conditions to be placed on any future application to "preserve the street physically" and to also ensure the street "does not become the preserve of the rich". These demands included restoring all buildings, ensuring any infill building was no higher than the existing terraces and not allowing any lifts in new buildings.[5] In addition, Nielsen called for the "social mix" of future building occupants to be strictly controlled, so that 40 per cent were for low-income residents, 30 per cent for middle-income residents and the final 30 per cent high-income earners, with the low-income dwellings to include boarding house and transient-style accommodation. She also called for the development to not have off-street parking, given that it was so close to public transport and because of the ramifications of a 400 parking spaces.

Nielsen's objection was having an impact. On 21 May, Theeman and fellow Victoria St developer Paul Strasser met with the NSW Planning Minister Sir John Fuller. A briefing note prepared for Fuller by one of his department staff referred to, and attached, Nielsen's objection and also agreed with its claim that the project would cause over-shadowing. "It is considered that the scale of development constitutes a severe over-development of the site and could tend to severely over-shadow … the Woolloomooloo basin," the briefing note said. The briefing note also said Nielsen's objection "indicates continuing opposition to the proposal".

On 23 May, Theeman was sufficiently concerned by Nielsen's objection letter to write to the Sydney Lord Mayor Nicholas Shehadie, listing points rebutting Nielsen's claims in the objection letter. "We

---

5   This has partially come to pass, with many of the apartments at the Victoria Point site having no lifts

intend to rehabilitate the street with first-class accommodation and not to make it an area for transients, unemployed and prostitutes," he said. "We intend making a decent, modern living area out of a slum area. Objectors desire to retain a slum area for purely political reasons." Based on the tone of the letter, Nielsen's objections cleared appeared to be getting under Theeman's skin. The fact that, at the time, Theeman was continuing to lose thousands of dollars per day in interest payments could not have helped his demeanour.[6]

It was three days later, on 26 May, that Theeman initiated a payment which remains the source of speculation to this day. Theeman handed Kings Cross nightclub manager Jim Anderson a cheque for $25,000. According to author Peter Rees, Theeman almost immediately had second thoughts about the transaction, calling Sydney nightclub owner Abe Saffron to say he had "done a very silly thing" and asking Saffron if he could provide $25,000 in cash so Theeman could withdraw the cheque and pay Anderson in cash instead. Saffron said he didn't have the money, and Anderson went on to deposit the cheque at the Kings Cross branch of the ANZ Bank, thereby establishing a financial transaction between the men which would have been avoided if the payment was in cash.[7] Theeman later stated the money was intended to help Anderson establish a new nightclub business. Over the years, the bona fides of this payment have come under intense scrutiny.

An investigation by an Australian Parliament committee in 1994 concluded that "the evidence on the Theeman-Anderson links is capable of supporting the conclusion that, if Theeman wanted assistance in 1975 to deal with Nielsen, it would not be surprising if he had turned to Anderson. The evidence also appears to be capable of supporting the conclusion that, at the time that Nielsen disappeared, Theeman paid money to Anderson for a purpose that may have been other than its stated purpose. This invites the question as to whether the true purpose

---

6   The National Crime Authority and James McCartney Anderson, A Report by the Parliamentary Joint Committee on the National Crime Authority, March 1994, page 162
7   *Killing Juanita*, page 97

was to pay Anderson for dealing with Nielsen's opposition to Theeman's Victoria St plans."

"The committee has been told that there is a view that Anderson was blackmailing Theeman in the late 1970s and into the 1980s, that Theeman was paying him, and that somehow this was related to the disappearance of Nielsen."[8]

As Nielsen continued to campaign, and following the $25,000 payment, individuals associated with Anderson suddenly began to show an increased interest in arranging meetings with Nielsen.

A man who was employed at the Carousel Cabaret at Kings Cross – which Anderson managed – was instructed to invite Nielsen to a 16 June press conference for a new show at the club. This was despite the fact Nielsen would not ordinarily have been invited, as she did not give free publicity and, in fact, Anderson had previously vetoed advertising in *NOW*.[9] The inquest was told that when Nielsen did not arrive at the press conference, Anderson apparently "blew his top".

On 29 June, the same man again tried to meet with Nielsen, this time by calling her while she was staying at her parents' Northern Beaches home and, on the pretext of booking advertising for landscaping, trying to set up a meeting at the Camperdown Travelodge (now an apartment building). Nielsen was suspicious of the call and refused to meet.

The next contact was on 30 June, when Eddie Trigg, who worked as the night manager of the Carousel Cabaret's second floor VIP Lounge, visited Nielsen's home at 202 Victoria St. There, Trigg told Nielsen's partner Farrell that he wanted to organise advertising for businessmen's lunches at the VIP Lounge, even though the kitchen was not on the same floor as the lunch location and indeed the whole premises was not licensed for lunches.[10] Farrell gave some general details about the

---

8   The National Crime Authority and James McCartney Anderson, page 197-198
9   The National Crime Authority and James McCartney Anderson, page 164, also *Killing Juanita*, page 100
10 The National Crime Authority and James McCartney Anderson, page 166, also *Killing Juanita*, page 107

publication's advertising approach but said Trigg needed to speak to Nielsen to finalise the deal. On 3 July, Trigg phoned Nielsen and the two organised to further discuss the alleged advertising opportunity the next day, at the Carousel Cabaret.[11]

Around the same time, Nielsen was continuing to scheme against Theeman's proposal, while the political environment was also undergoing rapid change.

On 8 June, at a rally held at Bronte in Sydney's Eastern Suburbs, Nielsen had bumped into John Glebe, the secretary of the Water and Sewerage Employees' Union. The two spoke about the possibility of the union blocking water connections to Theeman's project. This led to Nielsen writing to Glebe about the project, as well as a featured interview with Glebe in her newspaper and a short-lived affair between the pair.

Published in *NOW* on 17 June, the interview was headlined "The facts of the impending disaster in Victoria St" and outlined Glebe's theory that the local aged water supply network would not be able to handle the increased pressure required once water was supplied to Theeman's project. It was another annoyance and potential blockage which Theeman could well do without.

Alongside the interview with Glebe, Nielsen also published a call from Professor Neil Runcie, the chair of the Coalition of Resident Action Groups, for a judicial inquiry into the "terrorisation" of the original Victoria St tenants, and an editorial by herself claiming a petition circulating in the area, which supported Theeman's project, had been achieved by paying the petitioners. "Once again the 20c petitioners are out in force," Nielsen wrote.

At the same time, the NSW planning system was continuing to encourage people such as Nielsen to take part in planning decisions.

On 4 June, the NSW Government released a further, more detailed document outlining proposed planning reforms. This document said a future law would be created that would allow objectors to development

---

11 *Killing Juanita*, page 111

proposals to appeal to overturn a council's development approval. This was another significant step forward for the right of communities to participate in the planning system, and was largely seen as a replacement for green bans.[12] The document also proposed the creation of a Historic Buildings and Sites Advisory Committee with the powers to declare historic buildings off-limits to demolition.[13]

However, in the same month, as the Victoria St debate and Nielsen's campaign was reaching its climax, Tom Uren once again entered the fray to support Theeman. In response to a letter from Neville Gruzman, Uren had written: "I am pleased to see [Theeman's] present scheme incorporates some 10 per cent of accommodation [for low-cost housing] and that the Housing Commission of NSW has expressed its interest in this aspect of the proposal … it appears to me that this could be a valuable precedent which other private developers may follow". Uren then went on to say: "I have also expressed my belief that we should encourage denser forms of development on land in close proximity and with easy access to public transport, such as will exist with the operation of the Kings Cross railway station".

Theeman's site was as close as 250m from the proposed station. Uren then said his support for this type of development was conditional on good planning outcomes being achieved.

In an interview for this book, John Mant, who had served as an advisor to Uren in 1973 and 1974, said he was surprised by the tone of the letter, given that his advice to Uren was to avoid getting involved adjudicating site-by-site development issues. "It was a bit more positive than I would have advised him to say," he said.

Theeman knew that receiving such a letter was a coup. He distributed it to the NSW Planning Minister Sir John Fuller – the man responsible for approving the council's proposed planning controls for the site – who then passed it immediately to his planning bureaucracy. After receiving the letter, the government's planners stood to attention.

---

12 Proposals for a new environmental planning system for NSW, Minister for Planning and Environment, June 1975, page 24
13 Proposals for a new environmental planning system for NSW, page 29

In a note attached to the letter, a senior Planning and Environment Commission official asked one of his planners to discuss the "present position" of the site with him "as soon as possible", including addressing "floor space ratio, height limits etc etc at this site". The words "as soon as possible" were underlined.

What's more, just two days after Uren's letter was sent, Theeman received another boost, in part courtesy of the Australian Government. At a gala ceremony at Sydney Town Hall on 27 June, Prime Minister Gough Whitlam joined Uren, Sydney Lord Mayor Nicholas Shehadie and NSW Premier Tom Lewis to sign an agreement relating to planning in the Woolloomooloo area, including Victoria St. This agreement finally killed off the 1969 Woolloomooloo planning scheme, but at the same time gave life to Theeman's plans.

The headline announcement was that, under the agreement, the Australian Government would give $17 million to the NSW Government to buy land in the Woolloomooloo basin for low-rise public housing, including land still owned by Sid Londish. This was effectively the polar opposite of the 1969 vision of the valley becoming a "mini-Manhattan".

The deal was embraced by Nielsen's supporters in the basin, including Nellie and Gerry Leonard, who finally had certainty that they could see out their days as public housing tenants without the threat of eviction or redevelopment. At the same time, it condemned Londish and a number of other developers in the Woolloomooloo basin to bankruptcy from 1976 onwards, after their land was resumed for just a third of the value they had paid for it in the boom times of the early 1970s.[14]

A less reported aspect of the agreement, however, was that it had also given a fillip to Theeman. Not only did the agreement expressly spare Theeman's land from government acquisition, it also included, as an attachment, draft planning controls which had been prepared by the City of Sydney Council. These proposed controls stated that a 30m high development (equivalent to around 10 storeys) would now

---

14 For Sale Again: Woolloomooloo, *The Sydney Morning Herald*, 9 May 1977, by Malcolm Wilson, page 8

How Juanita Nielsen covered the signing of the Woolloomooloo redevelopment agreement in 1975. Nielsen's friend Nellie Leonard is looking at the camera

be allowed on Theeman's site on Victoria St, compared to the miserly four storeys being contemplated in 1974.

As she left her home on the morning of 4 July 1975, it's entirely possible that Nielsen was unaware that her campaign had been secretly undermined by the Australian Government. Nielsen had covered the agreement signing on her 1 July edition of *NOW* – the last to be published – under the headline "A Day to Remember". "The day the people of Woolloomooloo have waited years for," Nielsen wrote. She did not mention the little-known attachment to the agreement, which had come to Theeman's aid.

As far as Nielsen was concerned, she was simply taking a short 300m stroll from her home to a local club, to discuss a potential advertising opportunity. It was to be the final walk that Nielsen ever made.

CHAPTER 32

"Let us not let the rich who live in these houses ... forget the tactics that were used to make way for them"

In April 1973, Mick Fowler had returned to his 115 Victoria St bedsit apartment after months away working at sea, only to find he had been evicted from his home of more than a decade.

"I walked to where I live and my mother was sitting on the front door step, and she was very upset, like most of the people I saw starting to come out of the woodwork, they were all dazed and upset, but sort of hopeless," Fowler said. "My mother has $50 in her hand, that Theeman had kindly given, to help pay for the storage of my life."[1]

Unlike many of the other tenants however, who had left quietly after similar harassment, Fowler had decided to fight for his rights and sought to return to his home. Fowler's first attempt at re-occupation was unsuccessful, after he claims Frank Theeman's security personnel recommended he be arrested. A second attempt a few days' later, made with the support of a group of builders' labourers, was successful.

Despite never supporting Fowler's claims that he was a protected tenant,[2] Theeman allowed him to stay in his apartment. Fowler said

---

1   Quote from film Woolloomooloo: A Redevelopment 1969-1977
2   In the 1970s, some tenants had protection from eviction under historic laws which were being phased out

Mick Fowler playing the banjo at a rally in 1974 (Photo: Andrew Jakubowicz)

he was subject to constant harassment, by gangs of men swinging pick handles and making late-night noise outside his door.

From that point forward, Fowler became the symbolic and defiant face of Victoria St's working class, if not the face of the working-class struggle across inner Sydney. With little or no prompting, Fowler would speak of the need for governments and organisations to do more to stop the working class from being moved on from the inner suburbs in the face of rapid gentrification. "I thought that the guiding figure in Victoria St was Mick Fowler," former Builders Labourers' Federation (BLF) secretary Joe Owens said in a 2016 interview. "Undoubtedly, Mick Fowler … epitomised all of what Victoria St was about. It was a place of old musos, old workers, old seaman, you know a rough-and-ready street that had been there for years. It was part of the bohemian Cross, not the sleazy Cross like it is now … a sleazy place now."[3]

---

3   This information is taken from an interview between Joe Owens and Ann Turner, August 1996, National Library of Australia Oral History Section

With his rasping smoker's voice, thick moustache and a bent nose which had seen too many brawls, Fowler's appearance matched his mission. Aged in his 40s, he looked every bit the knockabout worker and the outspoken larrikin.

Fowler's working-class pedigree was also backed by deep left-wing convictions and creativity – facets that made him even more attractive to Sydney's activist class. As an accomplished jazz musician, song writer and poet, his skills and talents were valued within in the protester community.

In 1966, Fowler's ship had been fired upon by American soldiers when he and his crewmates had decided to provide food to Vietnamese women and children. The following year, Fowler and his crewmates had refused to ferry supplies to Australian troops in Vietnam, as part of a protest against the war. The Australian Government then took over the vessel as a naval ship.[4]

A scan of the trade union archives, located in Canberra, shows however that Fowler's working class hero image didn't always match reality.[5] Fowler could be a highly strung and agitated individual, who swiftly wore out welcome mats.

One welcome mat which quickly became threadbare was metaphorically located outside the office of Fowler's union, the Seamen's Union of Australia. In mid-1973, the union had attempted to help Fowler by writing to Premier Robert Askin and Police Commissioner Fred Hanson to complain that Fowler had been subject to an unlawful eviction, and harassment and intimidation. The union had also provided $512 towards Fowler's legal costs to fight his eviction, an amount that led to a heated dispute as the union considered it a loan and Fowler considered it a donation.

Fowler however wanted the union to do more to help his cause. "It is doubtful that Mick Fowler will ever be satisfied with the union's

---

4   Mick Fowler - A Militant Record, *Tribune*, Tuesday 5 February 1974, page 12

5   These are the archives located at the Noel Butlin Archives Centre, at the Australian National University in Canberra

A campaign poster in support of Mick Fowler, date unknown

efforts, as he has become somewhat obsessed with his position and in any discussion frequently becomes agitated and intemperate in his assessment of his difficulties," said union Sydney branch secretary John Benson in an early 1974 letter to the union's Federal branch. "He has made no suggestions as to what action the union might take except that we 'do something'."

Hostilities flared into the open at a union stop-work meeting on 29 January 1974.

Fowler moved a motion calling for "all Australian shipping to stop" if any attempt was made to evict him. In response, Benson launched a personal attack on Fowler, stating that "union members had carried" him for the past six years, during which he had around 70 days off roster, including due to "sick leave, suspension [and] release from obligations". The clear suggestion was that, on a far too regular basis, Fowler was a liability on a ship and a burden on his crewmates. "Following the union's intercession, Fowler had been offered immediate alternative accommodation in his locality and new accommodation in the redeveloped area at the same rent," Benson went on to say. "He had also been offered $6,000 to move out, and had resisted both offers." Fowler's motion was voted down, with just two votes in favour and 155 against.

Irrespective of Fowler's varying private and public personas, by the time of Nielsen's disappearance, he was the only tenant left living in Theeman's Victoria St terraces.

Fowler had also been close to Nielsen and was distraught at the lack of progress in the police investigation. He was a frequent visitor to Sydney newsrooms, urging journalists to keep pressure on the police and government to find her killer.

On 6 July 1975, just two days after Nielsen's disappearance, police interviewed Eddie Trigg. At this interview, Trigg told police that Nielsen had left the Carousel Cabaret after "I had told her that the directors of the establishment had decided not to advertise at that time due to poor business." Yet, at an interview a day later, Trigg changed his story. At this interview, Trigg told police that after he gave Nielsen $130 for advertising, Nielsen had provided a handwritten receipt in return. In an interview on 13 July, Trigg further embellished his second story, stating that Nielsen had told him the receipt was "quite legal", before leaving to go to a luncheon event.[6]

---

6   The National Crime Authority and James McCartney Anderson, page 167

This significant change in story raised police suspicions, and rightly so. It has never been explained why Trigg altered his story, although it is reasonable to assume the first story needed to be changed because it seemed so implausible that the Carousel Cabaret would pursue Nielsen to buy advertising over several weeks, only to then tell her face-to-face that a decision had been made not to advertise. In addition to this, the fact that Trigg had a handwritten receipt seemed to provide some sort of evidence that Nielsen had left the club.

On 11 July, police announced that Nielsen's handbag, including identity papers and cosmetics but no money, had been found beside the Western Freeway at Penrith, in Sydney's far outer west. On the same day, it was also revealed that several calls had been made to a newspaper office demanding a $5,000 ransom to return Nielsen. The ransom money had been delivered as instructed, but never collected.

On 15 July, a Carousel Cabaret receptionist told police that Nielsen had left the club on her own, although the receptionist recanted this claim a year later and said Nielsen had in fact left the club with Trigg.[7]

On 18 July, a local real estate agent told police that he had seen Nielsen getting into a yellow Ford with two men on the morning of 4 July, around the same time she was meant to be leaving the club. Despite extensive inquiries, New South Wales (NSW) Police never found the car. However, in the mid-1980s, NSW Police discovered that the agent had helped Jim Anderson obtain finance for a 1983 luxury car purchase. The finance application included a bogus statement, which described the finance applicant as a "James McCartney", who had helped Theeman with his Victoria Point development.[8]

The evidence of Trigg, the receptionist and the real estate agent, along with the handbag discovery and ransom calls, were helping draw attention away from the Carousel Cabaret as a crime scene. Instead, an impression was being created that Nielsen had been abducted and taken

---

7   The National Crime Authority and James McCartney Anderson, page 176
8   The National Crime Authority and James McCartney Anderson, page 170

Pro-Nielsen graffiti, dated from early 1976, in the aftermath of her disappearance (Courtesy of Mitchell Library, State Library of NSW and SEARCH Foundation)

from the Kings Cross area after leaving the Carousel Cabaret premises, with money being the primary motive for the abduction.

On 13 July, the former squatters – including Wendy Bacon and Roelof Smilde – along with Fowler came to the conclusion that the police were being misled by these so-called clues and were not adequately focussing on the most obvious line of inquiry – Victoria St's history of violence and Nielsen's role fighting development in the street.

The activists issued a statement which said: "We believe [Nielsen's] disappearance and probable death should be looked at in the context of two-and-a-half years of violence and intimidation directed against people opposed to development in Victoria St. Since the eviction of the squatters, and since the lifting of the BLF green ban, Juanita Nielsen has been the most prominent and effective opponent of development in Victoria St. The police have expanded their energies on a ransom hoax and a physical search of the Penrith area. We believe the emphasis of any inquiry should be shifted to investigating those interests which stand to gain most from Juanita's disappearance from the Victoria

St conflict". Soon after, the former squatters published a newspaper called *Now or Never* which tied Nielsen's disappearance to a censorship-motivated assassination, and re-printed her previous Victoria St stories.

Theeman was furious about the slur. "It is all part of a vicious plan to stop the proper redevelopment of Victoria St," he said in response. "The tactics of these people are to be deplored. They have vilified me in a manner reminiscent of Nazi Germany." The activists' hunch, however, appears to have been correct, with a 1994 Australian Parliament committee report finding that the attempt by police to investigate the role of Jim Anderson in Nielsen's disappearance to be "cursory".[9]

Meanwhile, *Inner Sydney Action*, a publication produced by the Inner Sydney Regional Council for Social Development, lamented Nielsen's passing. Under a story headlined "Residents' Friend Missing", the newspaper stated: "Although supposedly a woman of means, there was none of that condescending 'fighting for you, the little people' in her writing. She believes that individuals of every socio-economic group should be welcomed to take part in community projects and participate in planning. Long live '*NOW*' and Juanita".[10]

However, Nielsen didn't return, and the police investigation moved no closer to determining the reasons for her disappearance.

Work continued on Theeman's development proposal. On 18 August 1975, Theeman's cause was assisted when the NSW Government officially published the new ten-storey planning controls for his site, which had been attached to the Woolloomooloo agreement signed with the Australian Government. On 22 September 1975, the 18-storey plans Theeman lodged earlier in the year were refused as they were inconsistent with these controls. However, Theeman now had what he needed – clear planning controls, with the opportunity to get a return on his investment, and a political environment relatively free of union green bans or activists. He worked to lodge a new application for

---

9   The National Crime Authority and James McCartney Anderson, page 193
10 From August 1975 edition of Inner Sydney Action, produced by the Inner Sydney Regional Council for Social Development

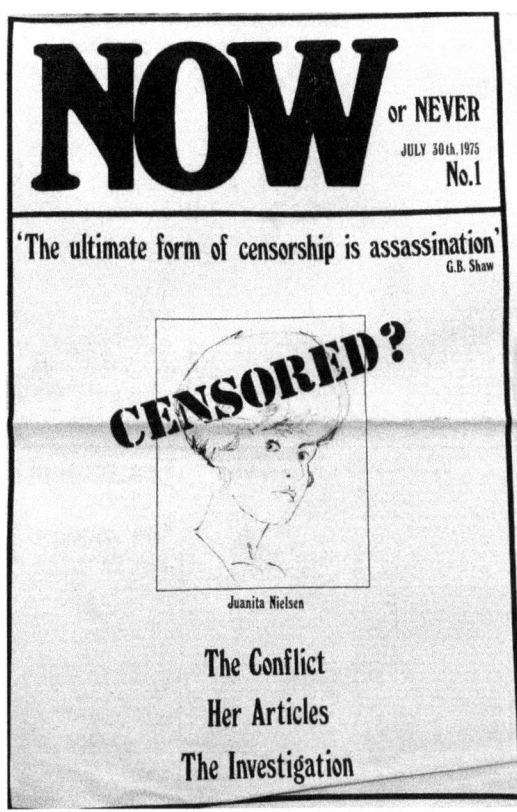

Now or Never, published in July 1975

643 units and 397 carparking spaces. With Nielsen no longer on the scene, the application proceeded with little fanfare and was approved by the City of Sydney Council in February 1976.

In May 1976, his legal appeal options exhausted, Mick Fowler was finally evicted from his apartment. Activists held a mock funeral, burying a coffin bearing the words "the right of low income earners to live in Victoria St" in the front yard of 115 Victoria St. Given the event happened around a year after Nielsen's disappearance, the coffin had a clear second meaning.

In her 'oration', activist Wendy Bacon predicted that, in the future, Victoria St would "become home of the rich". She went on to say: "We learned that to fight a developer is to fight a whole system of capital, property and State. We began by fighting Frank Theeman, but to fight Theeman we discovered was also to fight his thugs, to fight too … the

Wendy Bacon giving her 'oration' at the 'burial' of Victoria St's affordable housing, in 1976. Evicted tenant Mick Fowler stands at her right. (Courtesy of Mitchell Library, State Library of NSW and SEARCH Foundation)

big capitalists without which the speculators cannot operate. We were fighting the architects and lawyers who are conditioned to behave like neutral servants of property; we were fighting [the NSW Government] and judges and police who provided the legal muscles for Theeman.

"Victoria St changed some of us who began as protesters into revolutionaries. Let us not let the rich who live in these houses and the professionals who rent these offices forget the tactics that were used to make way for them."

CHAPTER 33

A club in Western Sydney

It's just ticked past 1pm on a warm Sunday afternoon and the Wests Tradies club in Western Sydney is beginning to hum.

In the main gaming room, around 20 people punch away on poker machines, hoping to win big on jackpots with come-on names such as Cash Express, Dollar Storm and Dragon Link. A few others sit in the TAB section, keeping a keen eye on the regional gallops and trots.

In the outdoor terrace, a group of parents watch their kids clamber over the new playground equipment, while casting a lazy eye towards the cricket on a large outdoor screen. The club manager, meanwhile, starts setting up for the meat raffle, while calling out members' names for the $10,000 lucky badge draw.

These are scenes which could be replicated in any club, in almost any part of New South Wales (NSW).

However, there is something unique about Wests Tradies, which sets it well apart from other clubs. West Tradies' founding story, in fact, has an unusual link to affordable housing issues in Victoria St, Potts Point – located a full 45km to the east.

In 1973, in an attempt to appease the Builders Labourers' Federation (BLF) and lift the green ban on his project, Frank Theeman first promised to set aside 10 per cent of new homes in his Victoria Point project for low-cost housing. At the time, Theeman said – and with some justification – that he was the first private developer to put forward such an idea. The problem was that he, or no-one else, really knew how such a concept could be achieved.

Today, there are myriad not-for-profit community housing providers who would gladly receive and lease affordable housing units. But in 1978, the only organisation in a position to accept Theeman's units was the NSW Government's Housing Commission, now Homes NSW. The Commission stated that while it supported the concept of "private developers including units for low-income earners", it hinted that it had concerns that the Victoria Point units to be set aside for affordable housing would not receive adequate fresh air or parking.[1] Eventually, the Commission backed out and said it could not accept the units due to "legal and administrative difficulties".

In early 1976, Theeman and the Building Trades Group (BTG), which represented a range of building unions, then agreed on an alternate model whereby 10 per cent of the project's units would be made available at a 15 per cent discount to applicants approved by the BTG. In 1978, the BTG realised this idea, also, was not practical, as it was difficult to determine who the approved applicants should be, and what their tenure should be, and there was also the distinct chance that the applicants could simply immediately re-sell the units for a windfall gain.

In October 1978, Theeman and the BTG agreed that $150,000 would be paid by Theeman, over three stages, to a union fund dedicated to the "recreation and welfare" of building workers. This fund was in turn used to help build a club, originally known as the Building Workers Club, on land owned by the Building Workers' Industrial Union in the Mount Druitt region in Sydney's west. This same club is now known as Wests Tradies.

There was a bitter irony in this decision. As part of the Victoria St campaign, activists such as Mick Fowler had sung about low-income tenants being forced out of inner Sydney and to Mount Druitt. The

---

1 Letter from Housing Commission chair J.M. Bourke to Sid Vaughan, secretary of the Building Trades Group, dated 13 May 1975

Wests Tradies: An air-conditioned box sitting in the middle of a carpark in Western Sydney (Photo: Mark Skelsey)

protest song 'Across the Western Suburbs' – sung to the tune of 'All for me Grog' – states that "before I even knew it, I was shifted to Mount Druitt, and the planners never gave me any say boys, now it really makes me weep, I am just at home to sleep, for it takes me hours to get to work each day boys". And now, the funds which were meant to be used to create affordable housing in Sydney's east were also forced out to Mount Druitt – to fund an air-conditioned mecca for drinking and gambling sitting in the middle of a giant carpark.

In short, West Tradies is where Victoria St's dreams of ongoing affordable housing went to die.

PART 5
THE LEGACY

CHAPTER 34

Victoria St hits the big screen

While the Victoria St struggle officially ended in 1976, the story certainly did not. The street's urban warfare, which to date had mainly been featured in newspaper stories and TV news bulletins, now found its way to the silver screen. Between 1976 and 1982, no less than four movies were made about Victoria St – two documentaries and two mainstream cinema fictional representations.

Street Music is a somewhat rushed and ramshackle 53-minute documentary released in 1976, which is centred around the day of Mick Fowler's eviction in May 1976 and the street party that night. "It was not a victory … but we are going out in style," one activist tells the documentary makers. The movie also records Fowler and others singing on the back of a truck as it drives around the Sydney Central Business District, while there are also repeated references to Nielsen's disappearance. *Street Music* helps capture the songs and colourful characters of the struggle, but ultimately falls short when it comes to telling the story of the struggle itself.

A more substantial piece of work was the 77-minute-long documentary *Woolloomooloo: A Redevelopment 1969–1977* which was released in 1978. Co-produced by Pat Fiske and Denise White, the documentary includes interviews with key players such as developers Sid Londish and Frank Theeman, former BLF secretary Joe Owens, tenant Mick Fowler, City of Sydney Alderman Andrew Briger and various activists. "The developer of course was usually considered to be the baddie in the piece, was in fact to my mind at a disadvantage, in as much as he had been invited to come into the area, he had been given a specification on which he could work, he worked accordingly to it and found – because of the shortcomings of the planning for the area – he was holding the baby," Briger says in the film.

The documentary also includes footage of Theeman's security personnel loitering in Victoria St and the dramatic eviction of the squatters, but curiously does not spend much time on Nielsen's disappearance. All in all, however, it truly is a remarkable piece of work which, apart from some minor factual inaccuracies, is an invaluable snapshot of the period.

The first of the fictional films, *The Killing of Angel St*, was largely filmed at Weston St, Balmain East, where a set showing the facades of traditional terrace homes was constructed on a harbourside park which fringes one side of the street. Released in 1981, the film picks up many elements of the Victoria St development saga.

It tells the story of residents, activists and unionists fighting a fictional development, known as Spectrum 2000, which seeks to demolish the terraces and instead build apartments with harbour views. "Those houses are obsolete, unhealthy, wasteful … what is there to conserve?" the film's developer says. "The 19th-century facades have been carefully copied, the high-rise set back discretely … there will be space for 10 times as many people to live and work in a beautiful precinct close the heart of the city. All this has been held up by a handful of old residents, sailors, waitresses, artists who don't pay their rent."

The film makes no secret that it is re-telling the Victoria St controversy, including directly naming Juanita Nielsen. "When the developers started to buy up property and kick the folks out, she started this little newspaper called *NOW*," says one of the film's characters. "By Jesus, she told it just as it is. The scandals about the developers, the thugs, the crooked coppers. And one day she just disappeared, never seen to this day. Everybody knows but nothing can be proved." In fact, the film's creative team said they were urged by a "knight of the realm" and a New South Wales (NSW) Government Minister not to

Juanita Nielsen's disappearance was called out in the 1981 movie, The Killing of Angel St (Image courtesy of the National Film and Sound Archive of Australia)

make the film, because of fears it would revive public interest into the disappearance of Nielsen.[1]

The film's script involves its main character, Jessica Simmonds (played by Liz Alexander), returning from London to support her father, B.C. Simmonds (played by Alexander Archdale), who is a stay-put resident fighting the Spectrum 2000 development. Just like in Victoria St, stooges representing the developer loiter outside the threatened homes, while street protests are held.

Jessica's father then dies in a suspicious fire, while another tenant is bashed and Jessica is kidnapped and threatened, before being wrongly charged by police. In the film, the clear implication is that the

---

1   The Killing of Angel St, Directory of World Cinema: Australia and New Zealand, Intellect Ltd, 2015, by Ben Goldsmith

developer may not be aware of the violence, but certainly is funding and condoning it, and has the support of corrupt police and government. The main union leader supporting Jessica's cause is implied to be a political opportunist. The film ends with the development being put on hold after Jessica exposes the violence on television.

Heatwave was released in 1982 and was largely filmed in and around picturesque Georgina St, Newtown which, like Victoria St, is known for its grand terrace homes. The film's lead characters are Kate Dean (played by Judy Davis), who is a tenant fighting a major redevelopment known as Eden, and the project's architect Stephen West (played by Richard Moir).

The film is set during a scorching heat wave during the Christmas-New Year period, in a nod to the mid-summer timing of the 1974 eviction of the Victoria St squatters. The film opens with Dean – just like the Victoria St squatters – tip-toeing across rooftops to avoid being evicted by a henchman working for the developer (who is known as 'Houseman' in a clear link to 'Theeman'). The film then focuses on the disappearance of leading female resident activist Mary Ford (a newspaper publisher), who is working with Dean to fight the project, and the pathetic police investigation into her disappearance, along with the frustrations of the idealistic architect West who is unable to consummate his masterpiece due to resident action.

"Why are we being forced out of our houses? Why is it that people who've lived here all their lives, are having their homes demolished by these arseholes," Dean says as she is being dragged off the rooftops. "The inner city is changing, everyone wants to live close to the centre and will pay to do it. I am sorry, it is a natural process," West retorts in another scene.

In a nod to the claims that the Victoria St squatters were not 'real residents', it's suggested during *Heatwave* that Dean is an imposter middle-class girl who sides with the working class to prove her socialist credentials. Also, and potentially building on media claims of sexual activity on the squatter site, Dean is shown sleeping with West and openly flirting with other men. The film ends in bloodied violence, as an underworld figure who takes over the site is gunned down on New Year's Eve and activist's head pops up on a building site, after a stormwater drain overflows during a summer storm.

Ken Woolley was interviewed by Moir before the movie was shot but says he was aghast at the final outcome, stating that it represented "scandalously conflated fiction and selective facts". "The relationship in the film between the architect and Judy Davis was the complete opposite of reality, beyond contemplation," Woolley said.[2] "The [building] design they produced was equally ludicrous. The architect was presented as a wimpish version of Howard Roark in the film *The Fountainhead*, with equally fatuous attitudes.

"The film set the murder much earlier than it is claimed to have been in reality. That was not in the period of either my design work or the site conflicts as far as I am aware. A final, possibly deliberate irony, the setting for the murder in the film was a real construction site in Cascade St Paddington ... its architects were [the same architects] who eventually carried out the present buildings in Victoria St, following Theeman's period."

While *Heatwave* is unquestionably a more creative and interesting piece of work compared to *The Killing of Angel St*, both films arguably fail to migrate the energy and passion of the Victoria St story to the big screen. The characters in the films seem shallow and self-absorbed, rather than fighting for a greater cause. The real story of Juanita Nielsen's energy-sapping campaign to preserve Victoria St, the haunting malevolence of mysterious figures loitering outside homes and the never-say-die party-like attitude of anarchist squatters seems so much more convincing and authentic compared to the films' fictional representations.

It's arguable that all four films, however, had a lasting impact on the public imagination, by generally casting developers as the baddies and the resident activists the goodies. The films suggested that developers were not to be trusted – motivated by profit rather than the public good

---

2 Draft memoirs prepared by Ken Woolley and passed to author, dated 2004

– and were mixing with criminals, and corrupt police and government officials. The films also glorified and promoted the concept of activists resisting development in their suburb, although it should be noted that *Heatwave* at least questioned the bona fides and motivations of the lead anti-development activist. This anti-development narrative came at a critical time as the State's new planning legislation was finalised and then implemented.

In March 1976, the NSW Liberal and National coalition government introduced new planning and heritage legislation into the State's Parliament. This legislation introduced new powers allowing objectors to both comment on, and appeal, major development, along with the creation of a new Historic Building Sites and Advisory Committee which had the ability to recommend interim and permanent preservation orders on buildings and areas. The proposed legislation prohibited owners from demolishing or damaging buildings or trees on sites where preservation orders apply, with up to six months in jail for breaching this requirement. However, the legislation was never passed, due to the government calling an election, which meant Parliament was suspended. On 1 May, the Liberal and National coalition narrowly lost the election to the Labor Opposition, bringing some 11 years of power to an end.

As is so often the case, the new State government took a different approach. It decided to create three new pieces of legislation – one focussing on heritage, another on all other planning and development issues, and a third establishing a new appeals court.

In September 1976, new Labor Premier Neville Wran hailed that the proposed Heritage Act would be the "most advanced and comprehensive legislation of its type in Australia", adding that it would "put an end to the destruction, by intent or neglect, of the State's heritage".[3] The legislation went even further than that of the previous government, by requiring minimum standards of repair for some heritage items and also

---

3   Government to Protect Historic Buildings, *The Sydney Morning Herald*, 23 September 1976, by Joseph Glascott, page 2

allowing the government to stop development on land in the event of illegal heritage item demolitions. The legislation came into operation in 1977.

Almost immediately, the legislation – which in part was sparked by Theeman's cavalier disregard for heritage – came in very handy at the Victoria Point site.

The Builders Labourers' Federation (BLF) green ban had forced Theeman into reluctantly retaining terraces at the site. However, as soon as Theeman had his development approval, and with the BLF now out of the way, he set about trying to get rid of the terraces, by any means possible. "Some of the listed buildings are not only quite unsafe, but it appears impossible to make them habitable," Theeman wrote to the National Trust in March 1977. "To preserve the character of the street, but produce habitable dwellings, we suggest that we carefully preserve the facades and replace the actual buildings behind with modern dwellings". The National Trust rejected the request out of hand. However, even worse still, the National Trust received information that Theeman was deliberately sabotaging the terraces. In April 1977, another Victoria St developer told the National Trust he had been told that Theeman had instructed a demolisher to "knock the remaining houses about a little, to make them look beyond redemption". Unfortunately, with the passage of time, it is not possible to know whether this claim is true.

By July 1978, the new Minister for Planning and Environment, Paul Landa, had had enough. He issued an order banning demolition of the terraces, given that many of them were looking increasingly neglected and rundown, even as construction work began on the site. Victoria St finally had formal, legislative heritage protection. However, it wasn't until the early 1980s, when a new developer took over the site, that all the terraces were preserved.

In the late 1970s, attention also turned to the best way to manage the entire planning system. In 1979, the Labor Government introduced the landmark Environmental Planning and Assessment Bill (which in a modified form remains in place today). In the legislation's

As construction started on the Victoria Point site in 1977, Theeman left the terraces in a rundown state, and schemed and manoeuvred to have them demolished (Courtesy of Mitchell Library, State Library of NSW and SEARCH Foundation)

second reading speech, Minister for Corrective Services Bill Haigh complimented the former government's 1976 bill – developed as the Victoria St battle was raging – stating that it "represented the first serious attempt to comprehensively replace existing town planning legislation with modern legislation appropriate to changed and changing circumstances in society" and "was to prove a fundamental source material for [this] Government's initiatives in reviewing existing town planning and environmental protection laws".

The many objectives of the new legislation included to "provide increased opportunity for public involvement and participation in environmental planning and assessment" and "to promote the sharing of the responsibility for environmental planning between the different levels of government in the State". It allowed members of the public to challenge the merits of some development approvals and the legality of all planning decisions, in a new Land Environment Court which had the same standing as the NSW Supreme Court.

The legislation also forced government agencies to more carefully consider the environmental impact of activities which previously did not need to receive planning approval, such as forestry, waterway dredging or the construction of new roads, bridges, marinas and railways. If the impacts of these activities were significant, an Environmental Impact Statement needed to be prepared and exhibited – allowing members of the public to participate in planning for these projects for the first time.

All up, then Minister for Planning Paul Landa said the new legislation "heralds a new deal for the public in a planning process by providing unprecedented opportunities for public participation".

Soon after the legislation was passed, several other important public events put a further spotlight on the Woolloomooloo and Victoria St situation.

In 1981, following a legal challenge by a landowner, Justice Ash in the Supreme Court of NSW found the 1969 Woolloomooloo planning scheme had been negligently prepared, particularly in planning for transport issues. "The requisite work – a deep quantitative analysis of this basic matter [transport] or of the retaining of consultants to do it – was not performed," Justice Ash said, while also commenting that "the consultations with the Departments [of Railways and Main Roads] were inadequate".[4] Peter Kacirek came in for particular criticism in the ruling, with the ruling saying his "evidence, whether considered individually or jointly with that of the other witnesses, has not provided an adequate defence to the plaintiff's claim of deficient preparation of this study" and that such a conclusion was "an unwelcome one in the light of the background of Mr Kacirek and his presentation in this case."[5] While the ruling of negligence against the NSW Government and City of Sydney Council was later overturned on legal technical issues, the criticism was stinging and stays on the public record.

Public interest and the justice system, meanwhile, continued to focus on Juanita Nielsen's disappearance.

---

[4] San Sebastian Pty Ltd and another versus the Minister administering the Environmental Planning and Assessment Act 1979, 17 December 1981, Justice Ash, page 80

[5] San Sebastian, page 56

In February 1983, the Carousel Cabaret's manager Eddie Trigg was sentenced to three years' jail after pleading guilty to conspiring – or in other words planning with others – to abduct Nielsen during June and July 1975. Another man, Shayne Martin-Simmonds, was found guilty of the same charge, and was sentenced to two years in jail, while a third man was acquitted of the offence.[6] In 1977, Martin-Simmonds told police in an interview that the advertising opportunity offered to Nielsen was a ploy to get her to come for a private conversation with someone. He said that if he and Trigg had been able to see Nielsen alone at her Victoria St home, and she resisted coming with them, they would have had to "put her in the back of [the car] on the floor with a blanket over her" and she "would have to be tied up". Martin-Simmonds said he did not know the identity of the person who wanted to speak to Nielsen, or the reason why.[7]

These court proceedings strengthened the link between Nielsen's disappearance and the Carousel Cabaret – but ultimately raised more questions than answers.

Meanwhile, in 1983, the coronial inquest was held into Nielsen's disappearance. Over a period of 13 weeks, a six-person jury at the NSW Coroner's Court delved into the events leading to Nielsen's presumed murder, creating headlines as Kings Cross figures such as Theeman, Jim Anderson and Abe Saffron were interviewed, and as Arthur King for the first time revealed his abduction.

On 7 November 1983, N.A. Newton, the counsel for the Nielsen estate, stated that Nielsen's campaign against Theeman's Victoria Point development – through her newspaper, letter writing and links to supportive union officials – provided the only possible motive for her murder. "At the time she disappeared, Ms Nielsen was probably the only possible bar to the work proceeding at that time," Newton said. "Hers was the voice that would not be stifled and hers were the hands that would not cease to write in opposition … basically it was the

---

6   Trigg Gets 3 Years for Juanita Conspiracy, *The Sydney Morning Herald*, 9 February 1983, page 10
7   The National Crime Authority and James McCartney Anderson, page 181

Victoria Point Pty Ltd development proposal which was the only one in which, at the time she disappeared, her opposition would have been of any importance at all. In other words, nobody else really had any motive to silence the voice and hands of Mrs [sic] Nielsen."[8]

During his time on the stand, Theeman denied that Nielsen posed a threat to his development. "She had no power, she was no problem," Theeman said.[9] Theeman said his letter to the Sydney Lord Mayor in May 1975, forcibly rebutting Nielsen's objections, and his decision to take Nielsen out to lunch in February 1975. had been done "merely as a matter of courtesy". On 8 November 1983, Theeman's lawyer John Dailly went further, telling the inquest "there is not one shred of evidence to directly link Frank Theeman with the disappearance of Juanita Nielsen".[10]

On 10 November 1983, the jury declared that Nielsen was dead, but it was unable to say how, when or where she died. The jury also added a significant sting to its finding by stating that, in its opinion, there was "evidence to show that the police inquiries were inhibited by an atmosphere of corruption, real or imagined, that existed at the time".

---

[8] The National Crime Authority and James McCartney Anderson, page 162
[9] Nielsen posed no threat, court told, *The Sydney Morning Herald*, 6 September 1983, by Neil Mercer, page 4
[10] Police not diligent, Nielsen jury told, *The Sydney Morning Herald*, 9 November 1983, by Neil Mercer, page 5

CHAPTER 35

Innovation comes from warfare

It only takes a quick scan of a City of Sydney Council planning map to show that Victoria St, north of its intersection with William St, has extensive heritage protection.

Along the street, there are more than 30 local heritage listings, covering about 60 properties with current uses as diverse as terrace homes, sandstone public staircases and a school. Among the listed terraces are 115 Victoria St, where stay-put tenant Mick Fowler lived, and 109 Victoria St, where artist John Olsen painted his famous *Spanish Encounter* in an attic room. As a consequence, demolition or major external changes to these buildings require approval.[1]

A further two properties – Juanita Nielsen's former tiny terrace at 202 Victoria St and a three-storey wide-fronted 1870s terrace alongside the McElhone Stairs at 55 Victoria St – have a stronger form of heritage protection, as they are also listed as State heritage items. As a result, the New South Wales (NSW) Heritage Council must be notified of applications relating to these items.[2]

In addition, the street – like so many others in inner Sydney – is covered by a heritage conservation area, a tool which usually ensures

---

1. See Clause 5.10 of the Sydney Local Environmental Plan 2012
2. See Section 57(1) of the *NSW Heritage Act*, also Section 4.41 of the Environmental Planning and Assessment Act 1979

that any new development (even if this development is not on a heritage listed site) is "sensitively accommodated" in the area.³

While the heritage listings and planning protections are broadly welcomed by the street's residents, there is also something strangely unsatisfactory about them. Protecting clusters of individual buildings, whether because of their beauty or social history, doesn't really reflect Victoria St's quite incredible contribution to society.⁴

Victoria St is really the social story of what this amazing place meant to people, rather than a group of historic buildings.

This place was so highly cherished that people were willing to fight, and even die, to protect it. The street's clifftop location, and its complementary and attractive buildings and trees, were one reason the street was so valued, particularly by artists. However, for many others, the street represented an ideal: that people on low-incomes should be able to live alongside the rich, that housing should be for everyone, and that developers who did not believe in this should be held accountable.

As a result of the fight for it, Victoria St became a crucible of innovation. It's often said that wars are a catalyst for innovation, with World War II leading to the invention of the home microwave and weather radar, and ushering in the space race. By the same token, the Victoria St war led to planning innovation.

Pressure from a union green ban forced Frank Theeman to develop the idea of setting aside a portion of low-cost housing in a private development, which at the time was a radical and new concept. Due to the immature status of the affordable housing sector at the time, these low-cost apartments were ultimately never delivered. However, Victoria

---

3. Guidelines for managing change in Heritage Conservation Areas, Heritage Office and Department of Urban Affairs and Planning, 1996, page 13. Note also the analysis about the impact of recent NSW Government planning changes affecting heritage conservation areas in Chapter 37.
4. Pro-development groups would probably also argue that the controls also mean the street is not helping to contribute needed new housing

St did seed the idea that this affordable housing concept could perhaps be delivered in the future.

Today, this concept is standard practice. In 2000, following a court challenge from a property developer, the NSW Government introduced legislation which gave it the power to establish a State policy which required developers to deliver, or fund, new affordable housing dwellings. It also preserved six existing Sydney council planning schemes which sought to deliver this outcome, in areas including Green Square, Pyrmont, St Leonards, North Sydney, Waverley and Randwick.[5] By 2019, the State policy was expanded outside of Sydney, with councils from rural and regional NSW allowed for the first time to create planning schemes which required private developers to supply, or contribute towards the construction of, new affordable housing dwellings.[6] The impact of these actions can be seen in the City of Sydney Council area. By July 2022, the council had collected about $378 million in levies from developers, with these levies contributing towards the construction of 1,427 affordable housing units, with a further 641 dwellings in the development pipeline.[7]

Victoria St also clearly illustrated to the world the need to work towards retaining existing affordable housing. The spectacle of hundreds of pensioners, unemployed people and low-income workers being subject to a mass eviction in Victoria St in 1973 was disturbing, particularly given these people also felt intimidated by agents of the developer. The situation highlighted that the planning system provided no safety net or compassion for people on low incomes. Partly in response to this issue, in 1984 the NSW Government introduced changes which sought to retain existing affordable housing. It did this by allowing councils to consider and respond to the loss of affordable housing when applications were lodged to subdivide and sell off existing boarding houses and residential flat buildings in 14

---

5   See *Environmental Planning and Assessment Amendment (Affordable Housing) Act* 2000
6   See State Environmental Planning Policy No 70 - Affordable Housing (Revised Schemes) Amendment (Application) published 25 February 2019
7   See report to City of Sydney council meeting of 26 June 2023 (Item 8.3)

Sydney local government areas, along with Newcastle and Wollongong. Once again, this typically led to the setting aside of levies to fund new affordable housing, or in some cases application refusals.[8] For instance, following the passing of this policy, North Sydney Council voted to levy developers who caused the loss of low income housing and to use these funds to build new housing.[9]

That's not to say that these policies have gone anywhere close to solving affordable housing issues faced by modern society – an issue further explored in the next chapter. Or that NSW could be regarded as a leader in this space. But Victoria St certainly played a role in attempts which have attempted in some way to deal with the issue.

The street was also linked to a range of heritage reforms.

At the time the Victoria St battle began in 1973, the State's heritage policy framework was in a rudimentary and disjointed state. The State Planning Authority (SPA) and its predecessor, the Cumberland County Council, had proclaimed just 15 historic buildings across Sydney. As a result of this action, the owners could demand the property be acquired by the NSW Government. Councils including Hunter's Hill and Windsor (now Hawkesbury) were also making attempts to prevent the demolition of groups of historic buildings, while the City of Sydney had proclaimed the suburb of Paddington as a preservation zone.[10]

Victoria St played a key role in the introduction of heritage conservation areas, which protected all aspects of precincts rather than just individual buildings.

On 4 May 1973, the heritage lobby group, the National Trust, placed the Victoria St precinct on its heritage list, which had no statutory effect but did tend to influence public debate and formal government action. Victoria St was the first precinct listed under a new National Trust

---

8   See State Environmental Planning Policy 10, printed in *NSW Government Gazette* on 6 July 1984 (page 3547-48).
9   Referred to in North Sydney Affordable Housing Strategy 1984
10 This analysis is taken from an internal report by SPA town planner Gabrielle Kibble prepared in 1974, in response to Cabinet discussions on heritage issues

classification system, which allowed the Trust to recognise the value of entire areas or places, rather than just individual houses or property.[11] This in turn has become the precursor for the concept of heritage conservation areas, which is now a standard feature in many statutory local plans. On the same day as its listing announcement in 1973, the National Trust announced it would press the NSW Government for new overall heritage legislation, linking Victoria St with the birth of modern heritage laws.

Victoria St was also a trailblazer in another innovative heritage reform, which helped preserve heritage buildings by allowing owners to sell the developable air space above these buildings to other property developers, while still retaining the heritage buildings themselves. The City of Sydney's landmark 1971 Strategic Plan had floated this idea, as it reduced the pressure to demolish and redevelop heritage buildings.

The reform was first used in Victoria St.[12] In 1973, a developer sought to demolish a row of 1880s Gothic-style terraces at 119–139 Victoria St for a 23-storey tower, as the site had been earmarked for significant development potential under the 1969 Woolloomooloo scheme.

However, as the Woolloomooloo scheme collapsed, the developer was unable to obtain planning approval and successfully applied to the council to instead sell the unbuilt and unrealised floor space above the terraces to other sites in the middle of the Sydney Central Business District. One purchaser of these air rights was a residential developer at York St who, as a result, was able to increase the building's height by around four storeys without having any discernible unwanted impact on the locality.[13] In turn, the original developer retained and restored the Gothic-style terraces – works which the National Trust oversaw and remarked represented "one of the first major rehabilitation projects in the inner-Sydney area".

---

11 Trust Joins Battle of Victoria St, *The Sydney Morning Herald*, 4 May 1973, page 1
12 Heritage Floor Space Update, July 2004, City of Sydney Council
13 Incentive for Restoration, *The Sydney Morning Herald*, 25 November 1982, by John Rich and Mark Coulton, page 2

HOW THE HERITAGE FLOOR SPACE TRANSFER SYSTEM WORKED IN VICTORIA ST

1 Historic terraces and shops at Victoria and Brougham St, and Rowena Place, are earmarked to be demolished for high-rise development in 1969 Woolloomooloo planning scheme. As support for scheme collapses, application for 23-storey tower on site not supported.

2 Council agrees to award developer around 16,000 sq/m of unused residential floor space above the buildings, if they are preserved and restored

3 Developer sells floor space to allow CBD developers in York and Market St to increase height and floor space of their residential buildings

4 23 terraces and two shops (now Butler Restaurant) sold by developer, following restoration work overseen by National Trust

An apartment tower looms behind retained terraces on the Victoria Point site (Photo: Mark Skelsey)

By 2018, the heritage floor space transfer reform had guaranteed the ongoing preservation and conservation of some 75 buildings across central Sydney, which would have otherwise been under significant demolition pressure, or too expensive to maintain.[14] The system has been used to preserve inner-Sydney heritage icons, including the Capitol Theatre, the distinctive 1930s AWA 'radio tower' building near Wynyard, St Mary's Cathedral and the Great Synagogue.

As a final point on heritage, the eventual development constructed on the Victoria Point site was also an early – although perhaps rudimentary – example of a major housing development retaining existing heritage buildings. Theeman's Victoria Point project involved building three ten-storey residential towers behind retained terraces. Such a blend of the old and new is now common practice in urban renewal, allowing both preservation and growth. While views on the quality of the final built form at the site are mixed, former activist Arthur King said that "the

---

[14] Sourced from report to City of Sydney Transport, Heritage and Planning Committee, 10 September 2018

preservation of the older buildings and the new infill development was probably the best you could have hoped for".[15]

Victoria St also helped prove that reforms needed to be made to ensure greater public participation in planning decisions. Victoria St was part of the broader 1969 Woolloomooloo planning scheme, which couldn't be implemented because insufficient consultation had taken place regarding how the scheme would be serviced by transport and other vital infrastructure, including water and sewerage. George Clarke, the urban planner who created the City of Sydney's famed 1971 Strategic Plan, later called the Woolloomooloo scheme the "archetype of all urban planning disasters".[16]

As outlined in Chapter 27 of this book, the Woolloomooloo debacle was cited by the NSW Planning Minister of the day, as well as a senior NSW Government MP, as an example of what could go wrong when there was a lack of public examination of planning schemes before they were adopted.

The Woolloomooloo scheme was also publicly called out as an example of what could go wrong when the needs and desires of private enterprise led the planning process. The Woolloomooloo scheme was unashamed in its rhetoric that private enterprise could implement the plan, without the guidance or oversight of a specific redevelopment authority, using what were later revealed to be excessive and flawed planning incentives. In fact, only property developers were really consulted before the plan was released.

As such, the failed Woolloomooloo scheme, which included the western side of Victoria St, helped usher in planning reforms which allow the public, government agencies and other stakeholders to have their say about planning issues in their community. The scheme also led to a turning point in the State's history, whereby community and environmental needs were prioritised, at the expense of individual landowner rights.

---

15 Interview with author
16 Planning Sydney: Nine Planners Remember, City of Sydney Council, 1992, page 22

With new legislation encouraging public participation in place, and with rising real estate values and movies and other public events focussing on planning issues, it's no surprise that Sydney experienced a boom in resident action groups in the 1980s.

Research found that 352 resident action groups were formed across Sydney in the 1980s, a sharp increase from 10 in the 1960s and 35 in the 1970s. The research found that, in 1991, some 51 per cent of resident action groups were in inner Sydney, with 42 per cent in middle Sydney and the rest (7 per cent) in outer Sydney. These groups were either formal associations looking at a range of issues, or were focussed on a single issue such as urban or industrial development, traffic or the environment.[17] Given the rise in anti-development activism, it's understandable that, during the 1980s, the acronym NIMBY – standing for 'Not In My Backyard' – also came into common parlance. The disparaging acronym – still divisive today – was intended as a criticism against residents thought to be motivated solely by self-interest, and being overly vigorous, when trying to stop development in their neighbourhood.

Of course, it's not accurate to state that Victoria St and Woolloomooloo were the sole forces behind these changes. At the time, there many other issues and controversies which built the case for change, including the highly destructive expansion of freeways through historic inner-city suburbs, The Rocks redevelopment scheme, the office tower boom of the late 1960s and early 1970s, and myriad other local skirmishes, both in urban and natural areas.

However, as sociologist Andrew Jakubowicz – a former Coalition of Resident Action Group chair – put it in an interview for this book: "There was a sort of wave, this sort of social movement wave that was going through and was clearly demonstrated in all sorts of ways. And Victoria St was like a sharp end of the [ship's] prow".

It should also be noted that Victoria St's legacy was not limited to planning issues.

---

17. Resident Action Groups in Sydney: People Power or Rat-bags? *Australian Geographer*, May 1994, by Lauren N. Costello and Kevin M. Dunn

Victoria St's squatting commune also helped inspire other politically-motivated Sydney squatting movements from 1974 onwards, some of which delivered significant urban and social change. For instance, research has found members of the Victoria St squat played a key role occupying vacant buildings to fight a proposed motorway running through Glebe. The success of this protest ultimately led to a decision by the NSW Government in 1977 to abandon a major inner-Sydney motorway construction scheme, which saved around 2,000 homes from demolition.[18] "I think we would have squatted anyway [in Glebe] but one of the things we learned [from Victoria St] was it was a lot safer squatting in a government-owned building than a privately owned one. We saw what happened [in Victoria St] and we knew the Department of Main Roads weren't going to bring thugs in on us," said Allan Rees, who was part of both the Glebe and Victoria St movements.[19]

Meanwhile, the Victoria St squat is also heralded as inspiring the occupation of other buildings in Glebe, to establish services for women. For instance, feminist Anne Summers led the charge to squat in a vacant church-owned building in Glebe to create Sydney's first hostel for women escaping abusive relationships (known as 'Elsie'). "I knew from the Victoria St experience how to do it," Summers said in an interview for this book. "If you established residency and you changed the locks, [that] gave you legal rights. I knew that from that experience. I think the lessons of Victoria St were very, very important."

The squat was also a formative experience for many other young left-wing activists. The list of people arrested during the 3 January 1974 eviction includes the names of many individuals who went on to have significant careers. Wendy Bacon became an award-winning journalist who exposed police and other corruption, and an academic teaching the next generation of journalists. Feminist Liz Fell became a journalist, public intellectual, teacher and activist, who campaigned and protested on behalf of women, indigenous rights and the rights of those

---

[18] Australian Urban Squatters of The 1970s: Establishing and Living a Radical Lifestyle in Inner-City Sydney, PhD thesis by Johanna Jane Trainor, August 2020
[19] Interview with author

in custody.[20] Teresa Brennan's career was as a feminist philosopher and psychoanalytic theorist, before dying in a 'hit and run' car crash in 2003. Sadly, Brennan is today better known as the person whom Australian judge Marcus Einfeld claimed was driving his car in Sydney in 2006 when he received a $77 speeding ticket, despite Brennan having been dead for several years. In 2008, Einfeld pleaded guilty to making a false statement on oath and attempting to pervert the course of justice, and served two years in jail. He has apologised and expressed remorse for his offence. Other high-profile names – on the arrest list – include Ian Milliss (contemporary artist), Jenny Coopes (political cartoonist and illustrator) and George Molnar (academic and philosopher).

Meanwhile, the failed investigation into Nielsen's murder – including the finding of the coronial inquest – helped build a community perception that endemic corruption was an issue in the NSW Police Force, although no officers involved in the case were ever found to have acted in a corrupt manner. The Nielsen case was cited by independent MP John Hatton in his 1994 speech to the NSW Parliament, leading to the creation of a Royal Commission into entrenched police corruption, which in turn played a landmark role addressing the problem.[21] Arthur King, who worked as an advisor to Hatton, said the Nielsen case "did bring about much more of an awareness of police corruption" but also noted that publicity about the case came at a time when governments around the world were already cracking down on corruption. "[The Nielsen case] brought the Cross to the notice of people, places like the Venus Room had been there forever, people had been shot in the Venus Room and coppers took no notice, licensing police had a rate card, based on your turnover," he said.

---

[20] Fearless Activist, Journalist and Teacher Influenced Many, *The Sydney Morning Herald*, 25 August 2020

[21] Speech by John Hatton to NSW Parliament, 11 May 1994

CHAPTER 36
"I love the plane trees ... terraces and the proximity to everything"

It's a glorious Sydney Saturday morning and I am sitting in the two-bedroom Victoria Point apartment of friends Richard and Susanne, enjoying a cup of coffee, a chat and uninterrupted views to the Sydney Central Business District skyline.

Six years ago, Richard and Susanne moved into the Victoria Point complex. First they rented, to see whether they liked the area and building, then after hearing an apartment was for sale, negotiated directly with the owner and purchased it for $2.1 million. The couple had both previously lived in standalone houses, and at first weren't sure whether they would enjoy apartment living. Now they wouldn't have it any other way.

"We absolutely love our view. We never get tired of looking at that. Particularly in the evening with the lights of the city coming on," says Richard. "Obviously, the fireworks are fun on New Year's Eve and other times of the year. And the proximity to almost everything that we need here, the railway stations, the shops. Virtually, all our shopping we do locally. We occasionally jump in the car and drive to Bondi Junction or Double Bay to go to bigger stores. But basically, everything we need on a day-to-day basis, we just walk to. And in a matter of 10 to 15 minutes, we can be in the city."

Despite being in the heart of the city, Richard and Susanne say their apartment is incredibly quiet, apart from the almost continuous sound

The view from Richard and Susanne's apartment in the Victoria Point project

of someone renovating in the complex, and the occasional yells and disturbances coming from the valley below.

Susanne, in particular, had always wanted to live in Victoria St. "When I thought about retiring, well, coming to live in the Cross, I'd always been fascinated by Victoria St. I'd often walked around here and I loved the trees and the buildings. And when I sold my house in Woollahra, I thought, 'that's the street I'd like to live in'. I love the plane trees and the terraces, and the proximity to everything. And I'd been volunteering at the Wayside [Chapel] for nine-and-a-half years so I knew the area quite well."

The Victoria Point apartment project is now home to many self-funded retirees, such as Richard and Susanne, alongside a healthy smattering of professional working renters and owner-occupiers. The complex appears to attract retirees who have had illustrious careers in government, such as senior foreign diplomats, a senior Federal Government bureaucrat, and a former State and Federal Minister.

When it comes to owning or renting, Victoria Point is anything but cheap. In October 2024, the record price for a Victoria Point apartment sat at $6.4 million, achieved in October 2022 for a 260 square metre pad described as an "exquisite penthouse [which] is an architectural ode to luxury, quality and entertainment excellence", which had been "transformed by a near-new cutting-edge renovation with no expense spared".[1] [2] Basic one-bedroom apartments with no views or parking typically to start at $800,000, with larger apartments with views and parking (such as Richard and Susanne's) likely to command well over $2.5 million. Renters, meanwhile, usually pay at least $700 a week for a one-bedroom apartment.

If the eye-watering rents and steep prices for apartments in the Victoria Point project weren't enough, the cost of terraces in the street itself are at the next level.

Also as of October 2024, the street record for a terrace sale was $12.5 million. That was the price paid in January 2024 for a terrace at 30 Victoria St containing two strata apartments, which its real estate blurb said was "immaculate and versatile". In 2021, a four-bedroom terrace at 154 Victoria St sold for $10.3 million. This terrace was described in its real estate ad as being "unparalleled in terms of grandeur, level of finish and unforgettable beauty" with a "striking one-of-a-kind architectural renovation".[3] Among some of the terrace's features included marble fireplaces, herringbone hardwood floors, "soaring" ceilings and of course an "award-winning Dolomite Marble kitchen [with] Wolf, BORA and Sub-Zero inclusions".

According to City of Sydney Council development application records, the terrace had undergone a $974,000 renovation from a vermin-filled backpackers' hostel – described as a "NIGHTMARE" and "worst experience ever" in reviews – into a palatial home. The terrace was allegedly purchased by a 'former Young Rich Lister' who is the co-head of an investment fund, before it could even hit the open market.[4]

---

1   Property price figures sourced from Zango
2   Real estate listing for 168/71 Victoria Street, Potts Point, NSW 2011
3   Real estate listing for 154 Victoria Street, Potts Point
4   Potts Point 1840s Terrace has $11m-$12m Price Hopes as Kings Cross Real Estate Boom Hits Overdrive, realestate.com.au, 4 March 2022, by Stephen Nicholls

As Richard and Susanne have discovered, the soaring value of Victoria St property means that homeowners seem to try to out-do each other with outlandish renovations. In October 2022, the vendors of a terrace at 81 Victoria St boasted that they had completed a $1.9 million renovation, which included a new basement level with its own study and cellar for 600 bottles. "It's a serious, temperature-controlled cellar with [a] Vintec fridge," the homeowner boasted. "We fell in love with the house and we've created this Potts Point jewel."[5]

In the 1970s, as the battle raged to preserve the street, Victoria St drew comparisons with the Parisian hillside suburb of Montmartre, due to its lofty location, providence as an artistic colony and proximity to a red light district. By the end of the 1970s, it was clear Frank Theeman's Victoria Point project was leading the area's gentrification.

In August 1978, the *Australian Financial Review* reported that apartments in Victoria Point were "selling like hotcakes", even before the sales campaign for the project's first stage had officially begun.[6] The paper reported that 60 out of the 72 apartments sold had been to owner-occupiers. "Agents in Kings Cross say there is a trend gathering momentum for owner-occupiers to move back into an area which has been predominantly a rental area for the past generation," the paper reported.

Now, in the 2020s, the street is being compared to London's most exclusive and expensive suburbs. "The prices being achieved locally are more like what you would expect in Knightsbridge in London than what we used to think of as the backend of Kings Cross," one real estate agent said in 2021.[7] In the same year, another agent said Victoria St should be regarded as the "Belgravia of Australia".[8]

---

5 Maurice Violani and Jessica Yates's stunning Potts Point Marble Palace Hits the Market, news.com.au, 21 October 2022, by Stephen Nicholls
6 Buyers Beat Path to Door of Controversial Victoria Point Project, *Australian Financial Review*, 11 August 1978, by Christopher Jay, page 18
7 Potts Point Makes like London's Knightsbridge as Terrace Sells for $10 million, domain.com.au, 11 June 2022, by Lucy Macken
8 Inner Sydney Prices Just Keep Rising, *The Australian*, 11-12 September 2021, page 32

The suburb's ongoing gentrification may also be related to the return of population decline, a problem identified by Juanita Nielsen in 1974.

From 2016 to 2023, the population of Potts Point and Woolloomooloo dropped by 3,697, or 16.2 per cent. Over the same time, Greater Sydney's population grew by 8.5 per cent.[9] Locals have stated that developers are assisting this de-population, and a related reduction in local demographic diversity. This is said to be happening by developers seeking to demolish existing buildings containing a high number of affordable single bedroom units, and instead building luxury complexes containing a small number of three- or four-bedroom apartments occupied by wealthy older couples. This trend appears to be confirmed by the fact that, in Potts Point between 2016 and 2021, all age groups recorded a population decline, with the exception of people aged 60 and over.[10]

In short, Victoria St has returned and most likely exceeded its heyday of the 1880s, when many of the most extravagant terraces were constructed and the street held pride of place as one of the best residential enclaves in Sydney. Terrace homes which in the 1970s were divided into low-cost flatettes, and more recently during the 1990s into jam-packed backpacker dormitories, are now being converted into single residences for the city's elite.

Meanwhile, just as in the 19th century, the valley below is now better known for its affordable housing. Thanks to the $17 million investment by the Whitlam Government in the 1970s, the 2021 Census figures show that 19.5 per cent of homes in Woolloomooloo (or around 400 homes) are rented as social housing, compared to 0.4 per cent (or 10 homes) in Potts Point, including the Victoria St area.

This means that, once again, there's a rich social divide between the valley and the ridge. The valley once again is home to many people on their only housing option, looked down upon by those who have the opportunity to select almost any housing option they like.

---

9. Sourced from Regional Population, Australian Bureau of Statistics, Population estimates by SA2 and above, 2001 to 2023, published 26 March 2024
10. See City of Sydney community profile for Potts Point

However, Susanne told me that, with the reduced number of backpackers, the Victoria St area no longer feels as safe at night. "If Richard was away and … I'd come home late, I'd wander down Victoria St," Susanne said. "And it was always full of young people and they're international students and they were lovely. And it felt incredibly safe coming home at 11 o'clock at night or later."

When walking home, Susanne almost certainly would have also wandered past the small brass plaque which greets locals and tourists about to scuttle down the Butler Stairs – the 1869 sandstone steps which link Victoria and the Woolloomooloo basin. The plaque commemorates Mick Fowler, who lived around 50m from the steps, for his "gallant stance against the demolition of workers' homes".

"They were hard old days, they were battling days, they were cruel times, but, in spite of it all, Victoria St will see low-income housing for workers again," the plaque reads.

Given recent trends, it's hard to imagine this prediction will ever come true.

CHAPTER 37
Sacrifices which should be recognised

In July 2021, the Australian Broadcasting Corporation (ABC) announced, with some fanfare, that it was going to publish a true crime television series and podcast which, yet again, delved into the enduring mystery of Juanita Nielsen's disappearance and presumed murder.

An ABC media release promised that the production "seeks to finally uncover the truth behind the heroic and glamorous figure's disappearance" and "uncovers strong leads exposing the failed police investigation into her disappearance". "Hear explosive revelations as the investigation unfolds … with new episodes releasing weekly," the media release promised, under the headline "What really happened to Juanita Nielsen".

In the end, the production's mooted "explosive revelation" nearly blew up the ABC, rather than cracking open the cold case. After going to air, serious doubts were raised about the accuracy of the production's star witness's claim that he had received a jail-house murder confession from Carousel Cabaret nightclub manager Eddie Trigg.[1] The TV series, and two podcast episodes, were yanked from streaming platforms. At a Senate hearing, the ABC's Managing Director David Anderson admitted "there is no doubt that they should have done more digging with regard to one of those participants that was interviewed

---

1   Makers of Pulled ABC Documentary Agreed not to ask Star Witness Key Questions, *The Sydney Morning Herald*, 10 October 2021, by Neil Mercer and Peter Rees

and the undertakings that they provided as part of that program; there's no doubt that that should have been better".²

The production was the last in a long line of journalistic efforts which characterised Nielsen as a victim of crime, rather than focussing on her public policy legacy. For decades, newspaper, radio and TV stories, along with books, art exhibitions and even movies, have trawled through the events leading up to – and following – Nielsen's murder, and have often tabled fantastic new theories about the reasons for her demise.

The prevailing view is that Nielsen was murdered because of opposition to the Victoria Point development. In *Killing Juanita*, Peter Rees states: "Juanita … died for one reason only – her strident and effective opposition to the redevelopment of Victoria St. An air of inevitability surrounded the events leading up to her death, metamorphosing the drama into a tragedy that is now part of Sydney folklore".³ In his 2008 book *Gentle Satan*, Alan Saffron – son of Kings Cross nightclub figure Abe Saffron – even goes as far as to recount the exact details of Nielsen's alleged murder. Saffron claims that Nielsen was taken by force to a North Sydney motel, where Frank Theeman offered her a "substantial sum of money" to drop her campaign. "Naturally, Juanita was extremely angry about being kidnapped and started to scream at the top of her voice." Saffron says Theeman associate Jim Anderson then hit Nielsen, causing her to fall and strike her head on a coffee table, which apparently killed her instantly. Nielsen's body was allegedly dumped in the harbour.⁴ Meanwhile, in the early 1980s, Sydney City Alderman Tony Reeves said he had evidence from three sources that Nielsen was murdered because she had come into possession of blackmail dossiers on 16 "prominent society figures",

---

2   ABC Managing Director David Anderson Admits to Editorial Failings in Juanita Nielsen Series, The Australian, 30 November 2021, by Sophie Elsworth
3   *Killing Juanita*, page 270
4   *Gentle Satan*, Michael Joseph / Penguin Books, 2008, by Alan Saffron, pages 133-34

including "knights, a judge and businessman".[5] None of these theories have been proven.

Often, in these true crime narratives, other participants in the Woolloomooloo and Victoria St saga (including the squatters and City of Sydney Aldermen) are characterised as bit players whose sole legacy was to create an environment of conflict and hostility which led to Nielsen's murder.

This book seeks to take a different approach. It outlines how Nielsen was far more than just another victim of Sydney's underworld, and in fact played a critical role in a social movement which represented a turning point in the city's history. This social movement was appalled by the greed, secrecy and incompetence of the Woolloomooloo scheme and the unrestrained actions of Kings Cross criminal figures, and inspired by Victoria St's beauty and social diversity. The resulting urban warfare between the forces for, and against, private property development left the New South Wales (NSW) Government with little choice but to strengthen laws and activities which better protected heritage, supported affordable housing gains and entrenched the right to participate in planning decisions. The same warfare also inspired later protests which resulted in the cancellation of inner-city motorways, and the opening of new women's shelters and centres. Nielsen's death only strengthened this movement, turning people against property developers for years to come and being cited as a reason to stamp out endemic police corruption.

And yet, some five decades later, the legacy of Nielsen and her contemporaries is more than ever the centre of public debate, and aspects of this legacy have either been reversed or are under threat. This is largely because the planning reforms which were introduced in the 1970s are now being blamed, by some, for contributing to the housing affordability crisis which has enveloped Australia following COVID-19.

---

5   $100,000 Offered for Juanita's Death, *Sun-Herald*, 11 July 1982, by Graham Gambie, page 6

This chapter seeks to briefly examine this issue, while also not pretending to represent detailed academic research on the vexed subject of housing affordability. To assist in this analysis, I conducted two interviews with figures with a strong interest in the planning debate. One of these interviews was with Peter Tulip, an economist for the 'free choice' public policy think tank the Centre for Independent Studies. The other was with Sue Weatherley, a long-term NSW planner and NSW president of the Planning Institute of Australia.

As outlined in this book, Nielsen was a passionate believer in the rights of people to participate in planning. Through her modest weekly publication, Nielsen played a crucial role spreading information about the events in various development battle-grounds around inner Sydney, including her home suburb. She regularly urged her readers to have their say about plans in their area and was also vocal in her opposition to the Victoria Point development in her street. In reality, it is very likely that Nielsen lost her life because of her unrelenting advocacy.

Tulip's view is that the planning system has, for many years, provided too much support for people who objected to development, and therefore have reduced the supply of new housing which in turn forced up prices. "Juanita Nielsen, and to an extent Jack Mundey and other campaigners at that time, established the story: the narrative of the heroic neighbourhood defender fighting against greedy – often corrupt – developers," Tulip said. "That seems to be a story that people love to tell and re-tell, and they look for other excuses for it. What we have is old wealthy Anglo residents, afraid of change in their neighbourhood, who don't like demographic change, fighting hard to keep out increases in density and to preserve their property values.

"The Cahill Expressway or Blues Point Tower would not be built now. They are almost universally regarded as eyesores. Part of that is with consultation. So there was a problem with a lack of consultation. Now we have different problems with consultation, in that it over-represents certain demographic groups and values, and greatly under-represents what I suspect may be majority opinion. It gives a loud megaphone to loud busybodies who want to keep their immediate neighbourhood exactly [the same]."

Weatherley believes that, while it is important that consultation seeks the views of a wide range of people, including young people and future residents, it's wrong to blame the legislation. Weatherley said the NSW planning legislation was always framed as 'make a submission', not 'make an objection', and noted that "submissions can be positive". "The NSW [planning] Act in terms of its general principles is fine," Weatherley said.

There are numerous recent examples of the NSW planning system moving back towards the 1960s, with community members being denied a say on planning issues in their area.

In 1998, the NSW Government introduced the concept of the complying development approval pathway. Under this pathway, a private accredited certifier, who is employed by the landowner, is able to approve development proposals. This can happen without the proposal ever being publicly exhibited, if the development meets a 'one size fits all' Statewide code. Over time, the complying development system has been expanded from small-scale house extensions, through to home demolitions and the construction of new detached houses, and more recently to semi-detached homes and small unit blocks.

Complying development is loved by home builders, renovators and developers, because it delivers a quicker and guaranteed approval – and therefore new housing. This is certainly a plus, at a time of a national housing shortage. Weatherley considers the complying system reasonable, given the codes which underpin the certifier's decision have been exhibited.

On the flipside, the complying development system can be contentious. One reason for this is because development proposals which were once exhibited are no longer open for feedback – leading to a retreat in public participation. A second reason is because development approved under this pathway isn't assessed on its merits or required to consider the surrounding area, which is a particular problem in existing and more historic urban areas, and therefore can result in

Example of an attached housing project in Marrickville (far right of photo) which was approved via the complying development pathway (Photo: Mark Skelsey)

new developments which are at odds with the surrounding streetscape. Thirdly, complying development decisions are made by people paid by an applicant – not independent experts or public servants.

Another example of reduced participation relates to appeal rights. The ability to appeal against a development approval is one way to participate in the planning system. The NSW Environmental Planning and Assessment Act, when introduced in 1979, gave any person the right to argue in court that the wrong steps had been followed when a planning decision had been made, and therefore that decision was invalid. However, in 2005, the NSW Government introduced laws which stopped these appeals if a project had been declared "critical infrastructure" which was "essential for the State for economic, environmental or social reasons".[6] This meant that objectors, including local councils or even other government agencies, could no longer argue that the correct process had not been followed in the approval of some

---

6   Via the Section 75T of the *Environmental Planning and Assessment Amendment (Infrastructure and Other Planning Reform) Act* 2005

Example of a new dwelling in Lewisham (centre of photo) which replaced a historic home and was approved via the complying development pathway (Photo: Mark Skelsey)

major infrastructure projects, such as a new road or railway line. This law remains in place today.[7]

Finally, a more recent example of public participation being denied relates to the creation of new Transport Oriented Development (TOD) precincts around Sydney train stations. In a bid to speed up the supply of housing, the NSW Minister for Planning in May 2024 exercised his right to rezone land in 18 precincts to deliver tens of thousands of new homes, without landowners in those areas having the ability to comment on draft plans.[8] The rezoning area was not decided on specific local characteristics of the precinct, but by a strict 400m radius around a railway station. This resulted in some landowners discovering they would now be living next door to a potential six-to-

---

[7] See Section 5.27 of the Environmental Planning and Assessment Act, also State Significant Infrastructure Guidelines, NSW Government, March 2024, page 29

[8] Only "targeted consultation" was undertaken with "affected councils, planning peak stakeholders, community housing advocacy organisations and community organisations" as referred to on page 5 of a document entitled What we heard Transport Oriented Development policy consultation, NSW Department of Planning, Housing and Infrastructure, undated but published in mid-2024

eight storey development site, while the height limit on their land was two-three storeys. A NSW Government planning official said the lack of consultation was because the TOD precincts were a "time-limited emergency measure" to deal with housing affordability issues.[9]

The debate about Nielsen's two other advocacy areas, affordable housing and heritage, remains equally fraught.

The preservation of affordable housing was a central plank in the arguments of Nielsen and other activists in the Victoria Point saga. Roelof Smilde, Wendy Bacon and other activists sought to argue the Victoria Point site should be purchased by the Australian Government and turned into co-operative housing, while Nielsen argued that strict controls should be placed on the income of future residents who could occupy the site. Both of these arguments could be considered radical, if not unrealistic, but they underscored a broader vision of equality. In response to union green bans brought about through community activism, Theeman was even willing to set aside 10 per cent of his future dwellings as affordable housing.

In reality, Nielsen and the squatters' dreams of an urban low-income utopia – a home for anyone on any income – has not been realised.

Sydney is stated to be the second most unaffordable housing market in the world, sitting only second behind Hong Kong.[10] The 2024 *State of the Housing System* report, published by the Australian Government in May 2024, found it takes the average prospective Australian homeowner around 10 years to save a 20 per cent deposit for an average dwelling, and even with a deposit, only 13 per cent of the homes sold in 2022/23 were affordable for a median income household. Meanwhile,

---

9   Email from Department of Planning and Environment Acting Executive Director Hanna Shalbaf dated 20 December 2023, which was included in response to a NSW Legislative Council resolution on 8 February 2024 requesting TOD documents from within government

10 Sydney Second-Least Affordable Place to Buy a Home in Study of 92 World Markets, news.com.au, 18 March 2022, by Melissa Iaria

rents across the nation increased by around 35 per cent from March 2020 to March 2024.[11]

The safety net meant to catch renters unable to afford the private rental market has also been becoming increasingly threadbare, allowing more to fall through it. Affordable housing – whether owned by governments or the not-for-profit sector – has been declining as a share of the nation's housing stock for three decades, from 5.6 per cent in 1991 to 3.8 per cent in 2021. This has resulted in waitlists for this type of housing increasing by 9.1 per cent from 2019 to 2023.[12] It seems as though the number of new affordable dwellings being produced, or retained, through planning regulation on private development, as discussed in Chapter 35, is by no means sufficient to keep up with demand. Neither is government funding, or other models intended to produce new affordable housing (such as working with private developers to redevelop existing public housing estates).

Co-operative housing – the resident-managed communal housing model promoted by the Victoria St squatters – has also unfortunately barely made a dent in the Australian housing market. A Western Sydney University report published in 2024 found that there were just 3,047 affordable co-operative housing dwellings across Australia, representing just 0.3 per cent of Australia's overall housing stock.[13]

The debate about how to deliver this badly-needed new affordable housing continues to rage.

In 2018, the NSW Government's Greater Sydney Commission released a new Greater Sydney Plan which recommended that 5–10 per cent of new residential floor space should be set aside for affordable rental housing, subject to a viability test.[14] This measure came close to the 10 per cent affordable housing target set on Theeman's Victoria

---

11 State of the Housing System report, by National Housing Supply and Affordability Council, pages 3 and 63
12 State of the Housing System report, page 5
13 The Value of Housing Co-operatives in Australia, Western Sydney University, 2024, page 20
14 Greater Sydney Region Plan: A Metropolis of Three Cities - connecting people, Greater Sydney Commission, March 2018, page 70

St site, and would help deliver the concept of communities with both market-priced and affordable housing. However, due to concerns about development feasibility in the high inflation post COVID-19 world, the NSW Government only required 2 per cent of new residential floor space in the aforementioned new TOD precincts to be affordable.[15][16] This means that, in a block of 40 new apartments, only one needs to be set aside for affordable rental purposes. Other two-bedroom apartments in the same complex are likely to cost at least $1.16 million, according to a development industry lobby group's analysis of development feasibility in these precincts.[17]

A range of peak bodies with an interest in NSW planning said the rate was too low.[18] "The sheer scale of uplift proposed in these reforms presents a one-off opportunity for meaningful policy reform to create significantly more affordable housing in perpetuity," the NSW Local Government and Shires Association said in its submission.[19] In addition, the Greater Sydney Commission has now been disbanded.

Separately, under a scheme introduced in December 2023, developers are allowed to breach building height and floor space controls by up to 30 per cent, if they provide up to 15 per cent of new dwellings as affordable housing for 15 years.[20] While this reform does deliver needed additional housing, including affordable housing, it also has some downsides. Firstly, in 15 years, these apartments will be returned to full market rentals, resulting in the potential eviction of lower-income earners. In addition to this, as was the case with Theeman's

---

15 See section 156 of the State Environmental Planning Policy (Housing) Amendment (Transport Oriented Development) 2024, published 29 April 2024. Also eight other larger TOD precincts have a base affordable housing rate of 3 per cent, with site-specific rates ranging from 4-18 per cent
16 The NSW Government says the rate may increase over time
17 Making the TODs work, Urban Development Institute of Australia NSW, June 2024, page 17
18 What We Heard - Transport Oriented Development policy consultation, report by NSW Department of Planning, Housing and Infrastructure, May 2024
19 Letter from David Reynolds, Chief Executive of Local Government NSW, to Department of Planning, Housing and Infrastructure Secretary Kiersten Fishburn, dated 23 February 2024
20 Available via Chapter 2, Part 2, Division 1 of the State Environmental Planning Policy (Housing) 2021

The Inner West suburb of Croydon, which has a high proportion of heritage areas, has been targeted as part of the Transport Oriented Development reforms (Photo: Mark Skelsey)

development and as noted by Nielsen at the time, the new affordable dwellings are often in the least salubrious parts of the developments, such as those with less sunlight or at lower levels of buildings.

A further issue relates to the evictions of low-income tenants, which played such a prominent role in the Victoria St saga. There has been public disquiet about a range of redevelopment proposals involving the eviction of low-cost housing tenants in inner-Sydney areas, at a time of great housing shortage. Sydney freelance writer Sue Williams reported in May 2024 that one of her Kings Cross neighbours committed suicide, after learning that his low-cost housing building was to be redeveloped into a smaller number of luxury apartments.[21]

The scheme introduced in 1984 giving councils powers to refuse, or levy, applications to subdivide and sell off low-cost accommodation remains in place, and has been extended to demolitions and refurbishments. The scheme is having mixed results.

---

21 My Neighbour Took his Own Life Rather than Face Homelessness: Will Anyone Bother to Notice? *The Sydney Morning Herald*, 14 May 2024, by Sue Williams

The scheme is continuing to be used for its original purpose. In August and again in December 2024, City of Sydney Council used the scheme's powers as one of several reasons to refuse a proposal at 117 Victoria St, only about 150m from Nielsen's former home. The proposal sought to demolish an older-style building containing 45 relatively affordable rental dwellings, and in its place build 25 larger and more expensive dwellings for private sale.[22]

However, the scheme does have its limitations, particularly in relation to boarding houses. Changes introduced in 2009 have had the effect of supporting the conversion of boarding houses to market-priced or luxury homes, if it can be proven that the boarding house is not "viable".[23] As this book was going to press, an applicant was using this argument to seek the proposed conversion of a 32-room boarding house at Paddington into four attached dwellings, resulting in the eviction of the boarding house's vulnerable and elderly tenants.[24] The council has reported that, since 2000, it has received 29 applications to convert boarding houses to other uses, including three in 2023 alone.[25] Similarly, at Dulwich Hill in Sydney's inner-west, a developer was able to demolish a boarding house and replace it with townhouses, after using the viability argument. Another boarding house owner in the same suburb evicted 75 residents, some of whom became homeless, after re-marketing the property to students – a process that did not require planning approval.[26]

---

22 Decision of City of Sydney Local Planning Panel for 117 Victoria St, Potts Point on 14 August 2024 and decision of City of Sydney Local Planning Panel for 117 Victoria St, Potts Point on 18 December 2024. The decision is under appeal.

23 Under Clause 50 of the Affordable Rental Housing State Environmental Planning Policy 2009, and pages 11-14 of the Guidelines for Retention of Existing Affordable Rental Housing, NSW Government, October 2009

24 Decision of City of Sydney Local Planning Panel for 58-60 and 62-64 Selwyn St, Paddington, 1 November 2023

25 Submission by City of Sydney Council to the NSW Legislative Assembly Select Committee on Essential Worker Housing, 12 September 2024, pages 18 and 19

26 How Sydney's Boarding Houses Evict Residents in Favour of Students, 'Millionaires' or Those able to Pay More, Australian Broadcasting Corporation, 17 September 2024, by Catherine Hanrahan

The City of Sydney Council refused a proposal to demolish and redevelop this building at 117 Victoria St, Potts Point

Several Sydney councils are also now progressing local planning scheme amendments which will make it easier for them to refuse applications which reduce overall dwelling numbers.[27]

On the flipside, the NSW Government (as part of its 2024/25 Budget) announced a major funding package to construct new affordable housing. This includes $5.1 billion to construct 8,400 new social housing dwellings. Some 50 per cent of these homes will be set aside for victim-survivors of domestic and family violence. Separately, $655 million will be set aside for essential worker and rental housing. Only time will tell if these new funding pools, and new planning incentives, are able to deliver the affordable housing that Sydney needs.[28]

The decision-making on affordable housing targets goes to the heart of a national debate on the role and importance of subsidised housing – the safety net to catch those unable to afford private rent. Tulip argues

---

27 This is being done by the City of Sydney and Woollahra Councils
28 2024/25 NSW Budget page on housing and planning

the focus for the nation's housing affordability woes should be to relax planning restrictions to supply more homes.

"The mistake that many people make is to think that what changes the affordability of housing is the cost of the new housing you build, and people think it makes a difference if that is below or above average," Tulip says. "In fact that makes no difference at all, what makes a huge difference is the effect of extra supply … it is supply and demand, so if you stop new construction, and you restrict supply, you put up the price of housing throughout the metropolitan area, and it is of negligible effect whether that new housing is luxury or subsidised housing, and this is the way the planning system has made Sydney unaffordable – to everyone except the children of wealthy parents – by restricting supply. My view is the view of most economists, [which is] if you build a lot more housing, it will become affordable, if you veto it, it will become unaffordable."[29]

Weatherley sees it differently. "I can't see how we can build anywhere near enough houses or homes to have such an impact on price, so that a family on a total income of $60,000 a year could afford to rent in the private market," she says. "We can't get the price down enough in a free-market environment where 95 per cent of all sales are existing homes, and new homes are priced on what the 95 per cent are valued at … we've relied on the free market for some extent for 30 years, we now have a significant problem on homelessness, people who are couch-surfing. We do have to find a way to increase supply, to manage the increase in house prices, but we always need a safety net. In some countries the level of social and affordable housing is 40 per cent and we are running at 3 per cent."

The third issue pursued by Nielsen related to heritage. The Woolloomooloo and Victoria St development saga exposed the rudimentary and incomplete nature of the State's heritage protection system. This in turn spawned an entirely new regulatory structure, which again reduced private property rights and elevated the rights

---

[29] Further explored in Housing Affordability and Supply Restrictions, Centre for Independent Studies, February 2024, by Peter Tulip

of the community to stop valuable areas and buildings from being destroyed. By the time Nielsen entered the Victoria St debate, Theeman had already committed to preserving the terraces on his development site. Nielsen supported this preservation, although some prescient activists did have concerns that this could lead to the street becoming the enclave of the wealthy.

Since the 1970s, heritage protection has been a huge growth industry. There are now more than 30,000 local or State heritage items, ranging from international icons such as the Sydney Opera House through to obscure local features such as historic post boxes, street trees, waterfalls or footpaths. Many other homes, buildings and natural features are protected via statutory heritage conservation areas.

Tulip's view is that heritage protection has gone too far. "In principle, I am not aware of anyone who disagrees with the idea that we should protect unusually old or attractive buildings," he says. "But the heritage culture and industry that has developed has gone way beyond that and community values. There are a bunch of architectural obsessives who think [that] because some obscure architect designed something in a weird way, that it should somehow be preserved, regardless of its impact on affordability, or amenity or attractiveness. You have huge swathes of older suburbs [that] are heritage protected. A lot of it is indefensible."

Tulip cites a survey of 3,000 Australians, undertaken in August 2023, as evidence that many people hold his view. The survey asked Australians about their main concerns with increasing housing density in their local area. Only 2 per cent of survey respondents said "losing built heritage" was their main concern, and only 10 per cent placed the issue in their top five concerns. Heritage was well down the list of concerns, behind other issues such as traffic congestion and parking.[30]

Weatherley has a different perspective. "I think the notion we should tear everything down and build new, and lose the stories of our cities because we don't have any of the significant buildings ... left, that is the wrong way to go," she says. "We have to get the balance right. We need

---

30 Understanding attitudes towards housing in Australia, a poll by the Susan McKinnon Foundation, 23 October 2023

to preserve the heritage that tells the story of our cities, and maintain the character and future of our cities; we do need to make sure we look after the right things."

"You look at Parramatta, which has a lot of heritage. There has been a lot of growth in that area, you are talking about tens of thousands of new homes and the highest growth [rate] of any local government area for a long time. We still preserved areas around Harris Park, still preserved Elizabeth Farm and heritage buildings in the Western Sydney University … so I think it is possible, but also a great thing, so people can see how growth has occurred."

Again, however, heritage is in the cross-hairs of the development industry and those who believe a step-change in housing supply is required. There's an argument that excessive use of heritage orders is stifling much-needed new housing supply, the rights of homeowners and the natural order of change in cities.[31] Some commentators refer to a "heritage mafia" – a phrase first coined in the United Kingdom in the 1980s that was said to explain a "cabal or closed shop exercising a hidden or malign influence over cities and places".[32]

Victoria St played a key role in the introduction of heritage conservation areas, which protected all aspects of precincts rather than just individual buildings. It also helped trigger a major expansion in heritage protection laws, and was an early – if not the first – example of historic buildings being retained on a development site.

In late 2023 and early 2024, the NSW Government announced a wide range of planning reforms, including the aforementioned TOD precincts and other measures allowing greater housing height and density close to public transport and retail centres. Heritage conservation areas, which until this time had been off-limits to major change, were specifically targeted for redevelopment. At the time, the National Trust raised grave concerns about the reforms, stating they had the potential

---

31 Heritage Laws Should be Demolished, *The Sydney Morning Herald*, 4 November 2015, by Michael Pascoe
32 Establishing Australia's Heritage Mafia, *History*, magazine of the Royal Australian Historical Society, December 2022, page 7

to "result in the greatest level of heritage destruction in NSW since the Heritage Act 1977 was introduced by the Wran Government".[33] Since this time, the NSW Government has allowed councils to prepare alternative plans which do protect heritage conservation areas in TOD precincts and has argued that, irrespective of this, new housing and heritage can co-exist.[34] However, it is still possible that Victoria St will be affected by the reforms, as it is within the Kings Cross town centre which has been earmarked for potential change.

Another issue relates to the NSW Heritage Council. In 1977, the NSW Government created the council as an independent body to manage and oversee the State's heritage. At the time, it had unqualified powers to approve or refuse applications relating to State heritage items.[35] Since 2005, however, the Heritage Council has no longer had the final say if a development has been deemed as significant to the State.[36] This change has relegated the role of the Heritage Council to an objector or commentator in some major projects. The National Trust has long had a policy position calling for the Heritage Council to have its approval or refusal powers reinstated.[37]

It's reasonable that policy and legislative approaches shift over time, in response to new challenges, including the acute housing shortage in the post-COVID world. Indeed, as this book was going to print in early 2025, it was clear that there was bi-partisan support for a comprehensive review of planning laws introduced in the late 1970s, to respond to contemporary challenges.[38] It's also expected that the planning system has to manage enduring tension and conflict

---

33. Housing reforms in NSW, submission by National Trust of Australia (NSW), dated February 2024
34. Guidance to Transport Oriented Development, NSW Department of Planning, Housing and Infrastructure, August 2024, page 10
35. See Section 57 Heritage Act 1977 (as made)
36. See Section 4.41 of the Environmental Planning and Assessment Act 1979
37. NSW State Election 2023: Make heritage matter, policy platform by National Trust of Australia (NSW)
38. How a 45-year-old Act is Holding Sydney Hostage on Housing Reform, *The Sydney Morning Herald*, 4 January 2025, by Alexandra Smith and Michael McGowan

– between individual and community rights, existing and future residents, and preservation and change.

However, in considering these issues, we should firstly recognise and honour the work and sacrifices of people such as Nielsen and the other 1970s activists. Nielsen in particular knowingly put herself at great personal risk, and then almost certainly paid the ultimate price for participating in a planning debate, and fighting for heritage protection and affordable housing in her local area. Her legacy lives on, but remains under constant challenge.

We also need to consider the world which existed before Nielsen and others worked to change the system. It was a world in which there were limited or no opportunities for community members to participate in planning in their area. It was also a world in which there was no or little respect for the historic areas of our cities, and one in which low-income tenants could be evicted en masse without adequate systems in place to deliver new affordable housing for them. It was also a world in which a major expansion of the Sydney city centre was proposed, despite little consideration of the infrastructure needed to support this growth.

Today, we must ask ourselves – do we want to return to this world?

Author's notes and acknowledgements

It was in 2013, after finishing an eight-year stint as Media Manager at the NSW Department of Planning, that I decided to start researching a book about the history of Sydney planning. My first proposed topic was changing community attitudes, since the early 20th century, to high-rise development. In undertaking this research, I came across the Victoria St and Woolloomooloo development battles of the 1970s. As someone who is deeply interested in how public opinion and protest shapes planning outcomes, the street's urban warfare caught my attention and I quickly pivoted to this subject and *Views To Die For* was born. As *Killing Juanita* author Peter Rees told me, once Victoria St gets into your blood, it's hard to get it out.

I soon realised that, while this period had been covered from a true crime perspective, its public policy legacy had been largely left untouched. I set out to prove the period's influence on Sydney's town planning environment and future from the late 1970s onwards, and believe I achieved this. What I wasn't anticipating was the need to analyse the significant actual and proposed changes to this legacy in a bid to deliver more housing in the post COVID-19 environment.

While working full-time, I undertook interviews, writing and archival research whenever I could. I would like to thank the many people who have willingly and freely provided their time for this somewhat speculative project. I would also like to note that Sid Londish, John Mant, Ken Woolley and Jack Mundey have all passed away since our interviews. Their legacy and memory lives on. Woolley in particular provided great encouragement for this book as he, like myself, was frustrated that the non-crime elements of the story had not been adequately covered. Allan Rees and Andrew Jakubowicz were particularly generous in providing both time for interviews, along with photos and archival material. I would also like to thank the many library and archival staff who assisted my work and had to accommodate my repeated and sometimes confusing archival requests.

There were times when I thought it was unlikely this project would ever see the light of day. For this reason, I would like to thank the many people who advised and assisted its publication, particularly David Longfield from Longueville Media, and a number of colleagues and Potts Point locals. I would also like to thank the many people who encouraged me to keep going. This includes my family, particularly my wife Amanda, who has also provided such enduring emotional support over many years.

It should also be noted that, in January 2025, a NSW Government Transport Oriented Development (TOD) plan was released which, if implemented, would directly and negatively affect my home in Sydney's inner west. This book refers to the TOD scheme. I have also been active, since 2015, commenting on development issues around my home and in my suburb. However, as outlined above, the idea to write this book came well before any of these plans were released. Furthermore, in the final chapter, I have strived to deliver a balanced assessment of the current planning and development debate, which considers multiple viewpoints, and have sought to not be influenced by what's happening in my local area.

About the author

Mark Skelsey is a Sydney-based writer, and media and communications professional, with a strong interest in urban affairs issues. He is a former State Political Reporter, and City Editor, with the *Daily Telegraph*, and a former Media Manager at the NSW Department of Planning.

He has a Masters in Environmental Law from the University of Sydney (2010) and a Bachelor of Arts (Communications) from the University of Technology, Sydney (1990).

All opinions in this book are that of the author, and not of the author's employers or clients, whether past, present or future.

www.ingramcontent.com/pod-product-compliance
Lightning Source LLC
Chambersburg PA
CBHW061205070526
44583CB00025B/3125